Patricia Durisin
Editor

Information Literacy Programs: Successes and Challenges

Information Literacy Programs: Successes and Challenges has been co-published simultaneously as *Journal of Library Administration*, Volume 36, Numbers 1/2 2002.

Pre-publication REVIEWS, COMMENTARIES, EVALUATIONS . . .

"I WAS VERY IMPRESSED. . . . This volume should go far in addressing the concerns of instruction librarians seeking to develop their programs, whether they are searching for new ideas to improve and reinvigorate successful, established programs, or starting a new program from scratch. . . . Approaches a wide range of related issues from both theoretical and practical perspectives, and includes extensive references to sources of further professional development for instruction librarians."

Kendall Hobbs, MLS
Reference/Instruction Librarian
Olin Library
Wesleyan University

D0141140

The Haworth Information Press
An Imprint of The Haworth Press, Inc.

Information
Literacy Programs:
Successes and Challenges

Information Literacy Programs: Successes and Challenges has been co-published simultaneously as *Journal of Library Administration,* Volume 36, Numbers 1/2 2002.

The *Journal of Library Administration* Monographic "Separates"

Below is a list of "separates," which in serials librarianship means a special issue simultaneously published as a special journal issue or double-issue *and* as a "separate" hardbound monograph. (This is a format which we also call a "DocuSerial.")

"Separates" are published because specialized libraries or professionals may wish to purchase a specific thematic issue by itself in a format which can be separately cataloged and shelved, as opposed to purchasing the journal on an on-going basis. Faculty members may also more easily consider a "separate" for classroom adoption.

"Separates" are carefully classified separately with the major book jobbers so that the journal tie-in can be noted on new book order slips to avoid duplicate purchasing.

You may wish to visit Haworth's Website at . . .

http://www.HaworthPress.com

. . . to search our online catalog for complete tables of contents of these separates and related publications.

You may also call 1-800-HAWORTH (outside US/Canada: 607-722-5857), or Fax 1-800-895-0582 (outside US/Canada: 607-771-0012), or e-mail at:

getinfo@haworthpressinc.com

Information Literacy Programs: Successes and Challenges, edited by Patricia Durisin, MLIS (Vol. 36, No. 1/2, 2002). *Examines Web-based collaboration, teamwork with academic and administrative colleagues, evidence-based librarianship, and active learning strategies in library instruction programs.*

Evaluating the Twenty-First Century Library: The Association of Research Libraries New Measures Initiative, 1997-2001, edited by Donald L. DeWitt, PhD (Vol. 35, No. 4, 2001). *This collection of articles (thirteen of which previously appeared in ARL's bimonthly newsletter/report on research issues and actions) examines the Association of Research Libraries' "new measures" initiative.*

Impact of Digital Technology on Library Collections and Resource Sharing, edited by Sul H. Lee (Vol. 35, No. 3, 2001). *Shows how digital resources have changed the traditional academic library.*

Libraries and Electronic Resources: New Partnerships, New Practices, New Perspectives, edited by Pamela L. Higgins (Vol. 35, No. 1/2, 2001). *An essential guide to the Internet's impact on electronic resources management–past, present, and future.*

Diversity Now: People, Collections and Services in Academic Libraries, edited by Teresa Y. Neely, MLS, PhD, and Kuang-Hwei (Janet) Lee Smeltzer, MS, MSLIS (Vol. 33, No. 1/2/3/4, 2001). *Examines multicultural trends in academic libraries' staff and users, types of collections, and services offered.*

Leadership in the Library and Information Science Professions: Theory and Practice, edited by Mark D. Winston, MLS, PhD (Vol. 32, No. 3/4, 2001). *Offers fresh ideas for developing and using leadership skills, including recruiting potential leaders, staff training and development, issues of gender and ethnic diversity, and budget strategies for success.*

Off-Campus Library Services, edited by Ann Marie Casey (Vol. 31, No. 3/4, 2001 and Vol. 32, No. 1/2, 2001). *This informative volume examines various aspects of off-campus, or distance learning. It explores training issues for library staff, Web site development, changing roles for librarians, the uses of conferencing software, library support for Web-based courses, library agreements and how to successfully negotiate them, and much more!*

Research Collections and Digital Information, edited by Sul H. Lee (Vol. 31, No. 2, 2000). *Offers new strategies for collecting, organizing, and accessing library materials in the digital age.*

Academic Research on the Internet: Options for Scholars & Libraries, edited by Helen Laurence, MLS, EdD, and William Miller, MLS, PhD (Vol. 30, No. 1/2/3/4, 2000). *"Emphasizes quality over quantity. . . . Presents the reader with the best research-oriented Web sites in the field. A state-of-the-art review of academic use of the Internet as well as a guide to the best Internet sites and services. . . . A useful addition for any academic library." (David A. Tyckoson, MLS, Head of Reference, California State University, Fresno)*

Management for Research Libraries Cooperation, edited by Sul H. Lee (Vol. 29, No. 3/4, 2000). *Delivers sound advice, models, and strategies for increasing sharing between institutions to maximize the amount of printed and electronic research material you can make available in your library while keeping costs under control.*

Integration in the Library Organization, edited by Christine E. Thompson, PhD (Vol. 29, No. 2, 1999). *Provides librarians with the necessary tools to help libraries balance and integrate public and technical services and to improve the capability of libraries to offer patrons quality services and large amounts of information.*

Library Training for Staff and Customers, edited by Sara Ramser Beck, MLS, MBA (Vol. 29, No. 1, 1999). *This comprehensive book is designed to assist library professionals involved in presenting or planning training for library staff members and customers. You will explore ideas for effective general reference training, training on automated systems, training in specialized subjects such as African American history and biography, and training for areas such as patents and trademarks, and business subjects.* Library Training for Staff and Customers *answers numerous training questions and is an excellent guide for planning staff development.*

Collection Development in the Electronic Environment: Shifting Priorities, edited by Sul H. Lee (Vol. 28, No. 4, 1999). *Through case studies and firsthand experiences, this volume discusses meeting the needs of scholars at universities, budgeting issues, user education, staffing in the electronic age, collaborating libraries and resources, and how vendors meet the needs of different customers.*

The Age Demographics of Academic Librarians: A Profession Apart, by Stanley J. Wilder (Vol. 28, No. 3, 1999). *The average age of librarians has been increasing dramatically since 1990. This unique book will provide insights on how this demographic issue can impact a library and what can be done to make the effects positive.*

Collection Development in a Digital Environment, edited by Sul H. Lee (Vol. 28, No. 1, 1999). *Explores ethical and technological dilemmas of collection development and gives several suggestions on how a library can successfully deal with these challenges and provide patrons with the information they need.*

Scholarship, Research Libraries, and Global Publishing, by Jutta Reed-Scott (Vol. 27, No. 3/4, 1999). *This book documents a research project in conjunction with the Association of Research Libraries (ARL) that explores the issue of foreign acquisition and how it affects collection in international studies, area studies, collection development, and practices of international research libraries.*

Managing Multicultural Diversity in the Library: Principles and Issues for Administrators, edited by Mark Winston (Vol. 27, No. 1/2, 1999). *Defines diversity, clarifies why it is important to address issues of diversity, and identifies goals related to diversity and how to go about achieving those goals.*

Information Technology Planning, edited by Lori A. Goetsch (Vol. 26, No. 3/4, 1999). *Offers innovative approaches and strategies useful in your library and provides some food for thought about information technology as we approach the millennium.*

The Economics of Information in the Networked Environment, edited by Meredith A. Butler, MLS, and Bruce R. Kingma, PhD (Vol. 26, No. 1/2, 1998). *"A book that should be read both by information professionals and by administrators, faculty and others who share a collective concern to provide the most information to the greatest number at the lowest cost in the networked environment." (Thomas J. Galvin, PhD, Professor of Information Science and Policy, University at Albany, State University of New York)*

OCLC 1967-1997: Thirty Years of Furthering Access to the World's Information, edited by K. Wayne Smith (Vol. 25, No. 2/3/4, 1998). *"A rich–and poignantly personal, at times–historical account of what is surely one of this century's most important developments in librarianship." (Deanna B. Marcum, PhD, President, Council on Library and Information Resources, Washington, DC)*

Management of Library and Archival Security: From the Outside Looking In, edited by Robert K. O'Neill, PhD (Vol. 25, No. 1, 1998). *"Provides useful advice and on-target insights for professionals caring for valuable documents and artifacts." (Menzi L. Behrnd-Klodt, JD, Attorney/Archivist, Klodt and Associates, Madison, WI)*

Economics of Digital Information: Collection, Storage, and Delivery, edited by Sul H. Lee (Vol. 24, No. 4, 1997). *Highlights key concepts and issues vital to a library's successful venture into the digital environment and helps you understand why the transition from the printed page to the digital packet has been problematic for both creators of proprietary materials and users of those materials.*

The Academic Library Director: Reflections on a Position in Transition, edited by Frank D'Andraia, MLS (Vol. 24, No. 3, 1997). *"A useful collection to have whether you are seeking a position as director or conducting a search for one." (College & Research Libraries News)*

Emerging Patterns of Collection Development in Expanding Resource Sharing, Electronic Information, and Network Environment, edited by Sul H. Lee (Vol. 24, No. 1/2, 1997). *"The issues it deals with are common to us all. We all need to make our funds go further and our resources work harder, and there are ideas here which we can all develop." (The Library Association Record)*

Interlibrary Loan/Document Delivery and Customer Satisfaction: Strategies for Redesigning Services, edited by Pat L. Weaver-Meyers, Wilbur A. Stolt, and Yem S. Fong (Vol. 23, No. 1/2, 1997). *"No interlibrary loan department supervisor at any mid-sized to large college or university library can afford not to read this book." (Gregg Sapp, MLS, MEd, Head of Access Services, University of Miami, Richter Library, Coral Gables, Florida)*

Access, Resource Sharing and Collection Development, edited by Sul H. Lee (Vol. 22, No. 4, 1996). *Features continuing investigation and discussion of important library issues, specifically the role of libraries in acquiring, storing, and disseminating information in different formats.*

Managing Change in Academic Libraries, edited by Joseph J. Branin (Vol. 22, No. 2/3, 1996). *"Touches on several aspects of academic library management, emphasizing the changes that are occurring at the present time. . . . Recommended this title for individuals or libraries interested in management aspects of academic libraries." (RQ American Library Association)*

Libraries and Student Assistants: Critical Links, edited by William K. Black, MLS (Vol. 21, No. 3/4, 1995). *"A handy reference work on many important aspects of managing student assistants. . . . Solid, useful information on basic management issues in this work and several chapters are useful for experienced managers." (The Journal of Academic Librarianship)*

The Future of Resource Sharing, edited by Shirley K. Baker and Mary E. Jackson, MLS (Vol. 21, No. 1/2, 1995). *"Recommended for library and information science schools because of its balanced presentation of the ILL/document delivery issues." (Library Acquisitions: Practice and Theory)*

The Future of Information Services, edited by Virginia Steel, MA, and C. Brigid Welch, MLS (Vol. 20, No. 3/4, 1995). *"The leadership discussions will be useful for library managers as will the discussions of how library structures and services might work in the next century." (Australian Special Libraries)*

The Dynamic Library Organizations in a Changing Environment, edited by Joan Giesecke, MLS, DPA (Vol. 20, No. 2, 1995). *"Provides a significant look at potential changes in the library world and presents its readers with possible ways to address the negative results of such changes. . . . Covers the key issues facing today's libraries . . . Two thumbs up!" (Marketing Library Resources)*

Access, Ownership, and Resource Sharing, edited by Sul H. Lee (Vol. 20, No. 1, 1995). *The contributing authors present a useful and informative look at the current status of information provision and some of the challenges the subject presents.*

Libraries as User-Centered Organizations: Imperatives for Organizational Change, edited by Meredith A. Butler (Vol. 19, No. 3/4, 1994). *"Presents a very timely and well-organized discussion of major trends and influences causing organizational changes." (Science Books & Films)*

Declining Acquisitions Budgets: Allocation, Collection Development and Impact Communication, edited by Sul H. Lee (Vol. 19, No. 2, 1994). *"Expert and provocative. . . . Presents many ways of looking at library budget deterioration and responses to it . . . There is much food for thought here." (Library Resources & Technical Services)*

The Role and Future of Special Collections in Research Libraries: British and American Perspectives, edited by Sul H. Lee (Vol. 19, No. 1, 1993). *"A provocative but informative read for library users, academic administrators, and private sponsors." (International Journal of Information and Library Research)*

Catalysts for Change: Managing Libraries in the 1990s, edited by Gisela M. von Dran, DPA, MLS, and Jennifer Cargill, MSLS, MSed (Vol. 18, No. 3/4, 1994). *"A useful collection of articles which focuses on the need for librarians to employ enlightened management practices in order to adapt to and thrive in the rapidly changing information environment." (Australian Library Review)*

Monographic "Separates" list continued at the back

Information Literacy Programs: Successes and Challenges

Patricia Durisin
Editor

Information Literacy Programs: Successes and Challenges has been co-published simultaneously as *Journal of Library Administration,* Volume 36, Numbers 1/2 2002.

The Haworth Information Press
An Imprint of
The Haworth Press, Inc.
New York • London • Oxford

Published by

The Haworth Information Press®, 10 Alice Street, Binghamton, NY 13904-1580 USA

The Haworth Information Press® is an imprint of The Haworth Press, Inc., 10 Alice Street, Binghamton, NY 13904-1580 USA.

Information Literacy Programs: Successes and Challenges has been co-published simultaneously as *Journal of Library Administration,* Volume 36, Numbers 1/2 2002.

The development, preparation, and publication of this work has been undertaken with great care. However, the publisher, employees, editors, and agents of The Haworth Press and all imprints of The Haworth Press, Inc., including The Haworth Medical Press® and Pharmaceutical Products Press®, are not responsible for any errors contained herein or for consequences that may ensue from use of materials or information contained in this work. Opinions expressed by the author(s) are not necessarily those of The Haworth Press, Inc. With regard to case studies, identities and circumstances of individuals discussed herein have been changed to protect confidentiality. Any resemblance to actual persons, living or dead, is entirely coincidental.

Cover design by Jennifer Gaska.

Library of Congress Cataloging-in-Publication Data

Information literacy programs : successes and challenges / Patricia Durisin, editor.
     p. cm.
    Co-published simultaneously as Journal of library administration, v. 36, nos. 1/2, 2002.
    Includes bibliographical references and index.
    ISBN 0-7890-1958-2 (alk. paper) – ISBN 0-7890-1959-0 (pbk : alk. paper)
    1. Information literacy–Study and teaching (Higher)–United States. 2. Library orientation for college students–United States. I. Durisin, Patricia. II. Journal of library administration.
ZA3075 .I54 2002
028.7'071'173–dc21
                                           2002008879

Indexing, Abstracting & Website/Internet Coverage

This section provides you with a list of major indexing & abstracting services. That is to say, each service began covering this periodical during the year noted in the right column. Most Websites which are listed below have indicated that they will either post, disseminate, compile, archive, cite or alert their own Website users with research-based content from this work. (This list is as current as the copyright date of this publication.)

(continued)

Special Bibliographic Notes related to special journal issues (separates) and indexing/abstracting:

- indexing/abstracting services in this list will also cover material in any "separate" that is co-published simultaneously with Haworth's special thematic journal issue or DocuSerial. Indexing/abstracting usually covers material at the article/chapter level.
- monographic co-editions are intended for either non-subscribers or libraries which intend to purchase a second copy for their circulating collections.
- monographic co-editions are reported to all jobbers/wholesalers/approval plans. The source journal is listed as the "series" to assist the prevention of duplicate purchasing in the same manner utilized for books-in-series.
- to facilitate user/access services all indexing/abstracting services are encouraged to utilize the co-indexing entry note indicated at the bottom of the first page of each article/chapter/contribution.
- this is intended to assist a library user of any reference tool (whether print, electronic, online, or CD-ROM) to locate the monographic version if the library has purchased this version but not a subscription to the source journal.
- individual articles/chapters in any Haworth publication are also available through the Haworth Document Delivery Service (HDDS).

Information Literacy Programs:
Successes and Challenges

CONTENTS

ABOUT THE EDITOR

Patricia Durisin, MLIS, is Instruction Coordinator at the Massachusetts Institute of Technology Humanities Library in Cambridge, MA, and has been working in academic libraries for more than seven years. She also teaches as an adjunct faculty at Simmons College Graduate School of Library and Information Science. She has done interdisciplinary work with faculty and students, and has designed, conducted, and evaluated many library instruction programs. Ms. Durisin is interested in trends and techniques in library instruction and the use of technology to enhance educational services. This work was prepared while she was working at Simmons College Beatley Library.

Introduction

Patricia Durisin

Librarians have, for many years, been involved in teaching users how to find information and use library resources effectively. In this day and age, with the proliferation of information sources in multiple formats, that task is increasingly complex. Academic librarians in particular bear the responsibility of educating library users, as reference, instruction or information literacy librarians; and many are committed to revising their library instruction programs to meet components of the broad definition of information literacy, which is "a set of abilities requiring individuals to recognize when information is needed and have the ability to locate, evaluate, and use effectively the needed information."[1] Instruction librarians aim to instill in students a sense of life-long learning by infusing information literacy into the academic curriculum.

This volume is devoted to the information literacy movement, and to those librarians who have begun to address this issue on their campuses. Although many librarians have taken very different paths along the journey to successful information literacy integration, each has a unique perspective to share on how to best make the trip. These articles explore a variety of issues involved in teaching and managing library instruction or information literacy programs, from integrating technology to teaching credit courses to reaching first year students. Instruction librarians from colleges and universities across the country contribute their thoughts and experiences, successes and challenges, on how they manage the complexities involved in delivering information literacy instruction to students. Common themes across many of the articles presented

Patricia Durisin is Coordinator of Public Services, Simmons College Libraries, 300 The Fenway, Boston, MA 02115 (E-mail: durisin@simmons.edu).

[Haworth co-indexing entry note]: "Introduction." Durisin, Patricia. Co-published simultaneously in *Journal of Library Administration* (The Haworth Information Press, an imprint of The Haworth Press, Inc.) Vol. 36, No. 1/2, 2002, pp. 1-2; and: *Information Literacy Programs: Successes and Challenges* (ed: Patricia Durisin) The Haworth Information Press, an imprint of The Haworth Press, Inc., 2002, pp. 1-2. Single or multiple copies of this article are available for a fee from The Haworth Document Delivery Service [1-800-HAWORTH, 9:00 a.m. - 5:00 p.m. (EST). E-mail address: getinfo@haworthpressinc.com].

here revolve around ideas of collaboration, assessment, effective teaching methods, and learning styles, many stressing the importance of addressing information literacy standards.

It is my hope that library administrators, higher education faculty, and librarians of all types will benefit from the research, innovation, and dedication presented in these articles. My thanks go out to the authors, whose time, energy, and commitment to information literacy made this special issue possible.

NOTE

1. The ACRL uses this brief definition of information literacy in an introduction to the details of the Association's recently approved information literacy competency standards. The ACRL provides background information about information literacy and the creation of the standards; see Association of College and Research Libraries, "Information Literacy Competency Standards for Higher Education," [Web page], July 27, 2000 [cited October 3, 2001]; available from the World Wide Web at http://www.ala.org/acrl/ilintro.html.

Changing Landscapes, Enduring Values: Making the Transition from Bibliographic Instruction to Information Literacy

Elizabeth O. Hutchins
Barbara Fister
Kris (Huber) MacPherson

SUMMARY. Two liberal arts colleges in Minnesota are building on their longstanding commitment to bibliographic instruction to develop innovative information literacy programs. This article explores assumptions shared by the Earlham model of bibliographic instruction and the information literacy movement, outlines important differences, examines conditions that in-

---

Elizabeth O. Hutchins is Assistant Professor, Reference/Instruction Librarian and Coordinator of Library Instruction, St. Olaf College, Northfield, MN.

Barbara Fister is Associate Professor, College Librarian and Coordinator of Library Instruction, Gustavus Adolphus College, St. Peter, MN.

Kris (Huber) MacPherson is Associate Professor and Reference/Instruction Librarian, St. Olaf College, Northfield, MN, and Associate Director of Superior Studies, Wolf Ridge Environmental Learning Center, Finland, MN.

With permission of the Association of College and Research Libraries, this is a revised and expanded edition of a paper given by Barbara Fister, Elizabeth O. Hutchins, and Kris (Huber) MacPherson, "From BI to IL: The Paths of Two Liberal Arts Colleges," originally published in Hugh A. Thompson, ed., *Crossing the Divide: Proceedings of the Tenth National Conference of the Association of College and Research Libraries,* Chicago: ACRL, 2001.

[Haworth co-indexing entry note]: "Changing Landscapes, Enduring Values: Making the Transition from Bibliographic Instruction to Information Literacy." Hutchins, Elizabeth O., Barbara Fister, and Kris (Huber) MacPherson. Co-published simultaneously in *Journal of Library Administration* (The Haworth Information Press, an imprint of The Haworth Press, Inc.) Vol. 36, No. 1/2, 2002, pp. 3-19; and: *Information Literacy Programs: Successes and Challenges* (ed: Patricia Durisin) The Haworth Information Press, an imprint of The Haworth Press, Inc., 2002, pp. 3-19. Single or multiple copies of this article are available for a fee from The Haworth Document Delivery Service [1-800-HAWORTH, 9:00 a.m. - 5:00 p.m. (EST). E-mail address: getinfo@haworthpressinc.com].

hibit change, and profiles two approaches to developing information literacy programs with strong cross-campus collaboration. *[Article copies available for a fee from The Haworth Document Delivery Service: 1-800-HAWORTH. E-mail address: <getinfo@haworthpressinc.com> Website: <http://www.HaworthPress.com> © 2002 by The Haworth Press, Inc. All rights reserved.]*

KEYWORDS. Information literacy, research skills, bibliographic instruction, library-faculty partnership, collaboration

Liberal arts colleges were early adopters of bibliographic instruction as an effective means of integrating research strategies into the curriculum; in fact, the influential "Earlham Model" was developed in a liberal arts context.[1] Given that many colleges using this model for three decades have strong programs already in place that rely on collaboration with faculty and are tied to curricular goals, the rhetoric surrounding information literacy seems oddly familiar. Innovations being introduced on other campuses under the banner of information literacy sound like what we've been doing for years. Are they finally catching on? Is information literacy a new name for a philosophy and practice long established at liberal arts colleges?

Yes–and no. St. Olaf College and Gustavus Adolphus College are two Minnesota liberal arts colleges that have practiced the Earlham model for years with notable success. Yet the concepts embraced by information literacy do offer opportunities to refine our approach and renew our commitment to developing even more effective cross-campus collaboration.

Colleges employing the Earlham model locate bibliographic instruction at the intersection of the classroom and the library, where library research methods and materials are developed in response to particular disciplinary needs. This approach to bibliographic instruction depends on collaboration between the library and other academic departments.[2] In practice, the results of this collaboration may range from one-shot sessions, in which librarians plug resources and skills into a course without knowing how well-integrated they are, to sessions in which individual departmental faculty and librarians are equal partners in the development, presentation and evaluation of student research projects. Wherever bibliographic instruction lies on this spectrum, the ownership of the program has resided in the library, with outreach to other constituencies.

Information literacy continues the Earlham tradition by situating research skills in the broader context of articulating questions, finding information, and putting it to use in generating some new understanding. But it does so with some key differences. Development of an information literacy program relies on transforming a library-based program into a cross-campus enterprise with wider ownership, seeking not just buy-in but leadership and engagement beyond the walls of the library. Further, information literacy depends on collaborative pedagogy, embedding research competencies in individual courses and throughout the curriculum, and integrating skills developmentally into the entire learning process with the aim of creating informed and critical lifelong learners.

REMEMBERING THE ROADS TRAVELED

We have learned a great deal from the roads we have already traveled. As a case in point, the St. Olaf Libraries' mission statement reflects the centrality of teaching and learning with a firm commitment to "systematic instruction in the retrieval and evaluation of information from its many sources" and to having "library instruction complement classroom teaching."[3]

This commitment has been long-standing. St. Olaf received a grant in 1977 to develop a course-integrated bibliographic instruction program under the mentorship of Evan Farber and sent many of its librarians to the Earlham workshops during the early '80s. The initial program was grounded in a college-wide agreement to having both the required first-year English and Religion courses include student research and bibliographic instruction. Then, as early as 1983, the College's Bibliographic Instruction Advisory Committee, composed of both library and disciplinary faculty, encouraged departments to develop multi-tiered programs in order to embed critical thinking and independent library use throughout their curriculum in a sequential, developmental way.[4] This approach had particular success with the departments of Music and History; in other departments where courses were not taken sequentially (for example, Psychology, Social Work, Biology), strong faculty connections still enabled quality, course-related and course-integrated bibliographic instruction.

The Libraries participated in the development of a new curriculum in the late 1980s and chose to continue a tradition of integration and collaboration, rather than isolate library literacy as a competency to be "checked off." Once the new curriculum was in place, the Libraries received a Pew grant in 1992 to assess and revise the sequential course-integrated approach to research skills. Since then, the program has continued to develop, with bibliographic instruction classes ranging from the traditional 50 minute module to strongly collaborative, jointly designed series of classes and/or hands-on labs with active student-centered learning. In 1997, the Libraries partnered with the Psychology Department in a successful NSF grant to develop a new introductory course with a three-hour information literacy lab,[5] and in 1998 they organized and sponsored an Associated Colleges of the Midwest (ACM)-funded conference, "Bibliographic Instruction: An Opportunity for Collaborative Pedagogy." The next logical step has been to transform the bibliographic instruction program into a campus-wide information literacy initiative with an expanded focus on developmental research skills, critical thinking, and pedagogy.

Gustavus followed a similar path. Odrun Peterson, Gustavus librarian from 1944 to 1973, believed strongly in the educational mission of the library. As early as 1956, she described the library as an "instrument of instruction"[6] and in a 1965 planning document, she wrote "The library is primarily a teaching library."[7] The Earlham model embodied important and valuable assumptions about learning research skills that were easily embraced by Gustavus librarians. But, as at St. Olaf, changes in faculty, programs and the administration required continual reintroduction of those principles. Librarians at Gustavus tried many ways to work closely with the faculty but still felt dissatisfied with the results. Students were still having trouble integrating what they learned in the library with the whole process of thinking through a research task. Librarians had difficulty working within what was usually no more than a fifty-minute window of opportunity. Faculty were growing increasingly frustrated with students' difficulty in making critical judgements about their sources. And all of this was exacerbated by the increasing complexity of the hybrid world of print and electronic resources. In spite of all of our efforts, something wasn't working.

The Gustavus library developed a strategic plan in 1998 that reiterated the importance of teaching and learning as the basis of the entire library program.[8] With that in mind, the library held focus groups with faculty across the curriculum who said that electronic information formats and inadequate computer hardware were not the problem. The issue wasn't *technology*, it was *pedagogy*. One of the faculty members said bluntly "we have to change the way we teach." They felt that the most valuable thing the library could do would be to provide faculty a chance to work with librarians and other colleagues to retool courses so that their students would learn how to articulate good questions, seek information in both print and online formats, make intelligent choices, and use what they learned to create new knowledge–in short, they wanted help making students information literate, though none of them used that phrase to describe what they meant.

What they wanted to do–and what we had hoped to do all these years–had not really changed. In fact, this form of learning is integral to a liberal arts education. But they expressed a need to develop better ways to embed support for their learning of research skills into the curriculum. It wasn't up to us to point out the need and gain their approval–it was work they recognized *they* had to do.

EXPLORING THE LANDSCAPE

Much of the literature on information literacy suggests that transforming library-based bibliographic instruction to a cross-campus program of information literacy entails a major paradigm shift.[9] The Boyer Commission report,

Reinventing Undergraduate Education, urges research universities to change "the prevailing undergraduate culture of receivers into a culture of inquirers, a culture in which faculty (and students) share an adventure of discovery."[10] Many liberal arts colleges are fortunate in having already established such a landscape of inquiry. Gustavus, for example, sends 30 to 40 students annually to the National Undergraduate Research Conference to present their research. Many more students present their work at regional and national conferences and several have co-authored articles with faculty appearing in major scholarly journals. St. Olaf has a similar track record. However, on many campuses there may still be a need to do a better job of addressing the challenge of cooperation between librarians and teaching faculty.[11]

Where might this cooperation encounter stumbling blocks? Several possibilities come to mind: different disciplinary cultures, questionable status of librarians, differing agendas, and competition for college resources.

Faculty and library cultures often differ significantly. Faculty culture is concerned with disciplinary integrity, subject expertise, research, and autonomy, while the library's culture may be more committed to an interdisciplinary perspective, the research process rather than the product, and student-centered learning.[12] This is not an either/or situation, but it is important to assess where the balance of these priorities lies, for the faculty culture will shape the attitudes towards integrating information literacy into the curriculum. St. Olaf's and Gustavus's experiences illustrate that the more disciplinary faculty and librarians are engaged in a shared enterprise, with the focus on student learning and a climate of inquiry, the smoother the transition towards information literacy will be.

The status of librarians can also be a major stumbling block in creating mutually supportive partnerships. The work of librarians is often misunderstood and invisible. Colleagues in other departments may be unaware of librarians' areas of scholarship and expertise. In addition, on many campuses librarians do not have faculty status and do not serve on all-campus committees. If librarians can achieve high visibility and status, it will be a boon to establishing partnerships with other faculty.

At St. Olaf and Gustavus, librarians do carry faculty status, periodically teach credit-bearing courses in various areas, lead off-campus programs, receive internal grants for work in non-library as well as library disciplines, and are active in faculty governance. Librarians work with academic colleagues as peers and fellow educators. This mutual respect contributes directly to collaboration and, in turn, to students becoming more engaged in their research. Librarians and classroom faculty share the goal of preparing students to participate in scholarly conversations, to evaluate resources critically through a particular disciplinary lens, and to be capable of contributing to the discipline's scholarly discourses. In Joan Bechtel's words, "the focus is on the process of scholarly dialogue, not on the organization of the library or the production of term papers."[13]

Could it be we don't share the same agenda? In many higher education institutions there is, perhaps out of necessity, a somewhat utilitarian view of information literacy that claims it will prepare students for jobs in the workplace and help them become "information-savvy consumers."[14] On a liberal arts campus, librarians and faculty both agree that those claims are suspect; it is more important to create socially-engaged critical thinkers who are equipped not to be better workers (though they certainly may be, assuming critical thinking is of value in the workplace), but to engage in that ongoing curiosity and conversation that helps us understand the world.

Finally, there is the challenge that the integration of information literacy into the curriculum may be in competition with other worthwhile college programs and resources.[15] The number of worthy causes on our campuses–where all the faculty are committed, the students are above average, and curriculum debates can be eternal–makes it difficult for the best intentions to get the attention they deserve. This creates the need to build new coalitions and reaffirm old ones in order to get a broad base of support. The library must use a variety of strategies to bring together a number of college constituencies. Gustavus and St. Olaf are taking different paths toward information literacy–but in both cases, librarians and disciplinary faculty are focused on a shared curricular enterprise and are working together as peers and fellow educators. This mutual respect provides a landscape open to a collaborative journey towards cross-campus implementation of information literacy.

THE ST. OLAF EXPERIENCE

The challenge facing St. Olaf has been to expand a successful library-centered program into a cross-campus, fully-integrated information literacy program woven throughout the curriculum. In response, the Libraries have created an action plan with the goal:

> To design and implement an innovative information literacy program firmly grounded in an historically strong bibliographic instruction program, incorporating active cross-campus collaboration, and embedded within the framework of St. Olaf College's curriculum and overall mission.[16]

The Action Plan's priorities have been:

- To support a campus-wide focus on the research process.
- To develop and articulate a definition of information literacy appropriate for St. Olaf College and its students.

- To design and implement an information literacy program that is sensitive to disciplinary distinctions and builds on the earlier 3-tiered model of bibliographic instruction.
- To offer to faculty professional development opportunities to become familiar with a variety of information resources, explore different research strategies, and redesign courses with information literacy integrated into the course objectives.
- To collaborate with faculty and institutional offices to develop evaluation tools which allow for regular assessment of student learning outcomes and the effectiveness of the program.
- To develop a sense of shared ownership by participating constituencies.

The focus of the action plan has been to affirm, support, and integrate into a coherent program the components of information literacy that already exist at St. Olaf. Building consensus among a variety of constituencies has been key to this process.

INTERNAL STEPS

The Libraries began with several internal steps. A series of retreats was held for the library faculty to enable them to become familiar with the *ACRL Information Literacy Competency Standards for Higher Education*[17] and to discuss ways in which bibliographic instruction and information literacy are similar and/or different. Support was provided for one of the librarians to participate in the ACRL's Institute for Information Literacy's first Immersion Program. Information literacy was subsequently identified as a major focus of the Libraries' Self-Study and External Review. Librarians also crafted and adopted a draft definition of information literacy that matches the mission of St. Olaf College and specifically mentions the importance of inquiry, disciplinary perspectives, and student participation in scholarly conversations.[18]

CROSS-CAMPUS FACULTY COLLABORATION

While librarians were becoming increasingly fluent with the concept of information literacy, most faculty in other departments had yet to be introduced to it. It has, therefore, been extraordinarily important to situate the Libraries' program and the information literacy initiative in the larger landscape of the College. The Libraries recognize that a firm commitment to student-centered learning necessarily places the primary locus of an information literacy program within the disciplinary and interdisciplinary curricula. These are the vehicles through which student learning takes place. To be successful, an information literacy program must be embedded in the curricula and clearly enhance teaching and learning.

Establishing a wide-ranging, grassroots coalition among faculty is critical. To achieve this coalition, it has been important that librarians continue to be "visible and viable" in cross-campus programs and as members of major faculty committees.[19] The strong library liaison program, which is at the heart of the Libraries' instructional mission, has been key.[20] In addition, feedback and recommendations concerning information literacy have been solicited from the Faculty Library Committee, as well as campus centers and programs involved with the curriculum.[21]

Several case studies of successful partnerships illustrate the variety of routes taken to expand cross-campus ownership:

- Faculty professional development: Hands-on department specific workshops are being offered by librarians to update colleagues on information resources, Web evaluation, research strategies, and technology's impact on pedagogy.
- Departmental discussions: Liaisons have begun to meet with departments and programs that are undergoing self-studies to discuss the competencies they expect students in their major to have upon graduation. This naturally leads to a definition of information literacy from their disciplinary perspective, courses that incorporate this, assignments that support it, and areas of future library-department collaboration. With two departments, the library has been involved as an equal partner in the discussions of their redesigned majors and the revision of their research courses.
- Showcasing faculty success: In panel presentations sponsored by the Center for Innovation in the Liberal Arts (our teaching and learning center), disciplinary faculty modeled ways in which their existing curricula already incorporates most of the performance indicators of the ACRL's *Information Literacy and Competency Standards for Higher Education.* In so doing, they discovered many ways in which they plan to revise their courses and assignments.
- Curriculum development: Building on the successfully NSF-funded partnership with psychology, the librarians have been actively involved in the redesign of a second introductory course focused on empirical research.[22]
- Interdisciplinary partnership: In collaboration with the Center for Integrative Studies, which supports students with individualized majors, librarians not only serve as research mentors in the design of a major but

also collaborated with other faculty on developing a rubric for required capstone electronic portfolios and Web literacy.

- Grant-funded collaboration: As recipients of the ACRL/IMLS grant for Assessing Student Learning Outcomes in Information Literacy Programs, St. Olaf librarians will be collaborating with psychology, political science, music, and history faculty to find ways to assess how integrating information literacy into a course enhances student-learning outcomes.

In summary, partnership with faculty is essential to a successful information literacy program. Our preliminary success with this curriculum-centered initiative may be attributed to its affirmation of the ways in which information literacy is already embedded in the college's program, expansion of faculty ownership, and strengthening of library-departmental collaboration. We consider it imperative to start at a grass roots level with faculty.[23]

Why does this work? Because faculty see that this collaboration meets students' needs and enhances learning, uses their disciplinary language, not ours, and supports what they are already doing. It is worth the effort. Of particular importance is that information literacy is not an end in itself but rather one that enables other shared goals and initiatives to flourish. The advocacy and enthusiasm of faculty and students for what they have gained as a result of these initiatives and collaboration are the best testimonies possible.[24]

ADMINISTRATIVE SUPPORT

Support by the administration is integral to the success of any information literacy program, especially in terms of allocating additional resources towards a new initiative. Given the changing landscape of college programs and administrative priorities, it is essential that librarians keep administrators informed and solicit their feedback. Past St. Olaf administrations have offered significant support for bibliographic instruction. To bring the current administrators' understanding of information literacy together with library-generated initiatives, librarians have engaged in one-on-one discussions about the ways in which the current initiatives match and enhance those of the College. In addition, librarians have submitted several proposals for information literacy grants and have met with Information and Instructional Technologies personnel to discuss technological innovations and information literacy.

REALITY CHECK

The path taken has had its twists and turns. Within the Libraries, there continues to be a spectrum of opinion about the extent of library involvement with integrating information literacy into specific courses. Some library faculty believe that it may be inappropriate to launch an increased outreach program that involves librarians in curriculum development, assignment creation, and assessment. Will this be at the expense of offering quality reference service and bibliographic instruction? Is this truly an area of expertise we can offer? These opinions will vary. They may also reflect the library liaisons' differing relationships with departments.

The Libraries recognize that integrating information literacy more fully into the curriculum will differ from discipline to discipline. While the social science departments have been keen partners in collaborative curriculum development, partnership with other disciplines has been slower or taken a different route. Some disciplines may naturally use the Libraries more than others. Moreover, if library faculty are not careful to take a disciplinary perspective when discussing developmental research skills, the use of "information literacy" may be off-putting and viewed as jargon. Presenting the detailed *Information Literacy Competency Standards for Higher Education* as the answer to a department's research needs may not only be presumptuous but could result in confusion and/or resistance. With the wide spectrum of departmental philosophies and ever-present constraint of time, there is no need to attempt a total buy-in of faculty within or outside of the Libraries. Starting small and building on existing partnerships is key.

Availability of adequate staffing and funding (or lack thereof) also offers an important reality check. At St. Olaf, this initiative coincided with a cross-campus FTE cut that has affected all departments. The Libraries have been careful, therefore, to present information literacy as a program that supports and enhances faculty teaching and student learning, rather than being an add-on. However, it has been an add-on within the Libraries. Expanded collaboration has increased the teaching load and required considerable time and energy in cultivating partnerships, departmental discussions, and involvement in interdisciplinary professional development opportunities. Keeping the goals limited and manageable with the objective of showcasing successful partnerships will be important. Administrative support and assistance in procuring additional staffing and grant funding will be essential.

In summary, even with constraints and selected resistance, an information literacy program can be successfully launched if it is embedded within a disciplinary context and supported by collaboration among faculty, librarians, and other campus constituencies.

THE GUSTAVUS EXPERIENCE

Strategic planning and faculty focus groups helped shape a proposal for a National Leadership Grant from the Institute of Museum and Library Services.[25] The two-year grant, received in the fall of 1999, had two goals: first, to provide support for course design and instruction, and second, to study the results to understand the problems students encounter in a complex, hybrid print/electronic information environment. The project rests on five basic assumptions:

• Research is a valuable learning experience for undergraduates.
• Research practices are situated in disciplinary frameworks.
• Research is a complex and recursive process of discovery.
• Learning research skills is a developmental process.
• Research skills are not dependent on information formats. Critical thinking skills used in research are the same whether using print or electronic resources.

The program included three components. First, the Gustavus Library hosted two Summer Institutes for librarians from several liberal arts colleges in the region; the first focused on pedagogy and the second on assessing student learning. During the first of these institutes, librarians heard faculty perspectives from various disciplines, in small groups tackled common problems that had been gathered beforehand through e-mail communication, worked through case studies of difficult instructional situations, and brainstormed lists of active learning techniques. In the second institute, changes in the accreditation process were presented by faculty involved in a campus self-study, librarians learned how to gather and process empirical data, worked in small groups to design assessment measures, and drafted assessment plans for their libraries. Participants in both Institutes were given a packet of readings in advance and were asked to prepare reports on initiatives at their campuses. The focus was on learning from each other and collaborative discovery.

Second, the Library sponsored two intensive summer programs for a core group of Gustavus faculty chosen from across the disciplines who designed or redesigned courses with the intention of embedding in them a developmental process for learning research skills. During each of these workshop weeks, faculty discussed the problems students face and shared solutions, worked with librarians on developing resources and assignments for their courses, presented to each other ways they have sequenced activities to develop research skills, and worked with writing program and assessment experts. One of the most eye-opening activities in these workshops was learning to see from a student's perspective. Faculty jotted down a paper topic one of their students might be expected to tackle, then exchanged them, and were asked to find five good articles on the topic. This led to a lively discussion of evaluating information when the subject matter is unfamiliar–a common problem for their students. In addition to meeting all day for a week in the summer, the faculty members continue to share their transformed courses and the materials they develop and meet occasionally to continue the conversation. These faculty have become an informal but committed community that have enjoyed sharing both their frustrations and their successes. The majority of the participants reported after the workshops, that they have incorporated changes in most of the courses they teach, not just the one they focused on in the workshop. Several departments that had faculty members active in the program have begun to explore ways to create department-wide change. It is too soon to assess the long-term, campus-wide impact of this program, but initial results are encouraging.

Third, the Library is conducting research and assessment, using this collaboration as a laboratory for exploring how students negotiate their way through an increasingly complex information environment. For example, we are examining the process used by students who are successful at conducting research in a hybrid print and electronic information environment, using the protocol of a similar study conducted at Gustavus in 1990.[26] Another project underway is to develop a tool for assessing the quality of students' use of information in researched writing–not just the quality of the sources chosen, but how effectively the information is employed–with the hope that such a tool could be used by other libraries to assess their information literacy programs and document the library's impact on student learning, a challenging new focus for library assessment.[27] Finally, we hope to instill in librarians and faculty a healthy curiosity about how students learn, offer support for satisfying that curiosity through research, and create common ground where insights can be shared.

DISTINCT LANDSCAPES WITH PARALLEL PATHS

As with many liberal arts colleges, both Gustavus and St. Olaf have their own cultural landscape in which collegiality is tempered by individualism to varying degrees. Because of these distinct settings, it has seemed wiser to work within the curriculum rather than make information literacy a graduation requirement. Though faculty at both campuses subscribe to the principles of information literacy, lobbying to make it a requirement would pit those principles against many other worthy causes, and could subject already accepted values to unnecessary attack. Further, a general education requirement attached to a course or limited number of courses, counters the notion that research skills are embedded in disciplinary traditions and are developmentally built up throughout an undergraduate's career.

Another feature of the cultures at both campuses is that working from the top down is often unsuccessful. It has been important to begin at the grass roots with motivated faculty. Both colleges intentionally share ownership of information literacy with the faculty because its success will be assessed through the student learning that evolves out of their courses. The librarians will help–as they have for decades–but the faculty are the ones who will work most closely with students on the whole process of learning to ask good questions, learning to assess arguments, and learning how to turn what they've found into new knowledge.

Years ago, Joan Bechtel proposed that conversation could be a new paradigm for librarianship.[28] Promoting the conversation among librarians and faculty is a place to start. The ultimate aim of this process is to create conditions that enable students to perceive themselves as active players in the production of knowledge and to understand how, in fact, knowledge is produced so that they can continue active participation in it beyond their college years.

While the information literacy goals of both schools have concentrated on students' developmental research skills and close collaboration with faculty, their approaches have differed. St. Olaf's action plan both maps out a campus-wide program aimed at engaging students and faculty actively in disciplinary discourse, and simultaneously supports already successful partnerships so that they may serve as examples for others. The Gustavus project has a smaller focus: bringing all of the librarians and a select group of faculty across the disciplines into intense dialogue, with the anticipation that they'll learn together and be able to use the experience to infuse what they've learned into other courses and programs. Both colleges hope to share their insights about student learning with other institutions, as they take their own paths toward information literacy.

LESSONS FROM THE TRIP

Though St. Olaf and Gustavus have chosen different paths as we make the transition from bibliographic instruction to information literacy, there are some common features that any institution contemplating the trip might consider.

First, we both began by reaffirming the long-standing centrality of teaching and learning in our libraries. Information literacy is a relatively new name for a concept that has for years infused the importance of student learning into the entire mission of our libraries. With student learning as our focus, the library's mission and that of the institution fall into alignment. Sharing a mission is essential for collaborative leadership.

We built from strength. Our programs have evolved over the years; there is much to be learned from our past. Reviewing our programs' histories, we rediscovered things that would help us move forward. Embracing information literacy as if it is a new concept risks branding it as a passing fad and suggests to the very faculty who would be our staunchest allies, that libraries are just discovering values that, for many, have been intrinsic to their teaching for years. Acknowledging the past efforts of librarians and faculty in the disciplines honors those that set us on this path in the first place.

We planned our transitions with knowledge of our institutional landscapes. Each campus has its own culture, its own history, its own mission. We knew where we would find support and where we might encounter roadblocks before we started out, and mapped our paths accordingly.

We initiated conversations and we listened. If information literacy depends on cross-campus collaboration, librarians can't be the only ones doing the talking. In fact, faculty are deeply committed to student-centered learning and are often willing to go to great lengths to support it. We gave faculty an opportunity to talk to each other and to us about what their students need. This gave us a deeper knowledge of our local landscapes and helped us learn what faculty were already doing and how our work might support theirs. In turn, we discovered that faculty were willing to turn to us for help and honored our expertise. These conversations build the community feeling necessary for collaboration to flourish.

We invited the faculty to join us in modeling collaborative leadership. In the collegial environment of a college campus, leadership is a matter of starting conversations, nudging them along, and creating conditions for peers to share their expertise, their doubts, their concerns. The library is common ground for the multiple disciplines that make up an institution's culture. It is uniquely positioned as a place where such cross-campus conversations can flourish. Librarians have a crucial role to play in making collaborative leadership happen–but if we truly want our students to be information literate, we must share ownership with the faculty.

We have found at our institutions that information literacy is not new territory and that the collaborative leadership it requires is invigorating as we chart new routes toward effective student learning. It is too soon to know exactly where our paths are leading, or whether the roads we have chosen are the best routes to take. But for both institutions, information literacy has taken the road we've been on for thirty years into some interesting new terrain.

NOTES

1. Evan Farber and Tom Kirk, building on Patricia Knapp's Monteith College program, developed a strong model at Earlham College in the late 1960s. The model spread as many other librarians and faculty were trained at Earlham workshops. See Anne F. Roberts and Susan G. Blandy, *Library Instruction for Librarians,* (Englewood:

Libraries Unlimited, 1989), 2-3, and Larry Hardesty et al., *Bibliographic Instruction in Practice: A Tribute to the Legacy of Evan Ira Farber* (Ann Arbor: Perian, 1993).

2. For examples of collaborative work between librarians and faculty, see Kris Huber and Tom Kirk, eds, "Term Paper Alternatives [ongoing column]." *Research Strategies* 8 no. 1 through 11 no. 3 (1990-1993).

3. St. Olaf College Libraries, *Mission Statement*, 1994.

4. In 1990, the Libraries approved a document that defined the conceptual content of introductory, intermediate, and advanced levels of multi-tiered developmental bibliographic instruction program. This step anticipated the information literacy movement. For another example of this incremental approach, see the University of Rhode Island's program described in Mary C. MacDonald, Andree J. Rathemacher and Joanna M. Burkhardt, "Challenges in Building an Incremental, Multi-Year Information Literacy Program," *References Services Review* 28, no. 3 (2000): 240-247; see also University of Rhode Island University Libraries Instruction Services, "Plan for Information Literacy at the University of Rhode Island," [Web page], May 2000 [cited August 9, 2001]; available from the World Wide Web at http://www.uri.edu/library/instruction_services/infolitplan.html.

5. For a description of this course and lab, see Elizabeth O. Hutchins and Bonnie S. Sherman, "Information Literacy and Psychological Science: A Case Study of Collaboration," in *Library User Education: Powerful Learning, Powerful Partnerships*, ed. Barbara I. Dewey (Metchuen: Scarecrow, 2001): 183-192.

6. Odrun Peterson, "Report to the Academic Dean" (September 1956).

7. Odrun Peterson, *Library Building Program, Gustavus Adolphus College, St. Peter, Minnesota* (December 23, 1965).

8. Folke Bernadotte Memorial Library, "Strategic Plan," [Web page], January 1998 [cited August 9, 2001]; available from the World Wide Web at http://www.gustavus.edu/Library/Pubs/StrategicPlan.htm.

9. See, for example, Loanne Snavely and Natasha Cooper, "Competing Agendas in Higher Education: Finding a Place for Information Literacy," *Reference & User Services Quarterly* 37 no. 1 (1997): 53-62, and Patricia Iannuzzi, "Faculty Development and Information Literacy: Establishing Campus Partnerships," *Reference Services Review* (Fall/Winter 1998): 97-102.

10. Boyer Commission on Educating Undergraduates in the Research University, "Reinventing Undergraduate Education: A Blueprint for America's Research Universities," [Web page], 2000 [cited August 9, 2001]; available from the World Wide Web at http://notes.cc.sunysb.edu/Pres/boyer.nsf/.

11. Evan Farber, "Faculty-Librarian Cooperation: A Personal Retrospective," *Reference Services Review* 27 no. 3 (1999): 229-234.

12. See Snavely and Cooper; Larry Hardesty, "Faculty Culture and Bibliographic Instruction: An Exploratory Analysis," *Library Trends* 44 no. 2 (1995): 339-367; Gloria J. Leckie and Anne Fullerton, "The Role of Academic Librarians in Fostering a Pedagogy for Information Literacy," in *Racing Toward Tomorrow, ACRL 1999 National Conference Papers* [Web page], 1999 [cited August 9, 2001]; available from the World Wide Web at http://www.ala.org/acrl/leckie.pdf; Evelyn B. Haynes, "Library-Faculty Partnerships in Instruction," *Advances in Librarianship* 20 (1996): 191-222; Rosemary M. Young and Stephena Harmony, *Working with Faculty to Design Undergraduate Information Literacy Programs,* (New York: Neal-Schuman,

1999); and Patricia Senn Breivik, "Politics for Closing the Gap," *The Reference Librarian* 24 (1989): 5-16.

13. Joan M. Bechtel, "Conversation, a New Paradigm for Librarianship?" *College & Research Libraries* 47 no. 3 (1986): 223.

14. Patricia Senn Breivik, "Information Literacy and the Engaged Campus," *AAHE Bulletin* (November 2000): 3.

15. Abigail Loomis, "Building Coalitions for Information Literacy," in *Information for a New Age: Redefining the Librarian* (Englewood, CO: Libraries Unlimited, 1995): 128.

16. St. Olaf College Libraries, "Information Literacy: An Action Plan for Re-Visioning," [Web page], March 2000 [cited August 31, 2001]; available from the World Wide Web at http://www.stolaf.edu/library/instruction/infolit/action1.html.

17. Association of College and Research Libraries, "Information Literacy Competency Standards for Higher Education" [Web page], July 27, 2000 [cited August 31, 2001]; available from the World Wide Web at http://www.ala.org/acrl/ilintro.html.

18. St. Olaf College Libraries, "Definition of Information Literacy," [Web page], October 2000 [cited August 31, 2001]; available from the World Wide Web at http://www.stolaf.edu/library/instruction/infolit/definition.html.

19. Katherine Beaty Chiste, Andrea Glover, and Glenna Westwood, "Infiltration and Entrenchment: Capturing and Securing Information Literacy Territory in Academe," *Journal of Academic Librarianship* 26 no. 3 (2000): 207.

20. For more information on liaison programs, see Irene K. Risser, Marjorie White, and Geraldine Benson, "The Successful Liaison Program: Librarians and Classroom Faculty as Partners in the Instructional Process," *Against the Grain* 12 no. 5 (Nov. 2000): 22-24 and Helene C. Williams, "An Academic Liaison Program: Making It Work," *Against the Grain* 12 no. 5 (Nov. 2000): 1, 20-22.

21. Such centers and programs include the Center for Innovation in the Liberal Arts (focused on faculty development and technology), Center for Integrative Studies (focused on individualized student majors and interdisciplinary seminars), the Writing Across the Curriculum Program, and Information and Instructional Technologies.

22. For more information, see Chuck Huff, "A Student's Handbook for Chuck Huff's Introduction to Psychology in Great Books Format," [Web page], [cited August 9, 2001]; available from the World Wide Web at http://www.stolaf.edu/people/huff/classes/Intro/index.html.

23. David L. Smallen describes Hamilton College's grass roots approach to integrating the use of new technologies into its academic program in "Reengineering of Student Learning? A Second Opinion from Camelot," in Professional Paper Series, no. 10, *Reengineering Teaching and Learning in Higher Education: Sheltered Groves, Camelot, Windmills, and Malls,* ed. Robert C. Heterick, Jr. (Boulder, CO: CAUSE, 1993).

24. For other examples of library partnership with faculty see Hannelore B. Rader, "A New Academic Library Model: Partnerships for Learning and Teaching," *College & Research Libraries News* 62 no. 4 (April, 2001): 393-396; Mary Jane Petrowski, David Baird, and Karen Leach, "Building a Successful Collaboration: Colgate University's Collaboration for Enhanced Learning," *College & Research Libraries News* 61 no. 11 (December 2000): 1003-1005; and Dick Raspa and Dane Ward, eds, *The Collaborative Imperative: Librarians and Faculty Working Together in the Information Universe* (Chicago: Association of College and Research Libraries, 2000).

25. Folke Bernadotte Memorial Library, "Enhancing Developmental Research Skills in the Undergraduate Curriculum: A Project Supported by an Institute of Museum and Library Services National Leadership Grant," [Web page], August 2000 [cited August 9, 2001]; available from the World Wide Web at http://www.gustavus. edu/Library/IMLS.

26. Barbara Fister, "The Research Processes of Undergraduate Students," *Journal of Academic Librarianship* 18 (July 1992): 163-169.

27. For example, see Association of College and Research Libraries, "Standards for College Libraries 2000 Edition," [Web page], January 2000 [cited August 9, 2001]; available from the World Wide Web at http://www.ala.org/acrl/guides/college.html.

28. Bechtel.

The Sum Is Greater Than the Parts: Cross-Institutional Collaboration for Information Literacy in Academic Libraries

Charity B. Hope
Christina A. Peterson

SUMMARY. Collaboration for information literacy has been a strong theme in recent library literature, with much of the discussion centering on strategies for building collaborative partnerships with classroom faculty or other on-campus allies. In this paper, we explore the progress that academic libraries have made in building cross-institutional collaborations, focusing in particular on three collaborative arenas: (1) national collaborative efforts through professional organizations; (2) multi-type, local cross-institutional collaborations, such as K-12/academic library partnerships; and (3) cross-institutional collaborative efforts between peer institutions. We close with observations on how library administrators can foster collaborative initiatives through support, advocacy, and leadership. *[Article copies available for a fee from The Haworth Document Delivery Service: 1-800-HAWORTH. E-mail address: <getinfo@haworthpressinc.com> Website: <http://www.HaworthPress.com> © 2002 by The Haworth Press, Inc. All rights reserved.]*

Charity B. Hope is Science Librarian, San Jose State University Library (E-mail: cbhope@email.sjsu.edu).

Christina A. Peterson is Health Professions Librarian, San Jose State University Library (E-mail: peterson@email.sjsu.edu).

The authors would like to thank Patricia Sean Breivik, Susan Curzon, Elizabeth Dupuis, and Ilene Rockman for their participation in this investigation.

[Haworth co-indexing entry note]: "The Sum Is Greater Than the Parts: Cross-Institutional Collaboration for Information Literacy in Academic Libraries." Hope, Charity B., and Christina A. Peterson. Co-published simultaneously in *Journal of Library Administration* (The Haworth Information Press, an imprint of The Haworth Press, Inc.) Vol. 36, No. 1/2, 2002, pp. 21-38; and: *Information Literacy Programs: Successes and Challenges* (ed: Patricia Durisin) The Haworth Information Press, an imprint of The Haworth Press, Inc., 2002, pp. 21-38. Single or multiple copies of this article are available for a fee from The Haworth Document Delivery Service [1-800-HAWORTH, 9:00 a.m. - 5:00 p.m. (EST). E-mail address: getinfo@haworth pressinc.com].

KEYWORDS. Information literacy, information competency, cross-institutional collaboration, cooperation, partnerships, outreach

INTRODUCTION

Recently, collaboration for information literacy has emerged as a particular theme in the professional literature. The past year alone (2000-2001) has seen the launch of ALA past-president Nancy Kranich's "Information Literacy Community Partnerships Initiative," and the related "Community and Collaboration" series in *CRL News*, beginning with Betsy Wilson's inaugural essay, "The Lone Ranger is Dead: Success Today Demands Collaboration."[1] The sense of urgency conveyed by Wilson's subtitle perhaps resonates most strongly in academic libraries, where librarians' success or failure in helping students to learn information literacy skills depends on building and maintaining collaborative partnerships with classroom faculty. The title and content of another significant and recent publication, the collection of essays edited by Raspa and Ward entitled, *The Collaborative Imperative: Librarians and Faculty Working Together in the Information Universe*, underscores this point. In Doug Cook's literature review on librarian/classroom faculty collaboration, he notes that his literature search for librarian-campus partnerships in academic libraries revealed over 400 articles describing specific campus projects and initiatives alone (what he calls the "How We Done It Good" category).[2] Collaboration–especially collaboration on campus–is clearly a central and growing area of concern for advocates of information literacy.

Another sort of collaborative relationship–between different institutions or between librarians at different institutions–is less thoroughly addressed in the literature. It is true that a body of literature has emerged documenting local collaborative or outreach initiatives between academic librarians and K-12 teachers or school library media specialists, and that a scattering of articles have appeared in the last decade describing information literacy projects across university systems or consortia. However, in general, less attention seems to have been paid to collaborative efforts that extend beyond campus borders, perhaps because so much work remains to be done in partnership building on campus. In our opinion, however, this cross-institutional collaboration is a growing trend and an area of great promise that deserves the attention and support of librarians and especially library administrators. As Elizabeth Dupuis and Clara Fowler, speaking of possible ongoing cross-institutional development of TILT, note "Working collaboratively, sharing resources, and continuing discussions among librarians and other educators will improve our collective ability to teach our students to be information literate."[3]

This essay has two primary goals: first, to survey the cross-institutional collaborative landscape for information literacy, focusing particularly on collaborations involving academic libraries–what kind of collaborative initiatives are in place or emerging, and what these initiatives have accomplished or could accomplish. We will focus on three collaborative arenas in which academic libraries have been active: (1) national collaborative efforts through professional organizations, (2) multi-type, local cross-institutional collaborations, such as K-12/academic library partnerships, and (3) cross-institutional collaborative efforts between peer institutions, which often build upon preexisting relationships, such as programs between institutions within a system or consortium. Our second–but by no means secondary–goal is to help library administrators understand the potential benefit of cross-institutional collaborative efforts, and how to support and encourage them. In addition to the published literature and Web documentation, conversations with individuals who have shown leadership in cross-institutional collaborative efforts for information literacy augmented this work.

THE SPECTRUM:
A HOLISTIC VIEW OF CROSS-INSTITUTIONAL COOPERATION AND COLLABORATION

As we began our survey of the collaborative landscape, we uncovered what might be called a spectrum of partnering, coordinating, and collaborative activities. At one end of the spectrum we found the simple information and resource sharing activities in which librarians have always participated. At the other end: true collaboration, with common goals, shared commitment, joint work, and shared rewards. Moving across the spectrum, relationships between participants become more formal, commitments become stronger, and mutual benefit deepens.

Other writers have observed, described and distinguished between these different levels of cooperation or collaboration. For example, Doug Cook, drawing from social scientist A.T. Himmelman, identifies three distinct types of "alliances" or connections at work in libraries:

- *Networking,* an informal connection to facilitate information sharing and exchange, such as that which occurs at conferences and workshops, or through discussion lists or clearinghouses.
- *Coordination,* in which participants work separately to achieve a common, coordinated goal. In Cook's example of this level of connection, a librarian, sharing a common goal with a classroom faculty member to

teach students critical thinking skills, may work independently to develop a library instruction session for a course.

- *Collaboration,* in which participants work closely together, as a team, toward a common goal. True collaboration, according to the model Cook presents, is a more complex relationship than either networking or coordination, and "always needs some type of structure to be successful."[4]

John Graham and Ken Barter, writing in the field of social work, also define collaboration as a type of relationship that far exceeds information sharing or cooperation. A true collaboration, they write, is one in which stakeholders address common social problems and set mutually agreed-upon goals based on an articulated set of guiding principles, and in which shared resources, distributed power, shared authority and distributed risk are characteristic.[5] Betsy Wilson shares this definition, citing in particular the sharing of authority and accountability as essential elements of collaboration. It is different from cooperation or coordination, she argues, in fundamental ways: "in vision and relationships, structure, authority and accountability, and resources and rewards."[6]

However, these different levels of cooperative, partnering, and collaborative activity–Cook's *networking, coordination,* and *collaboration*–frequently overlap, and importantly, activities which could be described as simple networking or cooperation often provide a foundation for further, and more deeply collaborative activities. Therefore, although the heart of this paper is on collaboration, we also discuss this issue more holistically, and sometimes include sharing, partnering, and cooperative activities–especially those that may potentially provide a foundation or springboard for true collaborative activities–within the scope of this work.

NATIONAL COLLABORATION THROUGH PROFESSIONAL ORGANIZATIONS, COMMITTEES, AND WORKING GROUPS

In "The Learning Environment–Then, Now and Later," Hannelore Rader surveys three decades of changes in library instruction, from early work in the 1970s at Eastern Michigan University and Earlham College, to the current opportunities for librarians to "reach out to the faculty to form partnerships for collaborative teaching and integrating information literacy throughout the curriculum."[7] One aspect of the picture of the library instruction movement that emerges in her essay is the early–and growing–emphasis on information sharing and collaboration beyond campus boundaries. "Orientation Librarians" shared experiences, strategies, and teaching resources at annual conferences beginning in the 1970s and through the national Library Orientation Exchange (LOEX) clearinghouse, or through state library instruction clearinghouses.

Shared information became shared work to articulate definitions, standards, and goals for library instruction with the establishment of national and local professional committees devoted to instruction, including sections of the American Library Association and the Association for College and Research Libraries.[8]

These early trends have only increased in recent years. Rader's survey of the "national environment for information literacy" in 1999 reveals a strong emphasis on national collaborative leadership in the area of information literacy.[9] Multiple collaborative organizations are at work to, as in early days, develop standards, guidelines, and learning resources, but the scope of their contributions have now moved into the areas of support, training, research and advocacy as well. In addition, these working groups, committees, and forums are not only collaborative bodies in themselves–often with participants from industry, higher education administration, classroom faculty and the computer science field as well as libraries–they also frequently strive to spark, support, and strengthen local collaborative efforts.

Standards alone, such as those released in the past few years by the American Association of School Librarians (AASL) and the Association for College and Research Libraries (ACRL), can greatly facilitate local collaborative efforts by providing would-be partners with common goals, outcomes, strategies, and assessment tools.[10] Moreover, both AASL's "Information Power: Building Partnerships for Learning" and ACRL's "Information Literacy Competency Standards for Higher Education" explicitly promote collaboration in the adoption and implementation of the guidelines. "To provide leadership, collaboration, and assistance to teachers and others in applying principles of instructional design to the use of instructional and information technology for learning" is central to the mission and goals of "Information Power." Moreover, the call for collaboration extends beyond individual librarians or school media specialists. Local or regional organizations are expected to cooperate and partner with numerous groups for advocacy, information sharing, support and training, including "building level media specialists, state Department of Education, state government, and other state education associations and professional associations, state library and technical associations, and other groups of state-level stakeholders."[11] The ACRL Guidelines also promote a collaborative approach as the most effective: "Incorporating information literacy across curricula, in all programs and services, and throughout the administrative life of the university, requires the collaborative efforts of faculty, librarians, and administrators."[12]

Other national collaborative organizations and programs offer training and a framework of support for information literacy activities. One notable example is the Institute for Information Literacy (IIL), first envisioned in 1997 as a program of intensive education for instruction librarians, developed as a "collaboration among practicing instruction librarians, library school faculty, library directors and appropriate faculty drawn from other disciplines like computer science, psychology and education."[13] The Institute offers an annual immersion program and online "best practices" planning resources to further three goals, as outlined on the IIL Web Site. Importantly, the goals reflect the organization's commitment to furthering ongoing collaborative information literacy activities:

1. Prepare librarians to become effective teachers in information literacy programs
2. Support librarians, other educators and administrators in playing a leadership role in the development and implementation of information literacy programs
3. Forge new relationships throughout the educational community to work towards information Literacy curriculum development.[14]

Another support and training initiative, the Center for Networked Information's (CNI) New Learning Communities program, was formed to recognize, support and disseminate the work and working model of "pioneer teams" of librarians, classroom faculty, technologists, and others who are working collaboratively with networked information to develop "student-centered teaching and learning."[15] Conferences and workshops showcased the innovative teaching methods made possible through these partnerships, and, to support similar efforts on other campuses, CNI developed a workbook and video to guide the local development of New Learning Communities programs. A similar project first formed by the American Association for Higher Education and now organized and promoted through an independent, non-profit organization, is the Teaching, Learning and Technology Roundtable (TLTR) framework.[16] As excerpted from a report at Notre Dame, one of over 600 campuses nationwide to have instituted TLTRs, "A Teaching, Learning and Technology Roundtable is a large diverse group composed of those who teach, those who learn, and those who support them. This group comes together to collaboratively advocate, promote, advance, and facilitate the wise use of technology and information resources as a part of the educational mission of the University."[17] Although not explicitly tied to information literacy instruction, the TLTR Project "identifies information literacy as a building block for constructing a meaningful institutional vision for improving teaching and learning through technology,"[18] and one librarian participant noted that TLTRs offer an exceptional opportunity to participate in broad-based, sustained partnerships in which communication about instructional issues is a key benefit.[19]

One of the most far-reaching national collaborative groups–in terms of both the diversity of the participants and the potential impact of the group's activities–is the National Forum on Information Literacy (NFIL), a research, advocacy, and policy planning body composed of over 80 organizations in education, industry, government, and libraries. NFIL, which grew out of the American Library Association's Presidential Committee on Information Literacy, pursues four key areas of interest:

> The Forum pursues activities in four primary areas. Through its member organizations, the Forum examines the role of information in our lives and integrates information literacy into their programs. It also supports, initiates, and monitors information literacy projects both in the United States and abroad. NFIL actively encourages the creation and adoption of information literacy guidelines by such regulatory bodies as State Departments of Education, Commissions on Higher Education, and Academic Governing Boards. And finally, it works with teacher education programs to insure that new teachers are able to incorporate information literacy into their teaching.[20]

Of all of the collaborative working groups mentioned above, NFIL is the most inclusive. Patricia Sean Breivik, NFIL Chair, cites the diversity of the membership–and particularly the fact that most NFIL member organizations come from outside the library–as a particular strength, both in terms of the broader and more creative understanding of information literacy made possible by the intersection of multiple perspectives, and because the multi-sector endorsement increases the visibility and credibility of NFIL initiatives. "When you can give a list where the majority are not even library associations," she notes, "people listen to you in a different way."[21]

Perhaps most significant is NFIL's work to "capture the imagination"[22] of education regulatory bodies at all levels and of policy makers in local, statewide, national and international government. Widespread buy-in and support from leaders in education and government will raise the profile of information literacy nationally and open new windows of opportunity for librarians to build connections and implement programs locally.

MULTI-TYPE PARTNERSHIPS AND COLLABORATIONS FOR INFORMATION LITERACY

Cooperation between libraries of different types, such as school, academic, and public, provides information literacy programming that meets a wide variety of information needs across the lifespan. Multi-type library information literacy projects are directed at specific learning communities shared by the libraries involved in the partnerships. University libraries work with school libraries to enhance information literacy of future students, teachers and librarians. Public libraries partner with agencies representing the private sector, such as the Small Business Association, to improve information access on launching and running a business enterprise. Wide-ranging cooperatives bring educators, politicians, and community leaders together to learn about information literacy and its vital link to success in college and the workplace. Representative examples of multi-type collaborative projects are cited in the Rochester Regional Library Council (RRLC) bibliography of articles and web resources, in particular the section, "Collaboration."[23] The literature of collaborative multi-type library information competence initiatives is instructive and inspiring, offering a wide range of project descriptions, activities, tips for success, and tools for working in the community. Missing are models for assessment of the collaborative process, including needs assessment and summative or formative evaluation. These activities, which are intrinsically important to library administrators, must become key items on the research agenda of collaborative library partnerships for information literacy.

LEADERSHIP AND LEARNING RESOURCES

Nancy Kranich, past president of ALA, created a Special Presidential Committee on Information Literacy Community Partnerships (SPCILCP)[24] in 2000 to develop a level of national focus and support for multi-type collaborations. This group promulgated the charge to "bring together librarians and community members/organizations to help prepare the public to utilize information efficiently and effectively so they can fully participate in the workplace, education, community and family life."[25] An outgrowth of this initiative, the Web-based Community Partnerships toolkit, is described by Julie Todero[26] as a resource for developing, assessing, and advocating for information literacy collaborations. The toolkit describes community partnerships as collaborations that compensate for the inability of a lone organization to address problems that arise because of knowledge gaps, problem complexity, or cost-sharing needs. Attributes of best partnerships are listed, including presence of an organizational structure, shared vision, and sustainability. Kranich convened the ALA Information Literacy Community Partnerships Assembly in 2000[27] to bring together leaders in the field and librarians who are active in typical community partnerships for information literacy. Brief descriptions of selected partnership projects can be found on a related American Library Association (ALA) Web site.[28] These include stakeholders from the private and public sectors, whose objectives include increasing life-long learning skills, developing information literacy instructional guidelines, creating a continuum of information literacy standards for schools and universities, and providing in-service workshops for teachers. The Rochester Regional Library Council's (RRLC) "Information Literacy for Electronic Resources: Developing Information Literacy Skills Across Library Types,"[29] showcases models that can be used by many types of library partners. Most importantly, it includes model program statements and a detailed comparison of the ACRL and AASL information literacy standards.

RECENT EXAMPLES IN ACADEMIC LIBRARIES

Selected university library partnerships with community groups and school libraries illustrate important trends in collaborative activities for information literacy. Jill McKinstry and Anne Garrison[30] show how engaged campus initiatives for community outreach offer strong support for their libraries' programs to promote information literacy for middle school students, at-risk high school students, and community members. The evolution of academic library partnerships into collaborative programs that include activities such as audience needs assessment and identification of new constituents is described by Todero.[31] The collaborative nature of these types of partnerships, with shared goals and risk, calls for clear agreement between parties regarding responsibilities and expected benefit. For an extensive examination of one university library's partnership guidelines, see the University of Connecticut Libraries (UCL) Partnership Website[32] which includes a guide to forming partnerships, criteria for new partnerships, and a partnership proposal form.

COLLABORATION BETWEEN PEER INSTITUTIONS

Especially within the past five years, collaborative instructional initiatives and programs between academic libraries have emerged and grown. Usually, these peer-to-peer information literacy collaborations build on preexisting relationships, as libraries within a university system or consortium join together in a project to jointly address their shared objectives for student learning. That these collaborative projects have developed in parallel with the growing significance of the World Wide Web as a medium for instruction is not coincidental. Rather, the potential of Web-based instruction to transcend the physical space of a specific campus, classroom, or building seems to have provided an impetus for cross-institutional initiatives; most system-wide or consortium-wide projects and initiatives have in fact focused on the collaborative development of Web-based information literacy instruction. However, as the multi-dimensional program of the California State University Information Literacy Initiative indicates, the development of Web-based tutorials is only one area in which individual libraries can benefit from cross-institutional collaboration.

Two Web-based cross-institutional collaborative projects–one developed by a statewide consortium of academic libraries, and the other by a university system–have gained particular prominence, and serve to illustrate common characteristics and potential benefits of these initiatives. The Internet Navigator, developed by a team of librarians from the Utah Academic Library Consortium (UALC), was designed to teach college-level information literacy and Internet research skills in a student-paced, one credit course. As lead developer Nancy Lombardo writes, these skills were seen as a "ubiquitous priority at all Utah academic libraries," so it made sense to work together to craft a solution.[33] After successfully winning funding from the Utah State Higher Education Technology and Distance Education Initiative, Lombardo enlisted 13 volunteers from UALC libraries to form the development and implementation team. Lombardo notes that the strong support of UALC library directors made it possible to bring together participants from each of the 11 college and university libraries in the consortium. Participating librarians committed to the shared work of refining the course goals and content (working from a prototype developed for the initial grant application), developing the online course modules, and serving as local instructors during the implementation stage. The course, which has been offered at multiple UALC colleges and universities since it was first offered in 1996, is now in its second stage, and was revised and re-launched in January 2001 with additional grant funding from the UALC. Ongoing development remains a collaborative process through the Information for Life Taskforce, a UALC sub-group.[34]

Other than the obvious benefit that the creation of a "shared teaching resource"[35] offers in terms of each individual library's reduced development burden, the collaborative strategy undertaken by the Utah libraries offered several other advantages. As Lombardo and her co-collaborator Carol Hansen note, "the collaborative approach led to the identification of many more issues relating to Web-based and statewide course delivery than could have been identified by an individual instructor."[36] In addition, through formal and informal meetings, regular e-mail communication, and cooperative learning to build the technical and pedagogical skills needed for course development, participants experienced significant professional growth and laid the groundwork for future collaborative initiatives. Through collaboration, Lombardo and Hanson conclude, "librarians can learn together, share expertise, and develop future models for cooperative instruction."[37]

Another Web-based information literacy learning resource, the Texas Information Literacy Tutorial (TILT), was developed by the Digital Information Literacy Office at the University of Texas at Austin and funded by the University of Texas System Digital Library. In some respects, TILT is more accurately described as an example of resource sharing rather than true collaboration, as librarians and staff at the University of Texas at Austin served as the primary developers for TILT. However, there are strong collaborative elements in the development of TILT as well. For example, the development team sought system-wide input throughout the stages of development, first with an initial needs assessment survey, then through regular telephone and e-mail exchanges with instruction librarians and library administrators throughout the system. In addition, TILT was explicitly designed for potential use across the 16 universities in the University of Texas System, each with very different information environments in each library. The libraries utilize different library catalogs and subscribe to different databases. As TILT developers Clara Fowler and Elizabeth Dupuis write, "This situation had a profound impact on the development of TILT. We needed to find common ground to discuss library resources without highlighting specific interfaces, individual libraries, or campus situations."[38] As a result of this cross-library orientation, TILT focuses on general, transferable research skills, rather than specific library resources.

Within the University of Texas System, TILT is currently being used, in whole or in part, by about half of the 16 campuses. However, with the spring 2001 release of TILT under an Open Publication License, this once system-wide resource has become a tool to be freely used and adapted by librarians and educators all over the world. As of September 2001, over 400 institutions have downloaded TILT for potential use in their own instructional programs. Fowler and Dupuis comment on the rich possibilities for "future collaborations" between the growing number of individuals and institutions that are using and adapting TILT, including the creation of multiple language versions and the development of more advanced modules incorporating discipline-specific information literacy skills: "We hope additional development will be done in collaboration with other individuals and institutions . . . Among librarians TILT functions as a starting-point for conversations about new ideas in online instruction. We hope to create a forum for those interested in building upon what already exists to develop new models and methods. Collaboration among instruction librarians, other educators, and technical experts will make it possible to create the next generation of online library instruction."[39]

It is important to note that both of these collaborative Web-based products were developed to augment, rather than replace, local instructional programs. For example, The Internet Navigator is used by Lombardo's home library, the

Health Sciences Library at the University of Utah, as one component of a multi-faceted instruction program that also includes library classes and other online research guides.[40] In addition, The Internet Navigator learning experience for students includes not only online work, but also e-mail or face-to-face interactions with locally based instructors. At the University of Texas at Austin, TILT has been integrated into the library instruction program as a prerequisite to face-to-face sessions. This has allowed librarians in the classroom to focus on high-level, information literacy concepts and challenging learning activities: "We no longer have to exclude teaching certain concepts in library sessions to teach basic skills in the allotted time."[41]

Web-based projects have proven to be rich avenues for collaborative work; however, cross-institutional information literacy initiatives need not stop there. Working together, leveraging joint financial and staff resources, libraries can tackle projects that are too large, complex, or costly to approach independently. For example, both the California State University (CSU) system and the public universities in Washington State are implementing large-scale assessment projects to measure student levels of information literacy.[42] These projects go far beyond the pre and post library skills tests that librarians have commonly used, and would not likely be possible as stand-alone, single campus projects. In the CSU assessment project, for example, researchers measured information literacy skills within the context of realistic information seeking scenarios, by asking students to strategize about how they would solve hypothetical problems. The collection of this detailed data—let alone the analysis—would be a heavy burden for an individual campus.

Cross-institutional collaborative leadership, too, can have a significant impact on the effectiveness of a library's information literacy program. The CSU Information Competency Initiative, of which the assessment project is one aspect, describes a system-wide strategic initiative for information literacy. The CSU Information Competence Committee—composed of library, campus, and system faculty and administrators from a variety of levels within and across the system—drives this strategic initiative through system-wide policy planning and advocacy efforts, and through the support of campus and cross-campus information literacy projects. As an advocacy, outreach, and policy-planning group, the Information Competency Committee draws attention to and builds support for the importance of information literacy among different groups on and across the campuses, and with other educators and legislators. Through information sharing, networking, and crafting alliances with campus and system leaders, they seek to posit information literacy issues within campus and system guidelines for teaching and learning.

In addition, the Committee works with the Manager of the Information Competence Initiative—a recently established position in the CSU Chancellor's Office–to encourage the development of information literacy projects through competitive grants to fund "grass roots projects to be developed on the campuses."[43] Grant recipients are expected to share information about their projects broadly across the system–the hope is that projects will benefit from, and build upon, earlier work. The Committee funds a wide variety of projects each year, and seeks "To provide as much flexibility as possible, encourage as much creativity as possible, and not hamper the process, other than to have an accountability component built in."[44]

This system-wide collaborative planning group in turn sparks and encourages collaborative efforts on and between individual campuses. For example, despite the flexibility of the funding process, the Committee helps to steer the overall, system-wide information literacy program, by choosing to fund activities and projects with the most potential impact and cross-institutional relevance. In the past year, for example, many of the grants have gone to collaborative groups of librarians and classroom faculty working to define and integrate information learning outcomes within the departmental curricula. It is hoped that these projects will be discussed, shared, and further developed across the CSU campuses.[45]

A ROLE FOR LIBRARY ADMINISTRATORS

What does it take to build a successful collaboration? At root, the most fundamental requirements may be vision and commitment. As Steve O'Connor writes, "Any model of organized endeavor which we might care to draw up depends on the willingness of the players in that arena to agree to it. Any set of objectives will only be addressed or achieved if there is a willingness to bind together, to believe that more will be achieved through the efforts of the whole than at the individual level."[46] As Graham and Barter note, this vision and commitment needs to be shared by people with "authority and influence–power to commit resources as well as to be in a position to convince others to do the same."[47] The support of library administrators, therefore, is particularly important–"paramount," as Betsy Wilson writes.[48]

In preparing for this paper we spoke with four individuals who have shown leadership in cross-institutional collaborations in the area of information literacy: Patricia Sean Breivik, Chair of the National Forum on Information Literacy; Elizabeth Dupuis, the lead developer of TILT; Ilene Rockman, Manager of the Information Competence Initiative at CSU; and Susan Curzon, Chair of the CSU Information Competence Committee. We asked them to comment on what library administrators could do to promote and encourage these efforts. Three key issues emerged: support, advocacy, and leadership.

Support may involve the commitment of money and/or staff time to cross-institutional collaborative activities. The issue of sustained financial support may not be immediately apparent because many cross-institutional collaborative projects are initially funded through grants or one-time allocations. Sustainability becomes a question, however, and unless a commitment to ongoing support is made, an initiative may disintegrate, and gains in an information literacy program may be lost. The allocation of adequate staff time is also very important. As Elizabeth Dupuis noted, "If we start talking thinking about these bigger picture projects, there has to be an understanding that they take an enormous amount of time, not only to create, but also to sustain, and that communication takes so much time, and developing shared goals amongst all the groups that are going to use the resource and add to it."[49] Ilene Rockman and Susan Curzon also identified the provision of support as an important role for administrators. Although there may be competing priorities, Rockman noted, "We do need to realize that often resources–whether they're time, whether they're financial, whatever they may be–are a key ingredient to an initiative being completed in a timely fashion."[50]

Support may also be a matter of trust, encouragement, and appreciation. Dupuis observed that library administrators could support innovative projects through trusting in the vision and creativity of their staff, even when–or perhaps especially when–a proposed project breaks new ground or offers new kinds of benefits or outcomes that "aren't going to be the same kind of benefits we've had before."[51] Positive reinforcement, too, may support people who are already moving in the right direction. As noted by Patricia Sean Breivik, part of a library director's job is to "make sure that the people who are doing the good things feel that they're being appreciated."[52]

Advocacy, both within the library and across the campus or system, leverages the progress made in the national collaborative arena to promote local initiatives, and helps to develop an environment in which collaboration at all levels can grow. Curzon, Breivik and Rockman each stress the importance of getting wide buy-in and support for the concept of information literacy. To build this campus or system-wide commitment, library administrators need to meet with "deans, provosts, career center directors–anyone and everyone,"[53] bringing evidence–the research that has been published, the groups (especially non-library groups) that recognize the importance of information literacy, and the impact that programs can have on graduates. Library administrators have to "continue to be advocates, continue to be promoters, continue to be cheerleaders and champions of this initiative."[54] Only by working with and through other stakeholders on campus can progress be made. For example, as Curzon notes, if the goal is to form a broad-based collaboration between a high school district and a college system, allies in the university or system administration would need to be recruited to the cause:

> The question for me would be how, in the best ways, we can get the attention of the provost, and the campus president, to make this an issue, so that there is campus-wide support for this initiative beyond the library. Because obviously provosts and presidents are at meetings that library administrators are not at. When they're working with superintendents and other major educational leaders, if they are starting a discussion there, that would be very useful. Or even the chancellors of systems–dealing with the superintendents of schools, dealing with the boards of trustees of community colleges.[55]

Other aspects of a library administrator's leadership can further encourage collaborative activities, including cross-institutional collaborative activities. Collaboration for information literacy can be a part of the library's strategic or annual plans, a strategic direction that the library as a whole commits to. Leadership might include initiating and modeling cross-institutional collaboration, such as the CSU Council of Library Deans. Also, library administrators can help librarians to focus on the areas where a "window of opportunity" promises the best chance of success for a collaborative venture–perhaps the general education guidelines are up for revision, or a change in leadership on campus provides a new opportunity. Where an opening exists, an administrator's leadership and vision can help the librarian to be more effective by "facilitating their political connections to pull more off."[56]

Clearly, building successful collaborations–whether these collaborative initiatives are on campus or between institutions–may require a large investment in time, energy, and resources. The potential payoff, however, is equally large. Through collaboration we may be able to solve "the really big problems,"[57] problems like how to assess what information literacy skills our students have when they graduate, or what skills they will need on the job. Collaboration affords us the opportunity "to learn to do things better–to improve from collective experience."[58] Dialogue with those whose perspective and experiences are unlike our own allows us to gain a broader view of information literacy, and consider new, creative solutions to our shared challenges. And perhaps, as the following quote from Patricia Breivik suggests, joining in partnerships to meet our common goals has become as much a professional responsibility as it is an opportunity: "It's a matter of how we see ourselves as a profession. Are we the keepers of the library, or do we have something to offer to the larger good? If we really have something to offer, how dare we keep it to ourselves?"[59]

NOTES

1. Betsy Wilson, "The Lone Ranger Is Dead: Success Today Demands Collaboration," *College & Research Libraries News* 61, no. 9 (September 2000): 698-701.
2. Doug Cook, "Creating Connections: A Review of the Literature," in *The Collaborative Imperative: Librarians and Faculty Working Together in the Information Universe*, eds. Dick Raspa and Dane Ward (Chicago, IL: The American Library Association, 2000), 19-38.
3. Clara S. Fowler and Elizabeth A. Dupuis, "What Have We Done: TILT's Impact on our Instruction Program," *RSR: Reference Services Review* 28, no. 4 (2000): 344.
4. Cook, 26-28.
5. John R. Graham and Ken Barter, "Collaboration: A Social Work Practice Method," *Families in Society: The Journal of Contemporary Human Services* 80, no. 9 (January-February 1999): 6-14.
6. Wilson, 700.
7. Hannelore B. Rader, "The Learning Environment–Then, Now and Later: 30 Years of Teaching Information Skills," *RSR: Reference Services Review* 27, no. 3 (1999): 219-224.
8. Rader, 221.
9. Rader, 222.
10. Renee Olson, "New Info Literacy Standards Billed as Tool for Collaboration," *School Library Journal* 44, no. 5 (May 1998): 12.
11. Louise Costello, "Information Literacy Standards: FAME's Collaborative Role," *Florida Media Quarterly* 23, no. 4 (1998): 27.
12. AASL, "Information Power: Building Partnerships for Learning" [Web page] 2000-2001 [cited 16 September 2001]; available from the World Wide Web at http://www.ala.org/aasl/ip_toc.html; ACRL, "Information Literacy Competency Standards for Higher Education" [Web page] 2000 [cited 16 September 2001]; available from the World Wide Web at http://www.ala.org/acrl/ilcomstan.html.
13. Bill Miller, "A Vision for I.I.L." [Web page] 1997 [cited 16 September 2001]; available from the World Wide Web at http://www.ala.org/acrl/nili/vision.html.
14. "Institute for Information Literacy (IIL)," [Web page] 2001 [cited 16 September 2001]; available from the World Wide Web at http://www.ala.org/acrl/nili/nilihp.html.
15. Philip Tomkins, Susan Perry and Joan K. Lippincott, "New Learning Communities: Collaboration, Networking, and Information Literacy," *Information Technology and Libraries* 17, no. 2 (June 1998): 100.
16. G. Margaret Porter, "Campus-wide Partnerships Through Teaching, Learning and Technology Roundtables," *RSR: Reference Services Review* 22, no. 2 (2001): 116-121.
17. University of Notre Dame, "Proposal for the Formation of a Teaching, Learning, and Technology Roundtable at the University of Notre Dame," [Web page] 1998 [cited 16 September 2001], available from the World Wide Web at http://www.nd.edu/~tltr/tltr.htm, quoted in Porter, 117.
18. Cerise Oberman, "The Institute for Information Literacy: Formal Training Is a Critical Need," *College & Research Libraries News* 59, no. 9 (October 1998): 703.
19. Porter, 121.
20. "National Forum on Information Literacy," [Web page] 2001 [cited 17 September 2001]; available from World Wide Web at http://www.infolit.org.

21. Patricia Sean Breivik, interview by author, San Jose, CA, 24 September 2001.

22. Breivik, 2001.

23. RRLC, "Bibliography," [Web page] 2001 [cited 17 September 2001]; available from World Wide Web at http://www.rrlc.org/infolit/infolitbib.html.

24. SPCILCP, "Information Literacy Community Partnerships Initiative," [Web page] 2001 [cited 10 September 2001]; available from World Wide Web at http://www.ala.org/kranich/literacy.html.

25. SPCILCP, Charge.

26. Julie Todero, "The Community Partnerships Toolkit: A 'How To' on the President's Theme," *C&RL News* 61, no. 10 (2000): 905-907.

27. SPCILCP, Assembly.

28. ALA, "Examples of Partnerships Focused [sic] on Information Literacy," [Web page] 2001 [cited 10 September 2001]; available from World Wide Web at http://www.ala.org/kranich/examples.html.

29. RRLC, "Information Literacy," [Web page] 2001 [cited 17 September 2001]; available from World Wide Web at http://www.rrlc.org/infolit/infolit.html.

30. Jill McKinstry and Anne Garrison, "Building Communities @ Your Library," *C&RL News* 62, no. 2 (2001): 165-7, 186.

31. Julie Todero, "Reaching Out to the Community: Models that Work," *C&RL News* 61, no. 9 (2000): 789-792.

32. UCL, "Partnerships," [Web page] [cited 17 September 2001]; available from World Wide Web at http://spirit.lib.uconn.edu/information/PartnershipDocument.html.

33. Nancy Lombardo, "The Internet Navigator: Collaborative Development and Delivery of an Electronic College Course," *PNLA Quarterly* 63, no. 1 (Fall,1998): 12.

34. Nancy Lombardo, "About the Internet Navigator Online Course," [Web page] 2001 [cited 17 September 2001]; available from World Wide Web at http://medstat.med.utah.edu/navigator/about.htm.

35. Nancy Lombardo, "The Internet Navigator: Collaborative Development and Delivery of an Electronic College Course," 12.

36. Carol Hansen and Nancy Lombardo, "Toward the Virtual University: Collaborative Development of a Web-Based Course," *Research Strategies* 15, no. 2 (1997): 75.

37. Hanson and Lombardo, 75.

38. Clara S. Fowler and Elizabeth A. Dupuis, "What Have We Done: TILT's Impact on our Instruction Program," *RSR: Reference Services Review* 28, no. 4 (2000): 344.

39. Fowler and Dupuis, 348.

40. University of Utah, "Spenser S. Eccles Health Sciences Library: Educational Materials," [Web page] 2001 [cited 17 September 2001]; available from World Wide Web at http://medstat.med.utah.edu/library/edumaterials/edumat.html.

41. Fowler and Dupuis, 345.

42. "Information/Technological Literacy Assessment Group Home Page," [Web page] 2001 [cited 17 September 2001]; available from World Wide Web at http://depts.washington.edu/infolitr/; "CSU Information Competency Assessment Project Home Page," [Web page] 2001 [cited 17 September 2001]; available from World Wide Web at http://www.csupomona.edu/~kkdunn/Icassess/ictaskforce.html.

43. Ilene Rockman, telephone interview by author, San Jose, CA, 24 September 2001.

44. Rockman, 2001.

45. Rockman, 2001.

46. Steve O'Connor, "Beyond Cooperation in Australia," *Library Hi Tech* 17, no. 3 (1999): 266.

47. Graham and Barter, 9.

48. Wilson, 700.

49. Elizabeth Dupuis, telephone interview by author, San Jose, CA, 23 September 2001.

50. Rockman, 2001.

51. Dupuis, 2001.

52. Breivik, 2001.

53. Rockman, 2001.

54. Rockman, 2001.

55. Susan Curzon, telephone interview by author, San Jose, CA, 26 September 2001.

56. Breivik, 2001.

57. Wilson, 700.

58. Graham and Barter, 9.

59. Breivik, 2001.

Technology and Innovation
in Library Instruction Management

Beth S. Woodard
Lisa Janicke Hinchliffe

SUMMARY. Faced with new educational technologies, the changing nature of access to information, and advances in understandings of how people learn, instruction managers seek strategies for incorporating technology into teaching and learning. This article presents theoretical frameworks relating to technological change and innovation, and then discusses how those theories can be applied to the management of instruction programs in libraries. The theories are also applied to understanding the integration of technology into teaching and learning. Discussion of specific examples highlights both the incorporation of technology into teaching and learning, as well as the use of technology to manage instruction programs. *[Article copies available for a fee from The Haworth Document Delivery Service: 1-800-HAWORTH. E-mail address: <getinfo@ haworthpressinc.com> Website: <http://www.HaworthPress.com> © 2002 by The Haworth Press, Inc. All rights reserved.]*

KEYWORDS. Technology, innovation, library instruction, information literacy, management

Beth S. Woodard is Central Information Services Librarian and Associate Professor of Library Administration, University of Illinois, Urbana, IL 61801.

Lisa Janicke Hinchliffe is Coordinator of Information Literacy Services and Instruction and Associate Professor of Library Administration, University of Illinois, Urbana, IL 61801.

[Haworth co-indexing entry note]: "Technology and Innovation in Library Instruction Management." Woodard, Beth S., and Lisa Janicke Hinchliffe. Co-published simultaneously in *Journal of Library Administration* (The Haworth Information Press, an imprint of The Haworth Press, Inc.) Vol. 36, No. 1/2, 2002, pp. 39-55; and: *Information Literacy Programs: Successes and Challenges* (ed: Patricia Durisin) The Haworth Information Press, an imprint of The Haworth Press, Inc., 2002, pp. 39-55. Single or multiple copies of this article are available for a fee from The Haworth Document Delivery Service [1-800-HAWORTH, 9:00 a.m. - 5:00 p.m. (EST). E-mail address: getinfo@haworthpressinc.com].

The challenge facing librarians in the new millennium is not that new educational technologies are being created, nor that the tools used to access information are constantly changing in nature and scope, nor that enhanced understandings of how people learn has caused us to change the way we teach. The challenge is that all three areas are converging at once: the ensuing impact has made many of us reel as we attempt to manage the resulting changes in our instruction programs. While one can say that this convergence was predictable and that many good instruction programs already have been adapted, instruction librarians continue to struggle with these issues and feel an urgent need to adopt new educational technologies for instructing our users as quickly as possible.

This article will present theoretical frameworks relating to technological change and innovation and discuss how those theories can be applied to the management of instruction programs in libraries. The theories will then be applied to understanding the integration of technology into instruction programs. Specific examples will discuss both the incorporation of technology into teaching and the use of technology to manage instruction programs.

THEORETICAL FRAMEWORKS

Theoretical frameworks provide a powerful lens through which to make sense of everyday experiences and observations. They provide a way to organize and explain that which might otherwise appear mystifying or without reason. By providing this framework for understanding, such theories also then provide a framework for developing and implementing strategies to direct and manage our experiences. With respect to making sense of the incorporation of technology into instruction programs in libraries and how technology can be used to manage those instruction programs, two theories are particularly useful. The first is the theory of technological automation and the second is the theory of the diffusion of innovations.

Theory of Technological Automation

The theory of automation and its application to educational technologies was succinctly discussed by Steven W. Gilbert in his *Change* article "Making the Most of a Slow Revolution." Gilbert discusses three stages of technology integration into teaching: (1) automating administrative operations, (2) enhancing current tasks, and (3) changing core functions. In automating administrative operations, technology is integrated into management tasks such as scheduling in order to increase productivity. In enhancing current tasks, technological tools are found which improve activities that are currently underway but which do not substantially alter how the tasks are conceptualized and conducted. For example, one might create a computer slide show presentation to replace a series of overhead transparencies. In the final stage, changing core functions, tasks and activities are re-conceptualized and, indeed, new goals and activities are developed.

Theory of the Diffusion of Innovations

In the now classic text *Diffusion of Innovations*, Everett M. Rogers details how ideas and approaches come to be adopted by groups of people. Two components of this discussion are particularly useful for understanding adoption of technological innovations: (1) characteristics of an innovation that effect the rate of adoption, and (2) characteristics of those who adopt innovations.

The rate of adoption of an innovation is effected by many variables including the characteristics of the innovation. These characteristics are the relative advantage of the innovation compared with the status quo, the compatibility with the values, experiences, and needs of adopters, the complexity or how difficult the innovation is to understand or use, the trialability or degree to which the innovation can be piloted, and the observability or degree to which the results are able to be observed by others. While the relative advantage, compatibility, trialability, and observability of an innovation are positively related to the rate of adoption, the complexity of an innovation is negatively related to the rate of adoption.[1] Important to note is that these characteristics are to be understood as characteristics of the innovation as perceived by the potential adopters, and not necessarily the characteristics of the innovation as they might be determined through empirical research studies.

To further understand the adoption of an innovation, it is useful to also understand the characteristics of those who adopt innovations. According to Rogers, "individuals can be classified into adopter categories on the basis of when they first begin using a new idea."[2] The adopter categories identified by Rogers are as follows: innovators, early adopters, early majority, late majority, and laggards. Research studies have found that innovators are venturesome and bring ideas into a social system, are willing to take risks, and are able to cope with uncertainty when adopting an innovation. Early adopters function as opinion leaders within a social system and serve as role models for others when adopting an innovation. The early majority is characterized by deliberateness in adopting innovations and thinks carefully before adopting a new idea. The late majority is more skeptical and cautious in adopting innovations and waits to adopt until an innovation becomes the norm of the social system. Laggards are traditionalists and are the last to adopt an innovation; they may appear to be resistant to change but the decision to wait is based on the desire for certainty that the innovation will not fail.[3]

Though one must avoid the trap of oversimplification, instruction librarians should think about the relationships among the perceived characteristics of a given innovation, the adopter categories represented in their library staff, and the stage of technological integration relative to their instruction programs. Careful consideration of these theories can help one develop an understanding of how and why some technologies are quickly incorporated into instruction programs in libraries while other innovations languish and are not adopted.

TRADITIONAL INSTRUCTIONAL STRATEGIES

Though this article has thus far realistically assumed that it is desirable to adopt new technologies into teaching in order to improve instructional programs, it is worthwhile to reflect upon traditional instructional approaches. A good understanding of the traditional approaches is needed in order to discuss the relative advantage, compatibility, and complexity of any new innovation that might be introduced.

Library instruction programs have long offered library tours to introduce users to the physical organization of the library. Such tours, however, challenge the understaffed library as in-person tours consume large amounts of staff time relative to the learning outcomes attained. Attempts to alleviate staffing difficulties involving volunteers have mixed results, as volunteers may adjust the instructional content of the tour relative to their own comfort in the library. In addition, though the traditional tour orients users to the physical library, the library is increasingly less physical and more virtual, and so the tour of the physical facility is an increasingly anemic experience of the true extent of services and collections.

Classroom instruction sessions offer the opportunity to more fully present users with the services and resources which the library offers to assist them with their research needs. For academic librarians, the ideal is a classroom instruction session developed collaboratively with the instructor around a particular research project. Unfortunately, differences between faculty and librarian cultures, lack of shared learning goals, and time and staffing constraints limit the scope and depth of such collaborative relationships. True collaborative experiences with teaching faculty elude many librarians who then struggle with only fifty-minute sessions as the sole opportunity to present library instruction. Though librarians have been frustrated with the one-shot session for years, even before the advent of electronic resources, the changes in technology have only exacerbated this frustration. It was difficult to teach the use of the library card catalog and paper indexes in a fifty minute session and it is even more difficult, perhaps even impossible, to cover the full range of possibilities available in today's electronic environment in that limited amount of time. The challenge of this situation is increased when one considers that, even if a librarian is able to *teach* about all of the resources users might need, it is impossible for a library user to *learn* about all of the resources at the pace that such a presentation would demand. Active learning techniques, arguably necessary for learners to truly understand electronic information resources, will be neglected in the attempt to stuff as much content as possible into the one-shot session.

Personal assistance to individuals remains the reference librarian's stock and trade. This one-on-one encounter provides a tutoring-like learning environment during which the librarian can discern the learning needs of the individual and provide immediate instruction and guidance. The form that personal assistance takes, however, is changing. As more and more users access library information from outside of the library building, librarians are faced with the challenge of figuring out how to provide this one-on-one assistance through technology tools such as electronic mail and chat.

Handouts and guides have also been a standard instructional strategy in libraries for many years. Such handouts list sources on a particular topic, explain what indexes are available, describe how to use a particular source, or detail the steps to take in finding particular kinds of information, and are often distributed during classroom instruction sessions, as well as being made available throughout the library in display racks. The challenge of handouts as an instructional strategy is two-fold: keeping the information current and encouraging library users to consult the handouts at the appropriate times. Keeping handouts current and understandable is made more challenging by the rapid pace of change spurred by technological developments. For the user who accesses library resources from outside of the library itself, the challenge of providing the guides simultaneously with the electronic resources themselves can be daunting.

INFRASTRUCTURE AND SUPPORT

Many of the known limitations of traditional instructional strategies relate to issues inherent in the traditional approaches themselves. However, there are also limitations and issues which relate to the existing infrastructure and support which is found in a given organization. Innovators and early adopters who have a robust infrastructure, have at their disposal then, the necessary tools and resources to move forward with innovative practices and strategies. Unfortunately, in other cases, the needed infrastructure and support services are not provided–perhaps purposively, perhaps not–and so the individuals who are attempting to implement innovations are stymied in their efforts. A few examples will help make this more clear.

Fundamental to managing and teaching with technology is access to technology. Librarians who are fortunate to have the support of a well-staffed and well-trained systems department find themselves with access to ever-increasing technological options and opportunities to collaborate with other librarians in using that technology. Unfortunately, for many libraries, such technological support is not a reality. Lacking well-qualified staff internally, many libraries rely on campus technology support units for computing infrastructure and support. Too often, these campus units are unable to provide the intensive levels of support the library needs in order to innovate and so the focus becomes maintaining existing and important technological tools such an online catalog system and access to electronic databases. Programming resources for developing interactive instructional tutorials are not always available. In some cases, the technology may be available on campus, but because the library does not generate credit-hours, certain technologies, such as WebCT, may not be available to the library for use in its instruction programs. Such policies and procedures limit access as effectively as not having the technology at all.

Facilities also provide challenges for many librarians seeking out innovative practices. While many libraries have demonstration classrooms, many are not able to provide an active, hands-on learning environment for students. In other cases, the library does have sufficient space and technology for a hands-on classroom, but is unable to move beyond traditional classroom arrangements by using laptops and wireless network connections because the facility lacks wireless capabilities.

It is easy to see, then, how the theories of automation and the diffusion of innovations may be difficult to implement in actuality. Real-life challenges relating to infrastructure and support can make it difficult or impossible for a desired innovation to be implemented.

INTEGRATING TECHNOLOGY INTO INSTRUCTION PROGRAMS

Given the challenges found in traditional approaches to instruction, the changing ways that users conduct library research, and newer understandings of teaching and learning, it is not surprising that librarians are looking to new educational technologies to help instruct users. Depending on the characteristics of a particular technology, the characteristics of the instructors who are the potential adopters of the technology, and the degree to which a library's instruction program as a whole has integrated technology, a given technology may be easily adopted, be adopted slowly but steadily, or fail to be adopted beyond initial pilot attempts. A final complicating factor will be real-life limitations in infrastructure and support.

Integrating Technology into Managing

Looking back to the theory of technological automation and the three stages of technology integration discussed in the first part of the article is useful for identifying a common approach to technology integration for managing instruction programs. The first stage of technology integration, automating administrative operations, has the relative advantage over previous approaches of increasing both the efficiency and accuracy of management tasks. Scheduling rooms using a calendaring software program (e.g., meetingmaker) and keeping statistics in a spreadsheet (e.g., QuattroPro) or database (e.g., Microsoft Access) are two activities that have been automated in most libraries. These technological innovations have the relative advantage over previous paper-based systems of increasing the manipulations one can do with the data while at the same time increasing access to the data. As replacements which do not require a re-conceptualization of the instruction program per se, these technologies were easily seen as compatible with existing practices, and the results of using these technologies could be easily observed in other libraries or organizations. For some libraries, however, the complexity of utilizing a calendaring software program has proved a difficult or insurmountable hurdle for this technology innovation to be adopted. In such circumstances, unless the instruction librarian is an innovator who is willing to accept a high degree of uncertainty and risk, calendaring will likely remain a paper-based activity.

An area that has seen a fair amount of success with respect to innovation adoption is online registration for open workshops. Through either registration software programs or simple mailto links, online registration has made it easier for librarians to manage enrollment and more convenient for users to register. The ability to send out e-mail reminders of the workshops, create waiting lists, and offer online evaluation forms for workshops has further enhanced the library's ability to reach out to users who might not otherwise take advantage of open workshops.

By comparison, another component of managing an instruction program–staff development–has not been automated in most libraries. Though the content of such staff development programs includes technology (e.g., electronic databases, Web searching, and file transfers), the delivery of that content continues to use strategies and approaches developed before today's technology-intensive environment. Many technological tools exist which could be used to provide staff development in a library. Most obvious is online courseware. Software packages such as WebCT and Blackboard, which were developed as online learning environments and purchased by many campuses for teaching students, could be re-purposed to provide an online learning environment for staff development. What barriers exist to using these courseware packages to enhance staff development offerings? The primary barriers in this example relate to complexity and trialability. Such courseware packages can be difficult to learn and require a great deal of time to understand and then employ in developing staff training materials. Because of the learning curve, it is also not easy to experiment with or trial the courseware. Finally, these factors, combined with the relatively small population of learners for such staff development materials, indicate a relative advantage to existing practices rather than to the potential technological innovation.

A final area of technological innovation in managing instruction programs is still in its infancy but holds great potential for increasing the efficiency and effectiveness of instructional preparation. Library intranets have the potential of serving as repositories of instructional materials created by librarians for instruction sessions. A well-structured, easy to use repository can be an instructional knowledge bank that allows each librarian to utilize the instructional materials created by their colleagues. In some cases, a more expansive approach can be envisioned. A consortium of libraries could create a shared online repository. Or, a vendor could serve as a repository of instructional materials that relate to the company's products.

Managing the Integration of Technology into the Instruction Program

In addition to managing the instruction program through technology, the instruction librarian must also manage the integration of technology into the instruction program. The challenge here is that focusing on technology alone, with inadequate attention to other components of the planning process, will lead to marginal gains and individual and organizational frustration.[4] The instruction librarian must remember that technology is a means to an end and is not an end in itself. Planning for technology requires attending to the objectives of instruction, matching the technology to the instructional goals, and developing a learning environment which is conducive to the appropriate application of that technology.

Planning for technology integration comes down to answering the question–why are we adopting these new technologies and changing teaching strategies? What are we trying to do? We need to keep in mind that the goal is still to foster information literacy, to help people develop lifelong skills for seeking information. The challenge is to use technology that is true and honest to how people learn. There are many potential technologies–the key is to choose the appropriate ones. Instruction librarians must be certain to use technology because we *plan* and not just because we *can*.

The design of instruction, especially in determining the kind of instructional mix appropriate, depends on a number of factors: time, equipment, facilities, and personnel available; established short range and long range goals for technology; institutional support and communication patterns; and the objectives of the instruction. One must examine what technology might assist and what the institution must sacrifice to accomplish those goals. Which combination of face-to-face meetings, independent work, and telecommunications are best for what purposes? How can technology be used most effectively? What can be replaced or enhanced and what needs to be reconfigured? What often seems to work best is a mixture of conventional and new technological strategies. In creating a strategic approach to integrating technology into the instruction program, librarians need to remember the seven principles for good practice in undergraduate education: encourage contact between students and faculty; develop reciprocity and cooperation among students; use active learning; emphasize time-on-task; provide rich and rapid feedback; set and communicate high expectations; and respect different talents and styles of learning.[5]

Instruction managers need to recognize that there will be apathy and resistance toward change, partly because people fear that the skills they have worked so hard to develop and maintain will no longer be valid. Training staff in new instructional technologies is an important step in managing the transition of change. Establishing good patterns of communication to inform people of what is happening and allowing individuals time to ask questions is another step in managing change. Getting broad-based support for new approaches is critical to success.

Just as librarians and faculty must develop collaborative communities within the learning environment of the classroom setting, so must the institution develop a collaborative community for technology. System-wide reconfigurations of the learning environment cannot happen with fragmented support service. Technology experts, computer and network professionals, faculty, educational development experts, and librarians must work cooperatively to create an infrastructure and a plan that works for everyone. Kozma and Johnston note that innovations which are the most successful involve the participation of others and evolve from an identified organizational need.[6]

Instruction managers must learn to be advocates for users, and get involved in the selection of databases and software. This means getting appointed to committees that choose databases or at least developing mechanisms to provide input for decisions about database selection, especially if those decisions are made consortially. Instruction librarians and front-line reference staff know best how users approach research questions and the problems they encounter in conducting searches. Librarians also need to be more vocal in demanding online tutorials and help screens from database vendors and software developers, so that librarians do not have to develop "how to use this tool" tutorials, but can spend more time on conceptual instruction or problem-solving applications.

Librarians need to take a larger role in training each other and sharing tips for using technology. It is of little benefit to develop good learning communities for students if the librarians themselves do not have access to the same kind of environment to foster learning about what is good practice, what has been adopted successfully, and what has not.

Integrating Technology into Teaching

Integrating technology into teaching takes the integration of technology into the instructional program one step further. Individual instructors must make decisions about which technologies they will use and how. In making these decisions, the individuals may wholeheartedly embrace any new technology, may employ a more cautious approach but still experiment somewhat, or may wait until a technology is proven effective and widely-used before adopting it. An individual's approach to adopting technology will indicate which of the adopter categories most accurately describes that person. For the instruction manager, observing whether individuals tend to be innovators, laggards, or in between will help in deciding which individuals might be most comfortable testing out a new technology that is being considered for adoption.

There is a danger in taking on more than one can handle, spending enormous amounts of time with new technology which changes rapidly, and ignoring completely traditional methods and sources which may be more effective. Gilbert notes that "no form of distance education or any other widely applicable educational use of information technology has yet proved so much more effective and/or less expensive than 'traditional' forms of teaching and learning as to become a complete replacement for them."[7] Successful adopters of new technology are not likely to start out with sweeping or global goals. They usually start with a small, definable population and purpose, and standardized curriculum.

Those who resist change fear loss of their mastery of current systems and devaluation of their knowledge of traditional sources and teaching skills. Because of the high developmental costs of instructional technology in terms of time and effort, many are hesitant to be forerunners in implementing technology. Some individuals have developed tutorials for third party software, only to be frustrated by a complete revision of the end-user interface. For many reluctant adopters, the risks of investing heavily in learning new technology often appear to be too great. In a video titled *Tactics of Innovation*, Joel Barker goes through ten tactics or suggestions to get new ideas accepted and used. Essentially, the tactics focus on reducing risks of failure by making sure that advantages outweigh disadvantages, that the ideas are simple and divided into small segments, that ideas are comfortable to communicate, compatible with goals, and believably presented. He concludes that the innovation must be reliable, easy to try out and easy to back out of. Instruction managers should encourage first time technology adopters to start with relatively stable topics, and begin with replacement strategies.

The first strategy for adopting new technology is to substitute new for old by replacing existing programs and services. One must be careful to be sure that the glitz of the technology is not the primary reason for the replacement. Often the old technology or method is equally, or even more, effective. Very simple examples are the replacement of chalkboards with overheads, and overheads with presentation software and computer-drive projection systems. Note however, that chalkboards are still effective and allow for more spontaneity than instruction using presentation software programs. When an instruction manager asks an instruction librarian who tends to be a technology-adoption laggard to adopt a substitution strategy, he or she must be very clear to articulate the purpose of the substitution. What benefits will the librarian gain? What benefits will the student gain?

Those instructional events which call for relatively passive intellectual involvement by the user, employ screen events that are largely determined by the software developer, focus on developer-determined interaction between user and machine, or are aimed at rote memory are the easiest to incorporate into new technologies. For example, in-person tours are easily replaced with taped tours, video cassette recordings, or online tours, if all that is done is adapt an already established script in a linear fashion to a different medium. Existing handouts, bibliographies, course materials and so on can simply be modified for the Web, either as PDF files or with simple HTML coding. Placing an existing handout on finding statistical sources which is organized in two parts–by type of material and by subject–onto the Web is an easy replacement strategy. Similarly, asking librarians to add their e-mail addresses in addition to their phone numbers on an instructor's paper syllabus is another easy replacement strategy.

The linear, passive study of textual material, while an appropriate use of technology, does not utilize the full capacity of the medium. Computers should not be used merely as electronic page turners. Technology has the capacity to provide a guided exploration of a learning environment, giving multiple representations and dimensions of the content. The best use of technology provides non-linear access to information where students can enter the learning environment at any point, and criss-cross the conceptual landscape many times.

The next phase of adopting new technology is to more fully utilize the technology's capacity to make available new and better ways of teaching by creating cooperative and independent learning systems. Kozma and Johnston suggest seven ways that computers can change what students can learn in the classroom: from reception to engagement, classroom to the real world, text to multiple representation, coverage to mastery, isolation to interconnection, products to process, and mechanics to understanding in the laboratory. The instruction manager's challenge then is to help instruction librarians understand how the technology in question can be used to its best advantage. How can the technology expand the ability of the student to understand and comprehend?

While traditional models of learning emphasize students passively absorbing information from textbooks, professors, and computer screens, other models of learning emphasize active engagement in the construction of knowledge. Enhanced systems require relatively active intellectual involvement by the user and place much of the control of the outcome in the hands of the user. The goal of this kind of application is the accomplishment of relatively creative tasks. Many hours of use are required before a user experiences all the capabilities of this type of software. As stated by Poole, "Computer learning should invite interaction. This interaction can take many forms, among which might be: responding to questions; finding answers to questions; completing verbal tasks; reacting to, and interacting with, simulations; browsing databases containing textual, visual, and audial materials; accessing data for inclusion in other research products."[8]

The classroom environment does not necessarily facilitate the transfer of learning to a different context. In many educational settings, "the reality that all teachers surely recognize–that students do not transfer knowledge across different settings, that there is a problem in relating theory to practice, i.e., that knowledge does seems to be context-related"[9] is painfully obvious. Technology assists with this difficult challenge by simulating different contexts within the classroom. Educational technologies can provide access to multiple approaches through hypermedia linking. By using hypermedia, students can create meaning for themselves through the ability to move about, choose what to explore next, and put things into context. Poole states this well:

> Hypertext systems are intricate webs on connected electronic data, rather like the neural network that we call the brain. When we think, we often rely on association to direct us along the path that represents the development of our ideas or trains of thought. The more experience and learning we have absorbed in the past, the more associations we will be able to draw-on, hence the value of education. A hypertext system is designed in such a way that the user can jump from one data item to the next in a semi-random, *nonlinear* order.[10]

In addition to providing alternative avenues, a greater number and variety of case studies or examples can be made available to the learner who can explore those most meaningful to him or her.

Instead of focusing on merely covering a topic, educational technology can also help focus a student's time on task, allowing them to become masters of a subject area and improve their understanding. Providing supplementary time for practice increases a student's level of achievement. But simply allocating time is not enough; students need to be actively and productively engaged in appropriate tasks and they need to know if they are performing these tasks correctly. In a technological-rich learning environment, novices can be given extensive guidance and corrective feedback to reduce their errors, while competent students can hone skills and broaden their knowledge of new and unusual situations to master the material more completely. Since learners can absorb and integrate only a limited amount of new information at one time, electronic technologies can improve learning by distributing activities across time to improve long-term retention.

Though learning has often been considered to be a solitary act, educators now realize that learning is often a collaborative activity, and that ideas tend to be examined within the context of other ideas and events. Educational technology can support collaborative problem-solving and interactive decision-making. Electronic mail exchanges, bulletin board systems, voice messaging, and electronic mentoring are just a few technological advances that allow interaction among students and between students and teachers. About twenty percent of learners need verbal processing, talking, discussion, opportunities to learn with others, cooperative learning methods, role playing, and personification techniques in order to best learn material. Approximately another third of learners benefit from listening to a variety of viewpoints, so discussion is important to their learning as well.[11]

Instruction managers should challenge instruction librarians to explore ways that technology can enhance existing instruction through active engagement, through increasing time on task and examples, and by improving interactions with others. In the example mentioned above of the handout on statistical resources, the instruction librarian could create a procedural flow chart that would take a student step-by-step through the kinds of questions they need to answer and then link them to the appropriate part of the bibliography for their research question. For example, a Web page might say: "Do you need time-series data or cross-sectional data?" If the student chooses cross-sectional data, he or she would be taken to the part of the bibliography that would list resources which include statistics in cities, counties, and states. The librarian could create pop-up windows that would define unfamiliar terms. Students could more effectively use this kind of bibliography in comparison to the printed one. Similarly, the librarian who was asked to provide students with an e-mail address could include the electronic mail address on the class Web-based syllabus with a mailto link, making it easier for the student to contact the librarian. While these might seem like relatively small changes in the use of technology, they represent a big shift in using the capability of technology to enhance student access and learning.

The final phase of incorporating technology into instruction involves an enterprise-wide redesign of educational systems characterized by unmediated user access to source materials, data, and/or tools; opportunities for apprenticeships and cooperative learning; and opportunities for self-paced learning where appropriate.[12] What instructional technology does best is "deliver content and provide access to information and to other people. It allows students and faculty to find and manipulate information, to take new meaning, and to have new (learning) experiences. In the near term, however, the demand for faculty guidance and intervention, for faculty mentoring, is more likely to increase than to decrease."[13] These restructured environments require librarians and instructors to serve as mentors and guides for students. "Instead of being the expert, posing the problems and knowing all the answers ahead of time, the teacher helps students as they engage problems of their own choosing or problems with varying solutions depending on the parameters set by the student."[14]

There is a shift here in the learner's role from recipient of knowledge to constructor of knowledge. These reconfigured learning environments rely heavily on constructivist learning theories which emphasize student construction of their own knowledge and understanding of a topic. In constructivist philosophy, learning is a social, collaborative activity.

In this phase, the instruction manager needs to challenge librarians to think beyond the original context and fully explore the technology. In the example of the instructional handout for statistical information, the fully developed instructional Web site would bear little resemblance to the original simple bibliography, and might include a search function that would allow subject searching for the person who knows that he wants data on the automotive industry, as well as a sophisticated flow chart that requires the student to make knowledgeable choices and guides the student in his search for statistical information. This resource could be used again and again as the student has other statistical needs, not just for a particular course assignment. In the example of offering an e-mail address, the librarian could ask the course instructor if he or she could be added to the class discussion list and actively monitor questions about the research project and about finding materials. The librarian would actually be reaching out to the student in response to student needs rather than the student having to approach the librarian. In both examples, the technology has been more fully utilized to increase student activity and interaction with the content and/or with others, in a way that was not possible without the use of technology.

Technology as Content

When teaching technology as part of the instructional content, instruction librarians follow the typical adoption patterns previously identified. When technologies are replacements for resources that have traditionally been provided by libraries, the library profession has been quick to adopt these into the content of instructional sessions. Librarians have not argued about whether we should teach online catalogs, Web-based indexes, or even electronic books. We initially disagreed with those early adopters who taught searching the Web and evaluating Web resources as being beyond the boundaries of our library world, but even the most reluctant instruction librarian has been convinced that this is indeed our venue, as an extension of finding and evaluating information. Innovators and early adopters are now challenging us to consider whether we should teach the use of citation management software programs (e.g., EndNote), Web development, presentation software, or digitizing materials. Clearly the debate on whether librarians have a role in teaching users what to do with the information they have found and how to manipulate it is one that has not yet reached its conclusion. Whether these technologies that allow users to manipulate information will challenge us to change the core functions of a library's instructional programs is yet to be decided.

CONCLUSION

Research shows that technology, when applied correctly, can enhance learning. Technology transfers control to the learner by adding choices of how, when and where they can access learning opportunities. It can reduce barriers imposed by affective factors on a single time, place, and mode of learning. It allows learners to gain access to people, information, and experience and to make learning a personal experience.[15]

Some characteristics of correct application of technology for learning include engaging students actively in learning, providing context and real-life environments, providing alternative approaches to learning, allowing a variety of representations, improving opportunities for time-on-task to increase understanding and mastery, increasing student/faculty interaction as well as student/student collaboration, and emphasizing the process and problem-solving.

A continuum of approaches to adapting technology ranges from replacing discrete portions of current instruction to enhancing instruction, and ultimately, to restructuring the learning environment. This process of innovation is effected by the organization culture, support infrastructure, and individuals with different innovation characteristics. By following models proven effective elsewhere, librarians can begin immediately to use the replacement strategy and plan the enhancement of instructional activities.

The instruction manager has a crucial role in the adoption of technological innovations for instruction. At a basic level, the instruction manager must examine the existing technical infrastructure and support structure in order to determine whether it is adequate to support current projects while allowing innovators and early adopters to explore new uses of technology. As new projects are implemented, the instruction manager must carefully monitor support levels to ensure that innovations are sustainable, not only in a pilot project mode, but into full-scale implementation. Finally, keeping in mind the later adopters, the instruction manager needs to help reduce the perceived risks of adopting innovations. The theory of automation can serve as the basis for assisting the later adopters with slow but steady technology integration–starting with replication, then enhancement, and finally restructuring.

Developing new learning environments consistent with developing educational theories will require librarians to change their roles in instruction through the implementation of new technologies. The challenges mentioned in the introduction remain. What the theories detailed in this article enable is a systematic understanding of our response to those challenges and a roadmap for understanding how we can plan for meeting our learning goals.

NOTES

1. Everett M. Rogers, *Diffusion of Innovations* (4th Edition) (New York: Free Press, 1995), 204-251.

2. Rogers, *Diffusion of Innovations*, 252.

3. Rogers, *Diffusion of Innovations*, 252-280.

4. Kenneth C. Green and Steven W. Gilbert, "Content, Communications, Productivity, and the Role of Information Technology in Higher Education" [Web page]; available on the World Wide Web at http://www.aahe.org/technology/tltr-ch4.htm.

5. Arthur W. Chickering and Stephen C. Ehrmann, "Implementing the Seven Principles: Technology as Lever," *AAHE Bulletin* 19 (October 1996): 3-6.

6. Robert B. Kozma and Jerome Johnston, "The Technological Revolution Comes to the Classroom," *Change* 23 (January-February 1991): 20.

7. Steven W. Gilbert, "Making the Most of a Slow Revolution," *Change* 28 (March/April 1996): 12.

8. Bernard J. Poole, *Education for an Information Age: Teaching in the Computerized Classroom* (Madison: Brown & Benchmark Publishers, 1995), 414.

9. Diana Laurillard, *Rethinking University Education: A Framework for the Effective Use of Educational Technology* (New York: Routledge, 1993), 13.

10. Poole, *Education for an Information Age*, 342.

11. Charles Schroeder, "New Students–New Learning Styles," *Change* 25 (September/October 1993): 21-26.

12. Barbara O'Keefe, *Learning Communities*. Paper presented at the 1997 UIUC Faculty Retreat on College Teaching: Tradition, Innovation and Technology: Teaching for Active Learning. Urbana, IL: February 6, 1997.

13. Green and Gilbert, "Content, Communications, Productivity."

14. Robert B. Kozma and Jerome Johnston, "The Technological Revolution Comes to the Classroom," *Change* 23 (January-February 1991): 19.

15. Karen L. Smith, "Preparing Faculty for Instructional Technology: From Education to Development to Creative Independence," *CAUSE/EFFECT* 20 (Fall 1997): 36-44, 48.

BIBLIOGRAPHY

Barker, Joel. *Tactics of Innovation*. [Videocassette] St. Paul, MN: Distributed by Star Thrower, 1998.

Chickering, Arthur W. and Stephen C. Ehrmann. "Implementing the Seven Principles: Technology as Lever." *AAHE Bulletin* 19 (October 1996): 3-6.

Gilbert, Steven W. "Making the Most of a Slow Revolution." *Change* 28 (March/April 1996): 10-23.

Green, Kenneth C. and Steven W. Gilbert. "Content, Communications, Productivity, and the Role of Information Technology in Higher Education." [Web page]. Available on the World Wide Web at http://www.aahe.org/technology/tltr-ch4.htm.

Kozma, Robert B., and Jerome Johnston. "The Technological Revolution Comes to the Classroom." *Change* 23 (Jan-Feb 1991): 10-20, 22-23.

Laurillard, Diana. *Rethinking University Education: A Framework for the Effective Use of Educational Technology*. New York: Routledge, 1993.

O'Keefe, Barbara. *Learning Communities*. Paper presented at the 1997 UIUC Faculty Retreat on College Teaching: Tradition, Innovation and Technology: Teaching for Active Learning. Urbana, IL: February 6, 1997.

Poole, Bernard J., *Education for an Information Age: Teaching in the Computerized Classroom*. Madison: Brown & Benchmark Publishers, 1995.

Rogers, Everett M. *Diffusion of Innovations* (4th Edition). New York: Free Press, 1995.

Schroeder, Charles. "New Students–New Learning Styles." *Change* 25 (September/October 1993): 21-26.

Smith, Karen L. "Preparing Faculty for Instructional Technology: From Education to Development to Creative Independence." *CAUSE/EFFECT* 20 (Fall 1997): 36-44, 48.

We're All in This Together:
Planning and Leading a Retreat
for Teaching Librarians

Anna Litten

SUMMARY. Library instruction programs are undergoing a major shift as teaching models are revised and programs revamped in the move towards information literacy. These shifts are often difficult on teaching librarians who must now work in new ways with faculty, convey different concepts in sessions, and change the focus of library instruction. This article describes the process one library went through in approaching changes in the library instruction program. The Coordinator of Instruction led a retreat with the teaching team to solicit criticism, define goals, and devise strategies for improving the experiences of members of the teaching team. *[Article copies available for a fee from The Haworth Document Delivery Service: 1-800-HAWORTH. E-mail address: <getinfo@haworthpressinc. com> Website: <http://www.HaworthPress.com> © 2002 by The Haworth Press, Inc. All rights reserved.]*

KEYWORDS. Library instruction, information literacy, teaching librarians, teaching retreat, retreat

---

Anna Litten has been the Coordinator of Library Instruction at the Emerson College Library since 1997. Ms. Litten's primary area of interest is in guiding learners through the critical thinking process.

[Haworth co-indexing entry note]: "We're All in This Together: Planning and Leading a Retreat for Teaching Librarians." Litten, Anna. Co-published simultaneously in *Journal of Library Administration* (The Haworth Information Press, an imprint of The Haworth Press, Inc.) Vol. 36, No. 1/2, 2002, pp. 57-69; and: *Information Literacy Programs: Successes and Challenges* (ed: Patricia Durisin) The Haworth Information Press, an imprint of The Haworth Press, Inc., 2002, pp. 57-69. Single or multiple copies of this article are available for a fee from The Haworth Document Delivery Service [1-800-HAWORTH, 9:00 a.m. - 5:00 p.m. (EST). E-mail address: getinfo@haworthpressinc.com].

The shift from bibliographic instruction to information literacy has not been easy on instruction librarians. Librarians, administrators, professors and students have all struggled as we redevelop existing library instruction programs and bring the library's teaching mission into line with the Information Literacy Competency Standards for Higher Education adopted by the Association of College and Research Libraries in 2000. Appropriate planning to ease the transition and change in our library instruction programs will have a far-reaching impact on our ability to be effective teachers, leaders and information literacy advocates. In this article, I will discuss the bumps in the road as one library moves towards a student-centered information literacy program, and how we as a staff devised strategies for facing change.

SHIFTING MODELS FROM BI TO INFORMATION LITERACY

At Emerson College, students study filmmaking, journalism, writing, and other professions of the communication arts and sciences. The nature of these fields demand that practitioners be critical thinkers and questioners, and the Emerson community embraces these qualities. Joining the staff of the Emerson College Library as the Coordinator of Library Instruction in 1997, I was lucky enough to enter a community that values critical thinking and questioning. By the time I joined the library, all students in the required first-year writing program were required to participate in the program and many upper-level and graduate students participated in the program at the request of faculty members.

For a number of years, the library instruction program followed an existing model. The Coordinator of Library Instruction would assign sessions to the four members of the teaching team. The librarians who participated in the library instruction program were all members of the Reference Department, but their primary responsibility was not teaching. Using a prepared script and outline, teaching librarians would introduce students to library databases and reference sources. Participating faculty appreciated the sessions, but after teaching with this model, I began to feel that we could do more.

As I looked around at the reference desk, I wondered if students were taking lessons out of the library classroom. Clearly, students were using databases that they had seen in library instruction sessions, but were they then able to adapt their thinking process to identifying research tools for new questions? Was our program of introducing students to sources indeed the best way to help college students approach information? What models could I find in the information literacy field that could help students become active participants in the information-seeking process?

Information literacy was already a heady topic in 1997,[1] and like many instruction librarians during the late 1990s, I turned towards theories and models of information literacy for ways to make our program meaningful, applicable, and far-sighted enough to help students who would leave ready to become journalists and documentarians. By 1999, I was ready to introduce the team of teaching librarians to new methods for working with students and professors to make our experiences in the library classroom as rich as possible for all participants.

THE GROWING PAINS OF AN INFORMATION LITERACY PROGRAM

Before the beginning of the 2000/2001 academic year, teaching librarians met to discuss new designs for library instruction sessions. Under our new model, library research sessions would be student-centered. I asked teaching librarians to focus less on the tools that we thought students needed to use, and more on the concepts of information literacy. Instead of following a prepared script, we would now tailor sessions to respond to student needs in the research process. We would work with professors to design assignments and sessions that would help students to understand information resources, determine information needs, find and evaluate information, and finally, effectively use information.[2]

Regardless of the planning during the summer of 2000, the 2000/2001 academic year was difficult for the members of the teaching team at the Emerson College Library. Preparing for classes under our new model was time-consuming. No longer relying on scripts and outlines, librarians needed to spend more time working with faculty members and researching to prepare for a class. Even more difficult, building a program around student questions meant that teaching librarians found that they were giving up some of the control in the classroom. Often, we would ask a class a question, without knowing where we would end up. Faculty members were impressed by our new model, as was evidenced by our year-end statistics. The number of sessions taught through the instruction program was up dramatically, from 127 during the 1999/2000 academic year, to 214 during the 2000/2001 academic year, an increase of almost 60%.

Members of the teaching team had legitimate complaints. We were teaching more sessions than ever before while, at the same time, preparing for sessions was becoming more time consuming. Still, we had not changed structures in the program to make our job as information literacy leaders easier. We had not created new tools or resources to match changes in the instruction program. I feared I was about to face insurrection from the teaching team. My goal for the summer of 2001 was to better prepare the teaching librarians for the academic year ahead.

Supporting teaching librarians through the academic year would clearly involve a new communication system. Instead of relying on short or informal meetings and email, we needed structure and formal tools. Starting with a retreat for teaching librarians, we would begin a drive to create better tools and support systems for teaching librarians and the information literacy mission of the library instruction program.

BEGINNING THE PROCESS

Choosing the retreat as a means for coping with change was simple. A retreat seemed to offer a number of advantages as the teaching team recovered from the year behind and looked to the year ahead. Separate and outside of the realm of our usual workday, a retreat might allow us to reflect honestly about our joys and frustrations in our work. I wanted to hear from teaching librarians about what had worked for them under the new model as well as what had not worked. From their feedback, we would work together to build tools to help us all be better teaching librarians.

Retreats are common tools in business, but there are few examples in library literature of retreats as a tool for approaching difficult situations and preparing for change. Those librarians who had written about conducting retreats were enthusiastic about the process, and their models would be my starting place.

PLANNING FOR THE PARTY

Once I settled on a retreat to begin our process, I began culling the literature for advice. I chose to stay within the confines of the library literature, since the unique nature of academic libraries and non-profit institutions seemed alien to many of the references I was finding in business and management literature. I began by focusing on two issues that came up in almost every article I read: choosing a location and defining goals for the retreat.

"Retreat" brings to mind visions of spa-like conference centers. None of the members of the teaching team would have objected to such a setting, and the literature suggested it, but an exotic location alone does not make a retreat. I decided to hold our retreat in one of the college's meeting rooms. With only four librarians in the teaching team, we did not need a conference center. The literature does suggest that the retreat take place outside of the library itself, which did seem important. So, choosing a meeting room away from our immediate work area but within the college offered our small group the best option. Away from our desks, the phones, email, and students, we would be free to discuss and assess our program.

In the business world, a moderator often leads retreats. That model was less common in library literature. When planning our retreat, I did consider finding a moderator to lead us, but decided that I would lead the retreat myself. My qualifications as a retreat leader are nil, but I hoped that my experience in library instruction and knowledge of our community would be enough.

The size of our group raised another issue. Did we need an entire day to retreat with four librarians? Teaching librarians certainly can be a talkative group, but regardless, I felt that a half-day retreat would be sufficient for an initial retreat. With the location and length of the event set, the more difficult issues of content lay ahead.

WHAT ARE OUR GOALS?

Defining goals was more difficult than choosing a location. There were many possible solutions to the problems of the previous year. Outreach to faculty, creative research assignments, or professional development plans for the library are all issues that factored into our successes and failures during the past year. Focusing on any one of these issues could have been the basis for a retreat. All of these topics seemed too heady, not practical enough for our shell-shocked team. Following Linda Dobbs's advice that "a retreat must have a purpose, which must be understood by all of the participants,"[3] I settled on a concrete topic. We would use the retreat to identify tools and brainstorm systems that would enable us to be effective in the library classroom.

Reading after reading emphasized that the retreat was not a self-contained event. Participation should begin even before entering the retreat. Again, I turned to the literature. Through her experiences of leading four annual retreats, Dobb found that pre-retreat activities were vital to the success of the event. For one retreat, Dobb solicited discussion topics from library managers; for another, Dobb provided readings for participants.[4] Langley and Martinez asked participants to reflect on their own activities by filling out "cost-impact" forms.[5]

Using the examples of those more experienced than myself, I began designing activities and the agenda for the event. I suspected that one of the problems during the previous academic year was that I, as the Coordinator of Instruction, was decreeing changes in the library instruction program rather than working together with members of the teaching team. I did not want the retreat to be another example of edicts or explanations. I wanted to hear from the teaching librarians. While I did want to focus the day's activities and bring us to our goal of defining tools for better teaching, I did not want to assign readings.

More like Langley and Martinez, I would ask participants to think and write before the retreat. Using the pre-retreat activity as our focus, we could begin the retreat with an open discussion. Discussion seemed appropriate to the tone I wanted to set for the day. After an opening discussion we would move to another area that seemed crucial to me, collaboration with faculty. To be information literacy librarians, we would need to be sure that we were all comfortable and competent in discussing library instruction with key players outside of the library. Finally, we all needed to brainstorm together to create teaching tools and support systems. The final outline for the retreat seemed vague, but settling on an agenda that would be both flexible enough to accommodate issues that the teaching team needed to discuss, and issues that I knew we could not avoid, led to a loose agenda.

As the only member of the teaching team whose primary job responsibility was teaching, I wanted to use the retreat as an opportunity to raise issues that were common in the field of information literacy, but not as common in other areas of librarianship. I felt that the stated goal of the retreat, to identify tools necessary to make us better teaching librarians, allowed me to bring up issues such as defining information literacy for our community. If we were to become true information literacy librarians we would also have to build our own information literacy definition, so as to better deal with change.

A week before the event, I gave librarians three questions for the pre-retreat activity. Table 1 includes the questions that the teaching librarians answered before the retreat. The first question was based on an assignment that I did before attending the Information Literacy Immersion program in the summer of 2000. I hoped that the first question would allow us to open with a discussion of what information literacy meant, and how information users see the search process. The last two questions were designed to help us move to the goal of identifying tools that we could use to become better teachers. To further separate the retreat from our normal workweek, I left participants colored note cards for writing answers.

INFORMATION TALES

We opened the retreat by sharing stories. The information literacy tales we had collected, answering the first question of the pre-retreat activity, gave us a peek into how non-librarians see the information world. We brought stories back of spouses in graduate school searching for articles for a paper, schoolteacher friends looking for information for elementary school students, and more. After hearing the stories, we noted the themes that were emerging in Table 2.

The tales were humorous, occasionally disheartening, and made us proud of the research skills of our friends and spouses. Beginning with this discussion helped us to see what we do, what we don't need to do, and served as a place for us to begin thinking about what we as librarians offer to information seekers.

Our interviews reinforced faculty feedback; student researchers can find information, but evaluating information is another topic altogether. Our respondents told us in stark terms that users do not always need more information; instead, they need help in being critical and evaluating information. For all of the meetings we have had on this subject, we suddenly had a clear picture and example of some of the difficulties that students face in the research process.

TABLE 1

- Ask someone you know (not a librarian!) to tell you about the last time he or she needed some information. What type of information was he or she looking for? How did she find it?
- Write down three things you love about teaching.
- Write down three things you do not like about teaching.

TABLE 2

- None of the people we talked to sought out a professional such as a librarian or a travel agent in their search.
- Like reference librarians, all of our respondents enjoyed looking for information, and they enjoyed looking for information by themselves, without help.
- Many of our respondents returned to information sources that had been successful for them in the past, without seeking new information tools.
- Our unscientific respondent pool of friends and family felt as if they were finding what they needed online, without our help.
- Information seekers were not always critical, or were uncertain as to how to be critical of information.

WORKING WITH FACULTY

To my eye, one of the most challenging issues in working with faculty is that faculty members think that they are coming to a similar library to the one that they grew to love during their years in school. Librarians know that our very collections are different in today's libraries, as students get information easily and quickly. Under our former model, our knowledge of library resources was enough to let us reach our goals in the library classroom. In an information literacy program, we needed more. Success in the library classroom begins with our success in working with faculty members. Thinking back, we all took a few moments to jot down some notes about successful times that we had in the library classroom.

UP ON STAGE:
SUCCESSES AND FAILURES IN THE LIBRARY CLASSROOM

Many of us listed similar experiences as being crucial in successful classes we had led. We all enjoyed classes in which the course instructor was involved. Instructors needed to either co-lead the session, or to share designing learning goals for the session. In a smaller school, we often get to know faculty members well, and that continuity helped us be better teachers. All of us enjoyed sessions when we had been very comfortable with the content of the material. In a smaller library like ours, we do not rely on subject specialists. We are all generalists, but generalists with an in-depth knowledge of the subject matter of a course fare far better. One of the criteria that led to the most successful library instruction session was good timing. Or, as one of the participants said, "When we luckily manage to meet the class when the students hit panic stage."

Sharing stories of our success in the classroom led us to the second and third questions that librarians answered for the pre-retreat activity. Facing our joys and fears in teaching, we listed things we loved, and things we do not love about teaching. On the whiteboard we listed both, good for all members of the teaching team to see. Table 3 includes our responses. Looking at both columns together, our goal is to make the "Things I Don't Like" column disappear, and to make the "Things That I Love" column grow. What tools, systems, and fundamental changes could we make to the library instruction program and the way that information literacy is seen?

WHAT CHANGES CAN WE MAKE?

We listened to all of the members of the teaching team and brainstormed together to devise plans for our future. No suggestion or observation was out of bounds. We did not limit the conversation to rational suggestions, but allowed complaints. Regardless of whether or not we could do anything about the issues that arose, we wanted to hear comments on the library instruction experiences. The suggestions, observations, and comments were diverse and are listed in Table 4.

I wanted suggestions on what made our successes possible. How could we eliminate problems? Immediately, we started coming up with ways that we, as a team, could address these issues. Already, we knew that we could create better communication tools for members of the teaching team as they worked with faculty. We could create a library of activities for librarians to use in

TABLE 3

Things I Love About Teaching	Things I Don't Like About Teaching
• Energy! • Challenges • Thinking with faculty • When it works!	• Lacking confidence as a teacher • Needing to be **on** • Haven't had time and mental space to prepare • Repetition • Anxiety

TABLE 4

- Librarians need to have enough information about every class.
- What do instructors think that students should learn?
- We need to know what stage students are at in the research process.
- The instructor needs to understand what kinds of information the students should access, and that students get information from sources they did not use when they were in school.
- Instructors need to know what their responsibilities are in the library classroom.
- Students have low attention spans!
- Teaching librarians need evaluations of their session.

classes. We could observe each other in the library classroom. We could schedule planning sessions along with class sessions. None of the tools were fully envisioned, but we were moving towards picturing what our library instruction program could look like.

WHAT CHANGES SHOULD WE MAKE?

For our next activity, I asked the librarians, "What are the three things that we wish we could teach students?" As both teaching librarians and reference librarians, we want to put a human face to information literacy. What would an information literate undergraduate look like? What were some of the traits we would see in students who could define information needs, find, evaluate, and use information effectively? This topic raised issues about the content of our sessions. Moving towards a model of partnering with faculty does not mean that we will abdicate our responsibilities in designing content for library sessions. Instead, we need to build a model in which both the faculty members and the librarians define learning outcomes for sessions together. Our active role is vital, but we needed to pinpoint some of the suggestions we would bring to faculty members. See Table 5 for our wish list. As the major goal of the retreat was to create a library of teaching tools for librarians, this list of issues could serve as a beginning place to start collecting teaching tips and activities that we had used in sessions to teach these concepts and skills.

WHAT HAPPENS IN THE LIBRARY CLASSROOM?

The preponderance of end-user tools and the challenges of information literacy should allow us to think of new and different models for how we could use our time with students in the library classroom. We might not need to allocate as much time to using databases, using the time to address evaluation or other issues instead. Opening a discussion on changes that we would like to see in the library instruction program helped us to think critically about the overall program, and using our time in the classroom. Again, all suggestions and complaints were welcome. See Table 6 for the discussion points.

WRAPPING UP THE RETREAT

Retreats have a purpose, and as the participants in our retreat knew, our purpose was to build better tools and systems for the teaching team, as we continually develop the information literacy program. Already, I knew of a few changes we could make to the program. We did not brainstorm on this session, but instead, I mentioned some of the ways that we might begin to address issues and concerns that came up during the retreat, such as creating an online form for instructors who are requesting library instruction as a tool for collecting information about courses, and setting up a schedule so that we can all observe each other in the classroom. As Coordinator of Library Instruction, I did not want to leave development of the tools to the team. Instead, I would assume the responsibility for developing tools and systems.

We finished the retreat with a catered lunch. Many retreat leaders stress that the social aspect of retreats is as important as the practical business aspects. Without a trip to a retreat center, merely sharing a lovely lunch was a good way for us to chat and reflect on the morning's activities.

TABLE 5

- How we search depends on what and how much we are looking for.
- Searchers need to think about the amount and kind of information they want.
- Using library resources instead of just searching online can be faster.
- The process of finding journal articles in an online world.
- How to pick a research topic.
- Students should have time to look at library resources.
- Librarians have a lot of answers.
- Bias isn't always so easy to see, it's often subtle.

TABLE 6

- Do we always need an entire class? Could we schedule library instruction as part of a class, either in our library classroom or the regular space?
- Can we rearrange the schedule during busy times of the semester?
- Can we link library instruction to other work, such as linking LI to the print and online publications we create?
- Can we do more outreach and schedule sessions for classes to avoid repetition at the reference desk?
- Can we make better use of technology in library instruction, perhaps creating more Web tours?

LESSONS WE HAVE APPLIED

As of this writing, we are four months away from the retreat. Already, we have started to implement ideas generated at the retreat. Table 7 lists a number of the steps we have taken to improve library instruction and the lot of teaching librarians. The library instruction program is continually growing and changing, and we still have many lessons to learn from the retreat. Although we are sharing teaching tips, techniques and activities, we do not have shared computer files, Web sites, or vertical files. Sharing our resources needs to become formalized in our library, not haphazard or informal.

Participants felt that the retreat was a success that gave us all a chance to discuss our concerns and experiences as teaching librarians. More importantly, the structure of the retreat required that we all continue to follow up on lessons learned during the retreat. We have developed some better tools since then, and continue to create many more. The retreat process has led us to fruitful change, but we are certainly not done changing. We will continue to build on our successes in the experience of the first information literacy retreat by holding more retreats in the future. By giving us structures to deal with the changes and difficulties of leading information literacy, the retreat has allowed us to be more comfortable in our role as teaching librarians.

REFLECTIONS FROM THE RETREAT LEADER

Our small retreat had a big impact. Members of the teaching team, often excluded from discussion of changes in the program, were involved in charting our future. We see real progress from the retreat in the new tools and systems being developed for the teaching team. Continuing the retreats also means that

TABLE 7

- Library instruction sessions are now scheduled in a shared Microsoft Outlook Calendar, accessible to all of the members of the teaching team. Librarians are encouraged to add sessions to the schedule if need be.
- Faculty members now fill out an online form when they are requesting a library session. The form comes to the electronic mailbox of the Coordinator of Library Instruction who then schedules the session, and forwards the form to the librarian who will be leading the session. The form is available at: http://library.emerson.edu/bi/classrequest.html.
- For large, multi section classes, we have worked with instructors to institute a new model of instruction. Instead of one, long library instruction session covering all of the tools that students will need, we are offering shorter sessions, geared to specific research questions and assignments.
- Librarians are sharing successful activities. An evaluation activity that one librarian used with a class is being adopted for another class, taught by another librarian.

we have decided to invest in our growth as teaching librarians in a dynamic information literacy program.

Looking back, I was happy not only with the outcomes, but also with the process itself. I had worried that our location and leader were inappropriate. Were we too close to the library itself? The meeting room that we used was one that we use for monthly staff meetings. Ideally, a retreat should probably be a little further away from the workplace than we were. For our next retreat, I would like to use a meeting space that we do not use in our normal work life.

For our first retreat, I believe it was appropriate for a member of the team to lead the retreat. An outside retreat leader, although unbiased, would not have the inside knowledge of our department and our program necessary to speak our common language. For future retreats, I would certainly consider asking a moderator to lead our discussion. Regardless, our retreat was indeed successful.

PLANNING AND LEADING FOR CHANGE

Leading faculty and undergraduates in developing information literacy skills has not been easy for teaching librarians. We have moved away from the comfortable to the uncomfortable. My goal was to help the teaching team be comfortable in the library instruction program. I wanted to change our information literacy program, but I did not want to own the program. The program belongs to all who participate: teaching librarians, faculty members, administrators and students.

Over the next year, I hope to decide what type of retreat we will hold in the future. The possibilities are almost limitless, from an event similar in scope and size to our retreat of the past summer, to opening up an information literacy retreat to the entire library staff and key members of the Emerson College community. This retreat was a way to solicit practical feedback on the classes we teach, the concepts we emphasize, and ways to work with faculty. Now that we have conducted our first retreat, we are all looking forward to the retreats in the future.

NOTES

1. "The Presidential Committee on Information Literacy" was released on January 10, 1989.

2. The growth of Emerson College Library's instruction program is not the focus of this article, but to see information on the changes that took place in this program, see http://khobbs.web.wesleyan.edu/nelig/pres/12-1-00pres/.

3. Janice Kirkland and Linda S. Dobb, "The Retreat as a Response to Change," *Library Trends* 37 (Spring 1989): 495-509.

4. Linda S. Dobb, "Four Retreats and a Forum: A Meditation on Retreats as a Response to Change," *Library Trends* 47 (Spring 1999).

5. Anne Langley and Linda Martinez, "Learning Our Limits: The Science Libraries at Duke University Retreat to Respond to Our Changing Environment," *Issues in Science and Technology Librarianship* (Fall 1999).

BIBLIOGRAPHY

Dobb, Linda. "Four Retreats and a Forum: A Meditation on Retreats as a Response to Change." *Library Trends* 47 (1999): 699-710.

Foster, Constance L., Etkin, Cynthia Moore, Elaine E. Staebell, etc. "The Net Result: Enthusiasm for exploring the Internet." *Information Technology and Libraries* 12 (1993): 433-436.

Kirkland, Janice and Linda S. Dobb. "The Retreat as a Response to Change." *Library Trends* 37 (1989): 495-509.

Langley, Anne and Linda Martinez. "Learning Our Limits: The Science Libraries at Duke University Retreat to Respond to Our Changing Environment." *Issues in Science and Technology Librarianship* 24 (1999). [cited August 2, 2001]; available on the World Wide Web at: http://www.library.ucsb.edu/istl/.

Nofsinger, Mary M. and Mary Gilles. "A Faculty Retreat: Coping With Challenges." *College and Research Library News* 50 (1989): 484-485.

The Politics of Pedagogy:
Expectations and Reality
for Information Literacy in Librarianship

Rebecca Albrecht
Sara Baron

SUMMARY. The ways librarians learn to teach, their educational paths to the profession, and current employer expectations are significant aspects of an ongoing national dialogue on information literacy. For over 15 years, our profession has discussed information literacy in terms of how we can actively teach our students research skills. The authors illustrate the importance of instruction and information literacy skills in academic libraries on several fronts: market needs, literacy standards, and graduate preparation for meeting the needs and standards from the employer's perspective (as expressed in advertisements) and from the employee's perspective (as manifest in survey responses). *[Article copies available for a fee from The Haworth Document Delivery Service: 1-800-HAWORTH. E-mail address: <getinfo@haworthpressinc.com> Website: <http://www.HaworthPress.com> © 2002 by The Haworth Press, Inc. All rights reserved.]*

KEYWORDS. Information literacy, library instruction, pedagogy, graduate education, teacher training, continuing education

Rebecca Albrecht is Coordinator of Library Instruction, Purchase College, SUNY, 735 Anderson Hill Road, Purchase, NY 10577 (E-mail: rebecca.albrecht@purchase.edu).

Sara Baron is Instruction Coordinator/Instructional Technology Center Director, University of Massachusetts, Boston, Healey Library, 100 Morrissey Boulevard, Boston, MA 02125 (E-mail: sara.baron@umb.edu).

[Haworth co-indexing entry note]: "The Politics of Pedagogy: Expectations and Reality for Information Literacy in Librarianship." Albrecht, Rebecca, and Sara Baron. Co-published simultaneously in *Journal of Library Administration* (The Haworth Information Press, an imprint of The Haworth Press, Inc.) Vol. 36, No. 1/2, 2002, pp. 71-96; and: *Information Literacy Programs: Successes and Challenges* (ed: Patricia Durisin) The Haworth Information Press, an imprint of The Haworth Press, Inc., 2002, pp. 71-96. Single or multiple copies of this article are available for a fee from The Haworth Document Delivery Service [1-800-HAWORTH, 9:00 a.m. - 5:00 p.m. (EST). E-mail address: getinfo@haworthpressinc.com].

INTRODUCTION

Librarians are no longer keepers of information, but teachers of information. The ways librarians learn to teach, their educational paths to the profession, and current employer expectations are significant aspects of an ongoing national dialogue on information literacy. For over 15 years, our profession has discussed information literacy in terms of how we can actively teach our students research skills. However, given the constraints of tighter budgets, staffing challenges, and dicey scheduling issues, this requires the deft talents of a trained instructor. Often, librarians have little time to make an impact. Using the right teaching technique at the right time is critical. Traditional faculty members have an entire semester to guide their students, while librarians may have only an hour or two. Our objective is to illustrate the importance of instruction and information literacy skills in academic libraries on several fronts: market needs, literacy standards, and graduate preparation for meeting the needs and standards from the employer's perspective (as expressed in advertisements), and from the employee's perspective (as manifest in survey responses).

RESEARCH PROBLEM AND QUESTIONS

We know librarians learn to teach through professional development opportunities. We know the professional literature is brimming with research, analyses and examples of librarians teaching. We know a large number of library positions require teaching. With these factors in mind, our research asked the following questions:

- How are Library and Information Science (LIS) programs preparing information professionals for library instruction and information literacy training? Has there been some significant change in light of new standards?
- Do job advertisements over the last five years illustrate a rise in library instruction and information literacy positions? Has there been a rise in positions with library instruction and information literacy in the job title?
- How did current library instruction and information literacy librarians learn their instructional skills? How do they maintain proficiency in new pedagogies?

BACKGROUND AND LITERATURE REVIEW

Graduate training in library instruction and information literacy involves much more than simply "how to teach." We argue that effective teacher-training programs for librarians include skills in administration, marketing, pedagogy, and assessment. Such programs include not only those skills associated with classroom planning, but also skills that increase efficient planning, faculty negotiation and outreach, learning theory, and designing active assignments that meet immediate needs and promote lifelong learning. As Peacock argues "librarians must be strongly positioned as key educators in the teaching and learning environment, and empowered with an educational competence and professional confidence equal to that of their academic peers."[1] This literature review will focus on three areas: the need for pedagogical training; how librarians learn to teach; and accreditation expectations.

NEED FOR PEDAGOGICAL TRAINING

Librarians in the field working without the "educational competence and professional confidence" Peacock refers to may feel overwhelmed and likely to think the acquisition of pedagogical skills should have been a required component of their coursework. Shonrock and Mulder's extensive study on instruction librarians' proficiency acquisition was based on the hypothesis that "although most literature suggests that some form of library instruction is necessary, most librarians don't have the skills needed to provide this instruction effectively."[2] They found that "on-the-job training and self-teaching were the primary means of learning for eighteen of the proficiencies and the secondary means for twenty-one of the proficiencies."[3] While that may be the case, most librarians surveyed claim that "library school should be their primary place to learn thirteen of the twenty five most important proficiencies."[4] Implicitly, these librarians were not satisfied with the means by which they were encouraged to learn skills essential to their profession. Looking back, they lamented that those skills were not a core part of their training that could have easily been "learned in one or two instructional methods and curriculum development classes."[5] The data in Shonrock and Mulder's study, while gathered in 1989, holds true today as evidenced by our own data. Many librarians, who responded to our survey, specifically mentioned feeling a disjunction between what they believed they needed to know in order to complete their job duties and what they expected to need before attaining their positions.

Shonrock and Mulder note "library schools may include communication, planning, and promotion in other courses, such as management."[6] It is possible, as Aluri and Engle suggest, that "the integrated approach will do more to foster support for BI and to prepare effective BI librarians than the separate course so strongly supported by those who became our BI experts without (such a course)."[7] However, both Shonrock and Mulder's study in 1989 and our data from 2000 find that practicing librarians are not feeling the successful acquisition of management and learning theory skills in library school or continuing education activities. Shonrock and Mulder's call for a reexamination of "library schools and their curriculum [and] the types of continuing education available from all sources"[8] has largely been accomplished. But the active revision of those curricula and continuing education opportunities has either not been done or has not met the growing need evidenced by market trends, professional surveys, and feedback. Some graduate schools of library and information science have heeded the call, offering electives and special courses in information literacy to bolster the ability of new librarians to gain some pedagogical tools. More often than not, these classes are not an integral part of the core curriculum, though most librarians engage in instruction activities regardless of the library environment.

Shonrock and Mulder cite White and Paris' 1985 survey, claiming that directors of large academic libraries did not "recommend special area courses, such as BI courses" as part of professional preparation. They speculate that directors did not recommend such courses because they were not directly supervising instruction librarians and were not aware of the need for such advanced skills. Perhaps, though, it is because they were aware of the fact that so few schools would offer opportunities for such preparation. In addition, the need for instruction has changed dramatically since 1985, moving from tool training to training for more transferable information literacy skills.

Though the information literacy movement was well underway in 1992 (evidenced by ACRL's 1987 Model Statement of Objectives for Academic Bibliographic Instruction), Roma Harris discovered that "nearly all" of the librarians she surveyed had done "some bibliographic instruction."[9] Despite varied library types, most also participated in instruction despite the fact that "their preparation for offering this instruction was often inadequate."[10] Harris claims that her results confirm those of Patterson and Howell, who contend that training at the graduate level is woefully inadequate on the whole. In addition, "few instruction librarians have the necessary courses and practical experience in their formal library education programs to prepare them even minimally for what is encountered on the job."[11]

Anne Woodsworth and June Lester examine the results of three surveys addressing the various professional competencies needed during a library career. One such competency is in "instructional design and adult education programming (i.e., understanding the cognitive processes of traditional and nontraditional students in colleges and universities)."[12] Throughout their review of the studies and literature, Woodsworth and Lester focus much of their energy on looking at competencies as a matter of formal training and "changes in library and information science education" as well as the development of a "shared vision" between all stakeholders (deans, SLIS faculties, funding agencies, etc.).[13]

Herbert White responds to Woodsworth and Lester by asserting that library education programs are not the problem–that we are "speaking not of educational but of professional imperatives, and . . . educators have no choice but to prepare for the jobs that exist today."[14] Instead, White proposes that there are many ways we can negotiate a balance between new educational values and the dynamic needs of the job market. He insists that internships, continuing education programs, and on-the-job training are just a few of the ways to "close the gap." These tools are necessary because library education programs cannot splinter themselves to prepare graduates for every area of specialization. Rather, efforts towards reform must begin with "the university administration and the faculty, making them understand that the quality of this new breed of librarians is a far more important priority for the library than the bricks and even the material budget . . . that academia must make this commitment to the people we are going to attract."[15]

In an ideal world this would be true. But negotiating with administration is, we argue, a component of teaching skills. "Making them *understand*" is about persuasion, outreach, marketing, communication–all skills instruction librarians need. As a profession, we have been trying internships, continuing education and other training tools, but many are not taken seriously and are so watered down in terms of requirements, structure, and quality that they simply can't be effective surrogates for more formal training. How often do we sit through a conference presentation with a witty title and leave without a shred of new knowledge? The authors disagree with White on the grounds that pedagogy is no longer an area of "specialization" in librarianship. Just as graduate programs have ably incorporated new technologies, they must also incorporate a vision of librarian as teacher. Clearly, at least for professional academic librarians, instruction duties *are* what will be required in nearly 50% of today's professional academic library positions. As Harris discovered, instruction for all types of librarians is a common job duty. But in academic libraries, user education programs are a staple because they are so closely aligned with the values of academia.

In a 1990 *Library Journal* article, Tom Eadie questioned the value of user education programs as "a special service of questionable value that arose not because users asked for it, but because librarians thought it would be good for them."[16] A decade has passed since the article was published, and many librarians still quote it as indicative of the kind of resistance that user education programs face in gaining legitimacy on some campuses. Clearly, with the growth of the Internet and Web-based databases, user needs have changed and grown. In a 1992 article for *Research Strategies*, Eadie shifts his position to better fit the coming of the virtual library.[17] As the information literacy movement has taken hold and more librarians understand that it is not a matter of presenting information, but one of engaging in an active dialogue, instruction "more closely resembles reference." Eadie is less likely to take the position that instruction programs in general are "presumptuous" and "superfluous." Certainly, his role as devil's advocate was aimed at calling into question the kind of instruction that was "more prevalent in the 70s than the 80s and certainly the 90s."[18]

HOW LIBRARIANS LEARN TO TEACH

It is well documented that librarians currently attempt to gain some instruction skills through professional development and continuing education opportunities.[19] Donnelley notes that "teaching has become the focus of our professional development activities."[20] Many arguments have been made for librarians to take greater roles in technology training.[21] But technology training is only one aspect of a much larger professional challenge posed by the need for information literacy training. Gone are the days of "click here" or "save as text." Rather, librarians now find themselves in the position of bolstering the larger academic mission to hone critical thinking skills and help students build a foundation for lifelong learning.

Calls for information literacy training have become increasingly more prevalent in the literature. A 1997 survey of academic librarians noted, "almost all respondents admitted the need for more instruction–and more intense instruction."[22] One respondent insists, "Our bibliographic instruction programs require a more thorough tutelage on search strategies and information structure."[23] Clearly, the emphasis has moved from information provision and point-of-need training to the acquisition of skills that are more lasting. Pastine and Wilson note what has since become the profession's mantra: "The process of research is more important than the product. Educators need to teach users how to think, not what to think . . . The process of educating should focus on the development of the critical thinking skills and research strategies required to turn information into knowledge."[24] Mary Reichel talks about this shift in goals as being one "from a pragmatic approach of teaching . . . to a global approach of emphasizing the value of finding information and utilizing it."[25] She notes a shift away from tool training to tool gaining, one that places the onus back onto the learners who have "more control over decision making, because they can find and evaluate relevant information."[26]

National organizations have responded to this shift by designing curricula of their own and have created and sponsored such initiatives as the Association of College and Research Library's Immersion Institute for Information Literacy. The Immersion Institute was intended as a "program specifically targeted at preparing the librarian with the foundation tools needed to begin the process of becoming an effective teacher."[27] ACRL's Instruction Section Web site lists 7 national and over 44 state and regional organizations that offer continuing education opportunities in addition to those offered by SLIS programs.[28] These organizations sponsor annual conferences, many of which, such as LOEX and LOEX-of-the-West, focus exclusively on issues related to library instruction and information literacy. The programs at the 2001 Association of College and Research Libraries conference as well as at countless regional conferences and symposia have been overwhelmingly concerned with information literacy training and assessment strategies.

These numbers do not even begin to tell the story, for they ignore the hundreds of smaller networking groups, special interest groups, and local associations that actively assist librarians helping each other with teaching. Nor do those numbers take into account the BI-L discussion list, with over 2800 subscribers, which has acted (for over eleven years) as a support for thousands of instruction librarians struggling to network and share practical instruction tips and methods.

THE ROLE OF ACCREDITATION

Librarians who teach information literacy skills are not only helping students become more effective information consumers, but are also helping their institutions succeed in gaining recognition and/or accreditation. Accreditation teams are increasingly looking for evidence of teaching excellence from libraries during reviews. The ACRL Information Literacy Standards suggest that there should be an institutional approach to training students in the use of library materials, critical thinking and other transferable skills needed to create an information literate student population.

Most regional accrediting agencies are curious about the administrative commitment to instruction programs and often specifically address library instructors' expertise with regard to "learning theory and pedagogical methods."[29] While many of the accrediting commissions are now placing greater import on the institutional self-study, it is clear that some expectations will remain. A recent survey of librarians in the Middle States region confirms that there is "consensus and insistence that every institution of higher education should prepare students to become independent learners by requiring them to develop information literacy (skills of inquiry, information management, and analysis), and students absolutely should be expected to go beyond the basic classroom materials provided for any course of study."[30]

This same survey suggests that "systematic instruction must be offered, and the performance of the students must be evaluated." Questions provided from survey participants as essential include: "How is assessment accomplished?"

"How are students learning to evaluate information?" "What criteria are being used to assess the success of the program."[31] Librarians throughout the Middle States Association region seem to agree that questions asked by evaluating teams should include a specific examination of the library's teaching efforts. Furthermore, accrediting agencies are not just looking for numbers. They are looking for meaningful data from librarians' definitions of "the key functions and resources perceived to be directly (or indirectly) linked to valued outcomes, such as student learning, teaching, and scholarly activity."[32]

Middle States is not the only association aware of the impact of and need for instruction. The latest draft of new "comprehensive standards" by the Southern Association of Colleges and Schools Commission on Colleges suggests that institutions should "ensure that users have access to regular and timely instruction in the use of the library and other learning/information technology resources."[33] Their 1998 *Criteria for Accreditation* talks about library instruction duties as a basic library service which should include "an orientation program designed to teach new users how to access bibliographic information and other learning resources. Any one of a variety of methods, or a combination of them, may be used for this purpose: formal instruction, lectures, library guides, etc."[34] Perhaps this increased focus on standards comes from a greater understanding of a new dynamic in the world of information, a world that reflects more chaos than anything–the Internet.

The smaller, more organized environment of the library's walls and the free-for-all of the Internet has highlighted the distinctions between information and understanding. Understanding involves placing knowledge in a context. It requires determining how the information or data was produced, by whom, why, and whether or not it is relevant. Respondents to the Middle States survey "concurred" that "we know in our minds as well as our hearts that information is not knowledge, that information retrieval is not research, that undergraduates cannot always evaluate Web sites."[35] Modern academic librarians have become shepherds, expected to help users get from one place (information) to the other (understanding). As Gretchen Douglass states, "I believe my role of 'professor librarian' will become a commonplace role for librarians in the future."[36] Clearly, it is becoming just that.

As a profession, librarians seem to be in an era when merely communicating what the library has to offer and how one particular tool works in one context is insufficient and irresponsible in light of the skills necessary to evaluate and synthesize information appropriately. The New England Association of School and Colleges, Inc. studied the effectiveness of their standards for accreditation. Respondents emphasized the fact that "given the technology explosion" which makes so much more information readily available "and its relevance to education, there should be some consideration of information literacy as a course requirement."[37] Many institutions do require students to participate in a program designed to make them more effective users of information. Even in those environments where faculty are loathe to add more credit hours to the core curriculum, some schools emphasize the importance of such skills by offering an elective course. In December of 2000, one researcher noted the existence of at least 23 one-credit classes on the use of information resources and mentioned the names of at least 19 schools that offer anywhere from one to four credit courses.[38]

Though it seems evident that librarians realize there is a difference between information and understanding for our students, we seem to have significant difficulty accepting that there is a similar distinction between communication and teaching for ourselves. Job advertisements give the impression that anyone with communication skills can teach effectively. Yet, through this overview of the literature, we see that leaders in the field are pleading with graduate programs to provide pedagogical training. We see that information literacy standards require transferable critical thinking and training skills beyond the provision of information or spot training on one bibliographic tool or the other. We see that accrediting bodies expect libraries and librarians to take a more active role in academia. And we see that the majority of attempts at pedagogical training are coming, not from our graduate schools, but associations and organizations or the pages of journal articles.

METHODOLOGY

Four data collection projects were used to gather information on our research questions. To answer the question about SLIS programs' preparation of instruction librarians, we performed a content analysis of SLIS Web sites. This data was supported with a survey of SLIS program deans. An extensive content analysis of job advertisements was used to gather information about the numbers of instruction positions and presence of information literacy concepts in those ads. In an effort to gauge current library instruction and information literacy librarians' training, we distributed an e-mail survey. Methodology and results for each data set will be presented together.

Methodology and Results for SLIS Content Analysis and SLIS Dean's Survey

Methodology

While research over the last 25 years has examined SLIS programs and library instruction training, we wanted to verify how they are preparing librarians for increased library instruction and information literacy needs today. To determine this, we performed a content analysis of program Web sites. There are forty-nine American Library Association accredited graduate schools of library and information science. There are two reasons why we focused on the Web sites. First, the program's Web site is used as a primary marketing tool, and therefore, all important program emphases should be accessible on the Web. Second, we assume changes in the profession are largely due to technological advances. It seems natural to look at the Web site of each program as a vehicle for delivering information.

To supplement the Web site content analysis and confirm program requirements, we surveyed the forty-nine deans and directors of U.S. SLIS programs via e-mail. The survey contained three questions, asking if the program requires an information literacy course as part of the core curriculum; if an information literacy course is offered regularly (at least once per year); and if so, we asked for information about the course.

Results

Forty-one SLIS program Web sites were analyzed in the summer of 2000. Twenty-six offered a class or classes in bibliographic instruction, library instruction, user education or information literacy, though it should be noted that many of these are targeted to those librarians preparing to work as School Library Media specialists. The courses were presented in a variety of ways. Several courses specifically mentioned information literacy: "Practicum in Instruction for Information Literacy" (San Jose State University); "Information Literacy, Library Instruction" (University of South Carolina); "Teaching Information Technology Literacy" (University of Hawaii). Other courses specifically mentioned instruction: "Library Instruction: Philosophy, Methodology, and Materials" (University of Rhode Island); "User Education/Bibliographic Instruction: Theory and Technique" (UCLA); "Special Topics: Instructions in the Use of Information" (University of Michigan). Several courses were focused on general reading and writing literacies: "Perspectives on Literacy" (UCLA); "Literacy and Library Involvement" (Dominican University); "Literacy: The Issue and the Library's Response" (Simmons). Many programs offered pedagogy training as part of a reference course or as a continuing education course. Only four of the programs required the information literacy class as part of the core curriculum. Results from nine programs were inconclusive due to dead links or incomplete course lists and descriptions.

We followed the content analysis with an e-mail survey to the 49 SLIS program deans in August of 2001. There was a 53% response rate, with 26 respondents. Of those directors who responded to our survey, only one indicated that the program had some kind of requirement regarding instruction. The University of Puerto Rico requires its students to take a two-credit Information Literacy course. While this does not represent the sum total of information literacy or user education courses available at the various schools, it does speak to the glaring omission of separate course requirements, a subject of longstanding debate in the professional literature.

Our inquiry regarding the availability of instructional content (instruction as part of another class) was more positive. Many schools embed content regarding instruction in other core classes. It was clear that programs were more generous with instructional training, offering some elective or course component in 58% of programs surveyed via email. The content analysis revealed 63% of the programs include instructional training as part of another course.

While it can't be said that SLIS programs ignore the need for instruction, it is clear that most programs focus on the need for instruction skills as part of a separate course only when preparing graduates to work with children as school library media specialists. Outside of that specific track, most programs only prepare graduates to teach as a portion of a graduate course in library science, usually a reference or management course.

Methodology and Results for Job Advertisement Content Analysis

Methodology

A content analysis of job advertisements was performed to capture trends of the market with respect to library instruction and information literacy positions and duties. *American Libraries* and *The Chronicle of Higher Education* were examined from 1996 to 2000. Analysis was limited to the months of March, June, September and December for *American Libraries* and the first week of those months for *The Chronicle of Higher Education*. Data collected about each position included: job title; institution; faculty status/tenure track; presence of an emphasis on information literacy, library instruction or bibliographic instruction in the job title, duties, requirements or desired qualifications. If the job required the candidate to teach a credit-bearing course focused on information literacy or library research skills, this was noted as well.

Past studies have limited data to only Association of Research Libraries, but this study is meant to be broader in scope, examining the overall academic market needs for instruction skills and training. We limited the analysis to academic library positions, which include community colleges, colleges and universities, medical, and law school libraries. Positions excluded from the analysis were school library media specialist positions; SLIS faculty positions; seminaries, military and other special libraries; residencies and part-time or temporary positions. Positions for distance learning and instructional design were not included unless the position was clearly focused on instruction within the library. Curriculum and education library positions were also excluded unless it was clear that the position involved instruction within the library, information literacy training, or traditional bibliographic instruction.

Several obstacles with the analysis included "see" references and tenure/faculty delineations. Many job advertisements had minimal information and "see" references to URLs for the complete job description (most of which would have been dead links because of their ephemeral nature). Because costs for print ads can be prohibitively expensive, forcing some institutions to rely on these URLs, it is clear that some positions which may have emphasized information literacy were missed in the study. We simply couldn't look at these. We also assumed that, to some extent, emphasis was indicated by an institution's willingness to be specific in the ads and pay for that specificity.

Results

Thousands of job advertisements were analyzed as part of the content analysis. One thousand twenty-two advertisements ended up in the final data set because they had something to do with library instruction or information literacy. We discovered that there has been a slight increase in the number of job advertisements for library instruction, but that the percentage of total job ads hovers around 50% (see Figure 1). Furthermore, there has also been a slight increase in positions with library instruction and information literacy in the job title (see Figure 2). Positions with library instruction, bibliographic instruction or information literacy in the job title are 55% more likely to require pedagogical experience than those with more general titles like "Reference Librarian" or more subject specific titles like "Science Librarian" (see Table 1). It is noteworthy that 45% percent of the positions with library instruction or information literacy in the job title do not require experience or training. Overall, instruction positions (those asking for some experience or indicating some instructional duties) were only half as likely to require experience than those that suggested instruction in their titles.

Many of the job ads included in our content analysis required applicants to take on teaching duties without insisting on tools other than an ALA accredited MLS degree and communication skills. Market demand is also made manifest in the content of job advertisements over time. While there may not be more institutions requiring experience in instruction, there are certainly more positions that mention instructional duties. Nearly 50% of academic position announcements specifically note that instructional duties will be required of the candidate. Current emphasis in instruction programs is on assessment–an ongoing process that ensures libraries are not depending solely on participants'

FIGURE 1. Total Number of Job Advertisements and Total Number of Instruction Positions (Mar, Jun, Sep, Dec)

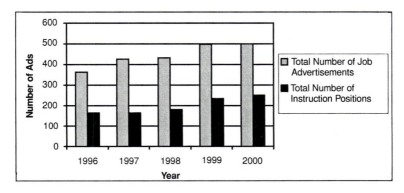

FIGURE 2. Information Literacy, Library Instruction or Bibliographic Instruction in the Job Title

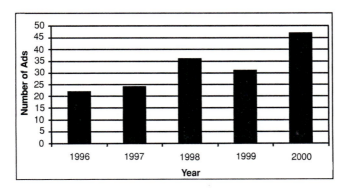

TABLE 1. Information Literacy, Library Instruction, or Bibliographic Instruction in the Job Title Crosstabulated with Positions Requiring Pedagogical Experience

| | | Required Experience | | Total |
		No	Yes	
IL/LI/BI in Job Title	No	654	196	850
	Yes	77	95	172
Total		731	291	1022

reactions to an instruction session, but on instruments and teaching strategies that extract real information from participants regarding the acquisition of transferable skills.

Methodology and Results for Survey of Practicing Instruction Librarians

Methodology

In an effort to gather data from practicing instruction librarians, an e-mail survey was distributed to two mailing lists. The initial survey was sent to Immersion '99, a mailing list of 120 graduates of the first Immersion Institute for Information Literacy, sponsored by ACRL (see Appendix 1). Survey questions asked about percentage of work spent on library instruction; anticipation of library instruction duties; reading and integrating ACRL Literacy Competency Standards; where librarians first learned to teach; how they enhance their understanding of library instruction and information literacy; and primary reasons for attending professional conferences. After adding a few questions (which we then asked of the Immersion group as a follow-up), the survey was submitted to BI-L, a national mailing list of over four thousand instruction librarians and anyone interested in library instruction. A friendly reminder was e-mailed to the list two weeks later. There were eight questions on the survey (see Appendix 2).

Several decisions about coding data are explained in detail. On questions where respondents answered with a percentage range (30-40%), the numbers in the range were averaged (35%). Question 2 asked for a percentage and a yes/no response. Some respondents answered the yes/no portion but not the percentage. As a result, complete data for 2A are not available. Question 5 asked where respondents first learned to teach library skills. If more than one answer was given, the first answer was used in the data analysis as the primary means of learning to teach library instruction, unless something else in the response implied otherwise. Responses to the open-ended survey questions were categorized into general and specific topics.

Results

A total of 80 surveys were analyzed. Respondents included participants of the 1999 Immersion Institute for Information Literacy (about 120 participants) and BI-L. When asked about their *first* library position, library instruction and/or information literacy functions accounted for only 22.4% of the duties.

Today, respondents reported that they spend an average of 50% of their time on library instruction and/or information literacy functions. Fifty-nine percent of the respondents expected that they'd be doing this amount of library instruction and/or information literacy training when they began this position. Conversely, over 40% of respondents did not expect to be doing as much teaching as they are presently doing. Often, they are not only responsible for training students, faculty and administrators, but also for teaching other librarians and library staff the importance of information literacy training skills. The notion of instruction librarians as advocates for information literacy and the ACRL standards was frequently mentioned.

The majority of our respondents primarily learned to teach library research through on-the-job training (84%). This was followed by SLIS courses, with only 19% learning to teach library instruction in library school. Secondary means of maintaining proficiency were on-the-job training, conferences, and the Internet (see Figure 3). Additional methods mentioned included programs outside the SLIS curriculum, professional literature, and conferences and continuing education (see Figure 4). In terms of maintaining proficiency with library instruction and information literacy training, professional literature was the top method (98%) followed by continuing education and professional development opportunities (74%). When asked why they attend professional conferences, most respondents stated they want to improve their skills (65%), get new ideas from colleagues (51%), and/or earn professional development points (43%).

Many respondents noted that they often felt that the ACRL Information Literacy Standards did not apply to them, making them difficult to integrate. Furthermore, networking and communication seemed to be major obstacles in incorporating standards. Within the networking/communication issues category (see Figure 5), time was cited as one of the biggest factors. Many librarians felt that they had difficulty prioritizing the standards among all their other instructional duties. They either felt that the standards were too broad or too narrow. Often, they cited assessment as a problem. They seemed to feel that it was simply "to early to tell" if the standards were having an impact on the efficacy of their instruction programs/approaches. Assessment efforts underway have not yet yielded anything conclusive about the effectiveness of instruction programs. In addition, time constraints (in combination with a lack of formal training) seem to strangle instruction librarians who are unable to integrate simple and crude assessment efforts that would, at a minimum, indicate a base level of success or failure.

Resistance to new types of library instruction and information literacy training on the part of immediate colleagues was cited as a key obstacle to integrating the ACRL Information Literacy Standards for about 5% of the respondents. For

FIGURE 3. How Librarians Enhance Their Understanding of Library Instruction and Information Literacy Since They First Learned About It

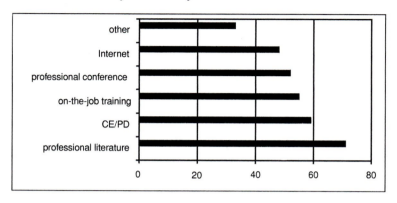

FIGURE 4. Where Librarians First Learned to Teach Library Research

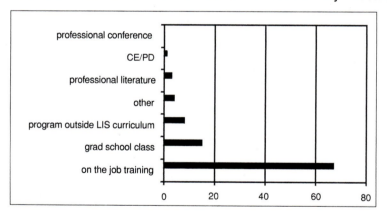

others, it was noted as an obstacle even when it was considered secondary to time constraints and other challenges of primary importance. In other words, for many instruction librarians, just getting the concepts of the information literacy standards across to other librarians was a fundamental issue. In these cases, the importance of strong teaching skills can be most effective. When dealing with faculty and administrators, strong teaching skills are central. Achieving a sense of buy-in is crucial when working off of a set of standards, like those created by the leadership of ACRL. Effectively teaching our academic colleagues to meet and use such standards is tricky, at best. One survey

FIGURE 5. Networking/Communication Challenges of Integrating the ACRL Information Literacy Standards

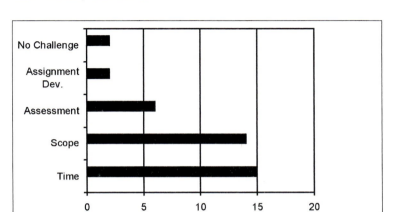

respondent stated that these are "our standards, not theirs, and therefore carry little weight."[39]

The most cited challenge to implementing the standards was communication. Networking with both faculty-at-large as well as one's library colleagues posed a significant obstacle to fulfilling basic requirements of information literacy programs–that the programs be well integrated into the curriculum. In some cases, this "campus wide effort" couldn't even get out of the library. In others, "getting people to understand the differences between computer literacy and information literacy" was the main challenge.[40]

Despite all the efforts to the contrary, many instruction librarians, even those who benefited from the best of the available training opportunities, such as the Immersion Institute, have felt overwhelmed by their perceived weaknesses. Of primary concern is their ability to negotiate the implementation of standards in an environment fraught with conflicting messages. They feel ineffective and, at times, impotent in taking an active role in training faculty, administrators, and even other librarians about the importance of information literacy skills training. Yet, most know that they will be expected to spark the growth of information literacy programs across campus. The negotiating, time management, and outreach skills aren't there. Clearly, this extension of pedagogical training continues to be a pressing need for our profession, as evidenced in national initiatives and the testimony of scores of individual librarians.

In a surprising number of survey responses (25 or 29%), librarians were clearly confused about the nature of the standards, their proper use, and implementation. Ironically, there seemed to be little difference between those who attended ACRL's Immersion Institute and those who did not, in terms of perceived success and challenges in integrating the ACRL Information Literacy Standards. One-third of the respondents from the first Immersion class cited faculty networking and outreach as the greatest obstacle to implementing information literacy goals.

In addition, it was clear that the very existence of the standards and their proper use/function stumped several respondents. One respondent stated, "We cannot implement all of the standards." The ACRL standards do not comprise a checklist that can be sequentially marked off. Rather, the standards are to be used as a guide, implemented, evaluated, and re-implemented at different stages of user education and by different stakeholders across the academic campus. Nowhere in the introductory comments for the standards do the creators suggest that the onus is fully on librarians. Nowhere does ACRL suggest that all the standards can, or should for that matter, be implemented at the library level.

Some felt that the standards simply did not apply to them, that their specific library context defied the very nature of the standards. This was particularly true of one respondent at the community college level who felt that the standards were simply too "esoteric." Another respondent felt that information was adequately covered in the general education curriculum and, therefore, outside of the library's scope. Clearly, our study reveals that more training on the use of the standards is needed.

It should be noted that the authors were surprised to learn that the survey itself became a vehicle for advertising the ACRL Information Literacy Standards themselves. Some librarians, despite their apparent participation in one of the most active and successful networking efforts, BI-L, did not know about the existence of the standards and read them only after receiving our survey via the listserv. While this was not widespread, representing just 2.3% of respondents, it is worth noting because it speaks to the training needs of those actively working in the field. A larger percentage of librarians stated that, though they know the standards exist, they simply didn't have the time to deal with them. Again, we suspect that this directly relates to training, if not in terms of the Standards, then surely in the absence of those teaching skills necessary to balance a large teaching load with continuing education needs.

DISCUSSION

Our findings bring up-to-date three decades of research on how librarians learn to teach. The "teaching library" and the "teaching librarian" are phrases we read repeatedly. With the passage of ACRL's information literacy competencies, we finally have standards to guide our library instruction and training. But we are still struggling with training librarians in pedagogy. Perhaps the new standards, coupled with national accrediting agencies' expectations, will finally help push pedagogical training into the SLIS requirements.

Our first research question about SLIS programs and how they prepare information professionals did not gather significant new information. We still find, as our colleagues did before us, that SLIS programs are reluctant to embrace the pedagogy as a core requirement of librarians. Though more programs than ever are offering rotational courses on library instruction and/or including it as part of another class, we argue this is woefully negligent. New graduates will enter a job market where they will be expected to teach. One of our colleagues anonymously told us, "I find grad students coming out of grad school (in the interview) are very positive about information literacy. However, once they get here, they freeze and don't know how to write objectives or clarify outcomes. More education courses need to be taught in graduate school and more experience with teaching needs to occur. Students know the theory of information literacy, but not the practical application." While we hoped new literacy standards would elicit a response from SLIS programs in the form of required–or even regularly scheduled–courses, we were not able to determine this.

Our second research question regarding the job market illustrated fascinating trends about instruction positions. While the rise in instruction positions has been small over the past five years, we did find a rise in quasi-managerial positions related to library instruction and information literacy as evidenced in job titles. The job of coordinating instruction and information literacy training was made the primary role of the individual, as opposed to a subset of reference duties. In addition, we found a slight correlation between those jobs and the requirement of experience in training. It was interesting to note, however, just how many positions required instruction as part of the job duties and yet did not require nor prefer any instructional experience.

We argue that required experience and training should be given prominence in job postings. Eadie also finds it puzzling that more advertisements don't call for experience and training, given the duties prevalent in the market. He speculates that this may be because librarian postings are affected by the "flavour" of faculty postings, which "seldom mention teaching experience or skills" and yet faculty engage in teaching.[41] For librarians among instruction circles, there is an understanding that legitimacy for user education programs cannot be established in the absence of appropriate pedagogical training.

Considering that librarians must assist faculty to become information literate before we can expect them to respect any literacy standards, we had to ask what skills and training they felt helped them the most. After all, today, librarians must "help faculty develop new pedagogical methods for the electronic age" and must be "active in curriculum design," according to Brendan Rapple in "The Librarian as Teacher in the Networked Environment."[42] But being active in curriculum design, we found, can be a politically fragile endeavor–even within the walls of the library.

We also asked practicing instruction librarians how they received instructional training and how they maintain proficiency. Due to the lack of SLIS commitment to pedagogical training, it was no surprise that most of our respondents first learned to teach library instruction on-the-job. We are not sure if this means their libraries had a training program, or if they were just thrown in the classroom and expected to survive. The trial-and-error training librarians have is supplemented heavily by conferences, continuing education opportunities and professional literature. But there are no standards for this training. It is a sink or swim proposition and a risk that most employers seem willing to take based on their job advertisements. It is a gamble that LIS programs make as well. Graduate students in those programs may not be aware of the odds.

CONCLUSION

Seemingly, the teaching skills of librarians essential to the success of instruction programs in academic libraries are often missing, and it is clear that legitimacy for user education programs cannot be established in the absence of appropriate pedagogical training–not on individual campuses and certainly not in a wider sense. Much of what we find, both in the literature and anecdotally, illuminates a process of librarians scrambling to acquire higher order teaching skills to help them manage overwhelming instruction loads and programs–after they find themselves overwhelmed.

While many aspects of our professional training are changing to meet the more pressing technological requirements of the job market, training for instructional skills remains the same overall. It seems as though some employers are "bargain hunting" in job ads, perhaps because they feel they will not find a candidate with the requisite skills or, perhaps, because they want more malleable employees whose approaches and opinions are not yet etched. Perhaps they know that graduate schools do not emphasize pedagogy. Why aren't employers demanding of SLIS programs what library practitioners have been of their graduates for thirty years?

Patricia Senn Breivik speculates that library schools "neglect" instruction in their course offerings for a number of reasons: there may be territorial issues with other professionals; library schools simply don't have room in the curriculum to address "training for teaching library skills"; and such training has historically been "disliked by the schools and students alike."[43] Yet, she insists that "library instruction should not be viewed as an end in itself in a library school curriculum anymore than the actual practice of teaching a library skill to an undergraduate should ever be viewed as an end in itself."[44]

Breivik recalls an ALA convention in Chicago with "an exhibit of library instruction materials from all types of libraries across the country" with a total anticipated audience of 500 librarians. She states "Within 15 minutes of the opening of the exhibit, more than 1500 people crowded into the [Use of Libraries Committee's] exhibit area, making it almost impossible to view the materials, but suggesting that many librarians were already well-motivated in this area."[45] That was in 1972. Breivik's "A Rose by Any Other Name" was published in John Luban's landmark work, *Educating the Library User*, in 1974. Three decades later, the same articles are examining the same challenges in the workplace. The same surveys are being reworked and mass distributed. While few attempt to debate the increased need for instruction in our libraries, many actively work to shift the onus from graduate programs to the workplace to national organizations and back.

Wherever the liability, however, several facts remain clear: librarians are being asked to take on more intense instruction duties with the understanding that doing so successfully does not require much, if any, preparation or experience. SLIS programs give this impression. Employers give this impression. Institutions reinforce this idea with small staffs and chronic under-budgeting. National organizations are not equipped to handle the influx of professionals who (aware of their knowledge deficit) flock to conferences in hopes of finding practical applications for largely theoretical pedagogical concepts that they have rarely seen employed or modeled. Perhaps the situation should not surprise us. The microcosm of the library reflects the methodological underpinnings of the larger world of academia. After all, it is clear from a recent study funded by the Pew Charitable Trusts that many doctoral students destined for full-time tenure-track positions as faculty "are not prepared for the various activities that most professors spend their time doing, especially teaching."[46] The dilemma is pandemic and seems to suggest that teaching children requires formal training, but teaching adults requires nothing more than general communication skills. But don't tell instructional librarians that. Most are too busy trying to play catch up.

NOTES

1. Judith Peacock, "Teaching Skills for Teaching Librarians: Postcards from the Edge of the Educational Paradigm," *Australian Academic and Research Libraries* 32, no. 1 (2001): 28.

2. Diana Shonrock and Craig Mulder, "Instruction Librarians: Acquiring the Proficiencies Critical to Their Work," *College & Research Libraries* 54 (1993): 137.

3. Shonrock and Mulder. "Instruction Librarians," 141.

4. Shonrock and Mulder. "Instruction Librarians," 145.

5. Shonrock and Mulder. "Instruction Librarians," 146.

6. Shonrock and Mulder. "Instruction Librarians," 147.

7. Aluri and Engle, quoted in Shonrock and Mulder, "Instruction Librarians," 147.

8. Shonrock and Mulder. "Instruction Librarians," 148.

9. Roma M. Harris, "Bibliographic Instruction: The Views of Academic, Special, and Public Librarians," *College & Research Libraries* 53, no. 3 (1992): 255.

10. Harris, "Bibliographic Instruction," 255.

11. Patterson and Howell, quoted in Harris, "Bibliographic Instruction," 256.

12. Anne Woodsworth and June Lester, "Educational Imperatives of the Future Research Library: A Symposium," *Journal of Academic Librarianship* 17 (1991): 208.

13. Woodsworth and Lester, "Educational Imperatives," 208.

14. Herbert S. White, "New Educational Values and Employability: Closing the Gap," *Journal of Academic Librarianship* 17 (1991): 209-210.

15. White, "New Educational Values," 210.

16. Tom Eadie, "Immodest Proposals: User Instruction for Students Does Not Work," *Library Journal* 115 (1990): 42-45.

17. Tom Eadie, "Beyond Immodesty: Questing the Benefits of BI," *Research Strategies* 13, no. 3 (1992): 105-110.

18. Tom Eadie, Personal e-mail communication with Author, September 7, 2001.

19. See Kilcullen; Shonrock and Mulder.

20. Kimberly Donnely, "Reflections on What Happens When Librarians Become Teachers," *Computers in Libraries* 20, no. 3 (2000); [Web page] March 2000, [cited October 4, 2000]; available on the World Wide Web at http://www.infotoday. com/cilmag/mar00/donnely.htm.

21. See Stoffle; Rapple; Rice.

22. Carol Tenopir and Lisa Ennis, "The Impact of Digital Reference on Librarians and Library Users," *Online* [Web page] November 1998; available on the World Wide Web at http://www.onlineinc.com/onlinemag/ol1998/tenopir11.html.

23. Tenopir, "Impact of Digital Reference."

24. Pastine and Wilson, quoted in Reichel, "Twenty Five Year Retrospective."

25. Mary Reichel, "Twenty Five Year Retrospective: The Importance of What We Do," *RQ* 33, no. 1 (1993).

26. Reichel, "Twenty-Five Years."

27. Cerise Oberman, "A Vision for I.I.L.," [Web page] July 17, 1997, [cited August 28, 2001]; available on the World Wide Web at http://www.ala.org/acrl/nili/vision. html.

28. Instruction Section, ALA/ACRL, "Sponsors of Continuing Education Programs for Library Instructors," [Web page] August 10, 2000, [cited September 5, 2001]; available on the World Wide Web at http://www.gwu.edu/~iseduc/sponsors. html.

29. Marilyn Lutzker, "Bibliographic Instruction and Accreditation in Higher Education," *College & Research Libraries* (1990): 14.

30. Oswald Ratteray, "Survey of Librarians in the Middle States Region on the Role of the Library, Electronic Resources, and Information Literacy Training in Higher Education," Draft document.

31. Ratteray, "Survey of Librarians," 2.

32. Bonnie Gratch Lindauer, "Defining and Measuring the Library's Impact on Campuswide Outcomes," *College & Research Libraries* 59, no. 6 (1998): 559.

33. Southern Association of Colleges and Schools, "Draft of Principles of Accreditation," [Web page], [November 11, 2000]; available on the World Wide Web at http://sascoc.org/COC/SectV.htm.

34. Southern Association of Colleges and Schools, "Draft of Principles," section 5.12.

35. Ratteray, "Survey of Librarians," 7.

36. Gretchen Douglass, "Professor Librarian: A Model of the Teaching Librarian of the Future," *Computers in Libraries* 19, no. 10 (1999).

37. NEASC, "A Study of the Effectiveness of the Standards for Accreditation," [Web page], [November 11, 2000]; available on the World Wide Web at http://www.neasc.org/cihe/effectiveness_standards.htm.

38. Susan Payne, "List of Credit Courses," [Listserv posting], February 15, 2001; available via email at bi-l@listserv.byu.edu.

39. Immersion participant and respondent 075.

40. Immersion participant and respondent 068.

41. Tom Eadie, Personal e-mail communication with Author, September 7, 2001.

42. Brendan A. Rapple, "The Librarian as Teacher in the Networked Environment," *College Teaching* 45, no.3 (1997).

43. Patricia Sean Breivik, "A Rose by Any Other Name–Or Library Instruction and the Library School," in *Educating the Library User*, ed. John Lubans, (New York: R.R. Bowker, 1974), 410.

44. Breivik, "A Rose by Any Other Name," 412.

45. Breivik, "A Rose by Any Other Name," 411.

46. Scott Smallwood, "Survey Points to Mismatch Between PhD Students, Their Programs, and Their Potential Employers," *The Chronicle of Higher Education* (January 16, 2001). See also http://www.wcer.wisc.edu/phd-survey/.

BIBLIOGRAPHY

Breivik, Patricia Sean. "A Rose by Any Other Name–Or Library Instruction and the Library School." In *Educating the Library User*, edited by John Lubans, Jr, 410-414. New York: R.R. Bowker, 1974.

Donnely, Kimberly. "Reflections on What Happens When Librarians Become Teachers." *Computers in Libraries* 20, no. 3 (2000). [Web page] March 2000, [cited October 4, 2000]; available on the World Wide Web at http://www.infotoday.com/cilmag/mar00/donnely.htm.

Douglass, Gretchen. "Professor Librarian: A Model of the Teaching Librarian of the Future." *Computers in Libraries* 19, no. 10 (1999): 24-28.

Eadie, Tom. E-mail communication with the author. September 7, 2001.

Eadie, Tom. "Beyond Immodesty: Questioning the Benefits of BI." *Research Strategies* 10 (1992): 105-110.

Eadie, Tom. "Immodest Proposals: User Instruction for Students Does Not Work." *Library Journal* 115 (1990): 42-45.

Harris, Roma M. "Bibliographic Instruction: The Views of Academic, Special, and Public Librarians." *College & Research Libraries* 53, no. 3 (1992): 249-256.

Instruction Section, ALA/ACRL. "Sponsors of Continuing Education Programs for Library Instructors." [Web page] August 10, 2000. [cited September 5, 2001]; available on the World Wide Web at http://www.gwu.edu/~iseduc/sponsors.html.

Kilcullen, Maureen. "Teaching Librarians to Teach: Recommendations on What We Need to Know." *Reference Services Review* 26, no. 2 (1992): 7-18.

Lindauer, Bonnie Gratch. "Defining and Measuring the Library's Impact on Campuswide Outcomes." *College & Research Libraries* 59, no. 6 (1998): 546-570.

Lutzker, Marilyn. "Bibliographic Instruction and Accreditation in Higher Education." *College & Research Libraries* (1990): 14.

NEASC. "A Study of the Effectiveness of the Standards for Accreditation." [Web page], [November 11, 2000]; available on the World Wide Web at http://www.neasc.org/cihe/effectiveness_standards.htm.

Oberman, Cerise. "A Vision for I.I.L." [Web page], July 17, 1997 [cited August 28, 2001]; available on the World Wide Web at http://www.ala.org/acrl/nili/vision.html.

Payne, Susan, "List of Credit Courses." [Listserv posting], 15 February 2001; available via email at bi-l@listserv.byu.edu.

Peacock, Judith. "Teaching Skills for Teaching Librarians: Postcards from the Edge of the Educational Paradigm." *Australian Academic and Research Libraries* 32, no. 1 (2001): 26-42.

Rapple, Brendan. "The Librarian as Teacher in the Networked Environment." *College Teaching* 45, no.3 (1997).

Ratteray, Oswald. "Survey of Librarians in the Middle States Region on the Role of the Library, Electronic Resources, and Information Literacy Training in Higher Education." Draft document.

Reichel, Mary. "Twenty Five Year Retrospective: The Importance of What We Do." *RQ* 33, no.1 (1993).

Rice-Livey, Mary Lynn and J. Drew Racine. "Role of Academic Librarians in the Era of Information Technology." *Journal of Academic Librarianship* 23, no. 1 (1997): 31-42.

Shonrock, Diana and Craig Mulder. "Instruction Librarians: Acquiring the Proficiencies Critical to Their Work." *College & Research Libraries* 54 (1993): 137-149.

Smallwood, Scott "Survey Points to Mismatch Between PhD Students, Their Programs, and Their Potential Employers." *The Chronicle of Higher Education*, (January, 16 2001). See also http://www.wcer.wisc.edu/phd-survey/.

Stoffle, Carla J. "Literacy 101 for the Digital Age." *American Libraries* 29, no. 11 (1998): 46-48.

Southern Association of Colleges and Schools. "Draft of Principles of Accreditation." [Web page], [November 11, 2000]; available on the World Wide Web at http://sascoc.org/COC/SectV.htm.

Tenopir, Carol and Lisa Ennis. "The Impact of Digital Reference on Librarians and Library Users." *Online* [Web page], [November 1998]; available on the World Wide Web at http://www.onlineinc.com/onlinemag/ol1998/tenopir11.html.

White, Herbert S. "New Educational Values and Employability: Closing the Gap." *Journal of Academic Librarianship* 17 (1991): 209-210.

Woodsworth, Anne and June Lester. "Educational Imperatives of the Future Research Library: A Symposium." *Journal of Academic Librarianship* 17 (1991): 204-215.

APPENDIX 1. SLIS Program Director's Survey

Your program's Web site was included in our research study on the curriculum of SLIS programs with regard to preparing students to teach in libraries. A content analysis of SLIS Web sites was inconclusive in trying to answer the following questions.

Your assistance will help us accurately represent SLIS program trends with regard to the emphasis on pedagogy/information literacy/library instruction.

Please take a moment to respond to the following questions concerning your program. Remember that we are looking at the preparation of academic librarians (NOT school library media specialists).

1. Does you program require students to take a course on pedagogy/information literacy/library instruction as part of the core curriculum? YES or NO

2. Does your program regularly offer (at least once per year) an elective course to teach students pedagogy/information literacy/library instruction? YES or NO

3. If you have answered YES to either 1 or 2, please provide the title of the course and a link to the course description on your Web site.

APPENDIX 2. BI-L Librarians Survey

1. What percentage of your work-time is spent doing library instruction and/or information literacy functions? (100%, 50%, etc.)

2. When you applied for your current position, did you anticipate that LI/IL (Library Instruction/Information Literacy) would be as big of a portion of your job as you noted in above? (yes or no)

   When you applied for your first position, what percentage of your job was LI/IL and did you anticipate that LI/IL would be as big a portion of your job as it was? (yes/no)

3. Have you read the ACRL Competency Standards?

   What attempt have you made to integrate the ACRL Competency Standards into your LI program? Please explain.

   Did you find the ACRL Competency Standards easy to integrate into your LI program? Please explain.

4. What have you found to be the most challenging aspect of incorporating ACRL standards into your LI program?

5. Where did you *first* learn how to teach library research? (Please check one)
   Graduate School Course (please list course name & core or elective)
   Continuing Ed/Professional Development
   Professional Conference Presentations (if so, what conference(s)?)
   Professional Literature
   On-the-job Training
   From the Internet
   Program outside LIS curriculum
   Other (please explain)

APPENDIX 2 (continued)

6. How have you enhanced your understanding of LI/IL since you *first* learned about it? (Check all that apply)

    Continuing Ed/Professional Development
    Professional Conference Presentations (if so, what conference(s)?)
    Professional Literature
    On-the-job Training
    From the Internet
    Other (please explain)

7. Please arrange in order the reasons you attend professional conferences on LI/IL

    To learn/improve my skills
    Professional Development points
    Tenure requirements
    To get ideas from colleagues
    Other (please specify)

8. My institution is located in: _____

9. My MLS is from: _____

Using the *ACRL Information Literacy Competency Standards for Higher Education* to Assess a University Library Instruction Program

Jeanne R. Davidson
Paula S. McMillen
Laurel S. Maughan

SUMMARY. The Reference and Instruction Department at Oregon State University (OSU) was charged with creating a vision and goals for its instruction program. This article describes how we used the recently published *ACRL Information Literacy Competency Standards for Higher Education* as a framework for an initial self-study of our instructional practice and for promoting the concept of information literacy at our institution. The process of assessing our current practice led to discussions with library and campus faculty about the value of information literacy and to a clearer articulation of our instructional mission. *[Article copies available for a fee from The Haworth Document Delivery Service: 1-800-HAWORTH. E-mail address: <getinfo@haworthpressinc.com> Website: <http://www.HaworthPress.com> © 2002 by The Haworth Press, Inc. All rights reserved.]*

Jeanne R. Davidson is Physical Sciences Librarian, Oregon State University, 121 The Valley Library, Corvallis, OR 97333.

Paula S. McMillen is Social Science Reference Librarian, Oregon State University, 121 The Valley Library, Corvallis, OR 97333.

Laurel S. Maughan is Humanities Reference Librarian, Oregon State University, 121 The Valley Library, Corvallis, OR 97333.

Acknowledgements: The authors would like to thank Wendy Smith for help in the literature review process, and JoLynn O'Hearn for assistance in creating visual representation of data.

[Haworth co-indexing entry note]: "Using the *ACRL Information Literacy Competency Standards for Higher Education* to Assess a University Library Instruction Program." Davidson, Jeanne R., Paula S. McMillen, and Laurel S. Maughan. Co-published simultaneously in *Journal of Library Administration* (The Haworth Information Press, an imprint of The Haworth Press, Inc.) Vol. 36, No. 1/2, 2002, pp. 97-121; and: *Information Literacy Programs: Successes and Challenges* (ed: Patricia Durisin) The Haworth Information Press, an imprint of The Haworth Press, Inc., 2002, pp. 97-121. Single or multiple copies of this article are available for a fee from The Haworth Document Delivery Service [1-800-HAWORTH, 9:00 a.m. - 5:00 p.m. (EST). E-mail address: getinfo@haworthpressinc.com].

KEYWORDS. Information literacy, library instruction programs, assessment, evaluation, self-study, *ACRL Information Literacy Competency Standards*

Information literacy competency is a more common element of general education requirements in higher education.[1] Consequently, an effective library instruction program will incorporate the concept. The Reference and Instruction Department at Oregon State University's (OSU) Valley Library was charged with preparing a vision statement for our instruction program with specific goals. In articulating our vision, we realized we must understand how information literacy competencies were being addressed. In this article, we describe the initial self-study of our instruction practice using the *ACRL Information Literacy Competency Standards for Higher Education*[2] (ILC's) as a benchmark. We discuss the results of our assessment, detail the follow-up to that effort, and describe the challenges and successes we experienced both within and outside the library.

EVALUATION OF INSTRUCTION

The motivation for evaluating library instruction programs is both internal and external. Library instructors desire to meet the needs of their students and want to know how effectively they do so. Accrediting agencies place increased emphasis on accountability for demonstrating student learning outcomes.[3]

Bober, Poulin, and Vileno [4] point out several compelling reasons for evaluating library instruction. One of these is to use the results for improving the quality of the program. A second reason is for professional development of teaching staff. A third reason is more strategic: proving the value of such instruction furthers the larger educational goals of the various disciplines and the institution as a whole. It is only this type of accountability that will result in institutionalized curricular changes. All of these reasons played a role in approaching our own program assessment. Evaluations of entire programs are not common.[5] Our review of the recent library literature found nothing similar to our initial self-assessment process. As Colburn and Cordell point out "assessment in library instruction programs most often means assessment of the instruction session . . . [which] has not, in most cases been particularly useful."[6] Our instruction program evaluation has been comprised of largely this type of "reaction" data from students and the requesting faculty member. The evaluation materials for library instruction programs created by the Research Committee of the Library Instruction Round Table[7] do not include any approaches similar to our standards-based program evaluation.

One means of assessing a program is to select benchmarks for comparison. One looks at the "gap" between existing practice and desired position, and analyzes what needs to be done to close that gap. Certainly standards for library instruction programs in academic institutions have existed for years. The ACRL ILC's seemed the logical benchmark, however, because it provides the most current model and has been adopted by several states' Boards of Higher Education.

We developed an assessment tool for our current instruction practices using the ACRL ILC's as a framework. The results served as the basis for discussions with the library's teaching faculty about our goals for our program and the measures needed to reach them. In addition, we identified "priority" competencies to use as a starting point for conversations with key faculty and programs on campus.

OVERVIEW OF THE EXISTING PROGRAM

OSU is a Carnegie I Research institution with Land, Sea and Space grant status. There are approximately 17,000 undergraduate and graduate students from every state in the nation and about 80 other countries. Instruction in the use of the library has been a part of librarians' responsibilities for many years here. Our "program" has consisted largely of individual sessions requested by faculty for discipline-based classes at all levels, from freshmen to graduate students. Classroom space has always been provided in the library. In the 1970s and 1980s, several credit courses were developed, usually 1 or 2 credit seminars, for various disciplines such as English, Chemistry, Engineering and Agriculture. Additionally, printed (and now Web based) materials, such as subject research guides and help pages for specific tools, have been provided. With the increase in electronic access and resources, online tutorials have also evolved. Although we have attempted over the years to include a more systematic introduction to research proficiency in fundamental areas of the undergraduate program, such as the writing intensive curriculum, we have been largely unsuccessful.

OSU does not currently have an information literacy requirement as part of its baccalaureate core program. Like many academic libraries, we would like to see information literacy instruction better integrated into the curriculum.[8] We believe we first need to raise awareness and promote the importance of this set of skills as an essential part of creating students who can be successful both during their academic careers and beyond. Additionally, we want to position the Library and its instructional program as a significant resource to achieve this end.

We can build awareness about the value of information literacy through our individual contacts with faculty and through our instructional work with students. To effectively articulate these ideas on campus, however, we needed to be clear among ourselves as a teaching faculty what we are trying to accomplish with our current instruction efforts as well as what we want to work towards.

ASSESSING OUR CURRENT PRACTICE

The assessment of our current instruction practice involved surveying and analyzing our library's instructors regarding their use of competencies in their teaching. We also produced a statistical summary examining our instruction over the past year.

In creating the survey instrument (see Appendix 1) to make this assessment, we tailored the ACRL ILC's to our institutional situation. We reordered them based on a more logical research strategy, dropped some which seemed inappropriate for our situation, and integrated some of our own competencies which had been developed during the revision of our online tutorial. We selected those ILC's which seemed most appropriate for introduction at the lower division academic level, and those which librarians seemed to be uniquely qualified to teach.

The survey was distributed to our library teaching faculty, who responded to the following questions based on the previous year's instruction in each discipline for which they were responsible. For each selected outcome/performance measure, we asked librarians to indicate:

1. How do you teach this? Choices included:

   a. one-shot general sessions
   b. one-shot subject specific sessions
   c. a credit course
   d. a Web-based tutorial
   e. one-on-one at the Reference Desk

2. At what level do you teach this? Choices included:

   a. lower division undergraduate
   b. upper division undergraduate
   c. graduate

3. Ideally, at what level would this outcome be introduced to students?

   a. lower division undergraduate
   b. upper division undergraduate
   c. graduate

Library instructors found the survey very difficult to complete. Difficulties arose from several factors. First, librarians tend to "teach to assignments"; that is, we teach what is needed for students to complete the research assignment as given by the classroom instructor. Identifying competencies within these very disparate types of assignments is difficult because assignments may or may not concretely address specific information literacy competencies. Conversely, assignments may address parts of multiple competencies. Second, inclusion of the "outcomes" with the competencies and performance indicators introduced duplications, discrepancies and contradictions that were difficult to reconcile. In many instances, librarians may have taught one of the outcomes or a piece of an outcome, but the majority of the performance indicator or the competency was not addressed.

PRIMARY COMPETENCIES DETERMINED

We analyzed 27 surveys in terms of the frequencies with which the ILC's were addressed.* Our survey results confirmed that our librarians felt the competencies and outcomes included in the survey are ideally introduced to students at the lower division undergraduate level. In spite of the "ideal" level of introduction to lower division undergraduates, much of our instruction on all these competencies takes place in upper division and graduate level sessions. Several competencies surfaced as "priorities" (see Figure 1). They are addressed more often than others and at all levels of instruction from lower division undergraduate to graduate students. The top eight competencies, in priority order as determined by their total frequency across all types of instruction, include:

1. 1.1.e. Identifies key concepts and terms that describe the information need.
2. 2.3.a. Uses various search systems to retrieve information in a variety of formats.
3. 2.1.c. Investigates the scope, content and organization of information retrieval systems.
4. 2.2.b. Identifies key words, synonyms and related terms for the information needed.
5. 2.2.d. Constructs a search strategy using appropriate commands for the information retrieval system selected.
6. 2.3.c. Uses specialized online or in person services available at the institution to retrieve information needed.
7. 1.2.c. Identifies the value and differences of potential resources in a variety of formats.
8. 1.1.c. Explores general information sources to increase familiarity with the topic.

---

*For additional information or copies of the raw data, please contact Jeanne Davidson; Jeanne.Davidson@orst.edu or 121 The Valley Library, Oregon State University, Corvallis, OR 97331.

FIGURE 1. Rank Order of Competencies by Type of Instruction

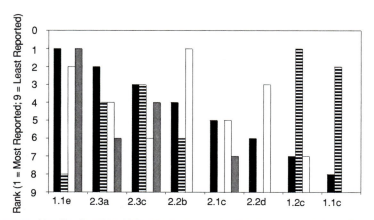

Competency Identifier (found in *ACRL Information Literacy Competencies for Higher Education*)

■ Grand Total	▤ Single Session– General	▢ Single Session– Subject Specific	▥ One-on-One at Ref Desk

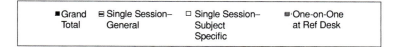

These priorities can be seen particularly in the one shot classes, both General and Subject Specific. The ordering of these competencies is not as clearly defined in the online tutorial or the credit courses. In these two categories, the majority of our "priority competencies" placed within the top 50%, but numbers 2, 3, and 6 fall very low in the frequency observations. These are also very small samples within the overall observations.

Four of the eight priority competencies are addressed substantially at the Reference Desk (see Figure 1). The top eight outcomes that are addressed at the reference desk, in priority order (competencies also identified as "priority" competencies are indicated by *) included:

1. *1.1.e. Identifies key concepts and terms that describe the information need.
2. 2.3.b. Uses various classification schemes and other systems to locate information resources within the library or to identify specific sites for physical exploration.
3. 1.1.d. Defines or modifies the information need to achieve a manageable focus.
4. *2.3.c. Uses specialized online or in person services available at the institution to retrieve information needed.
5. 2.5.a. Selects among various technologies the most appropriate one for the task of extracting the needed information.

6. *2.3.a. Uses various search systems to retrieve information in a variety of formats.
7. *2.1.c. Investigates the scope, content and organization of information retrieval systems.
8. 2.1.d. Selects efficient and effective approaches for accessing the information needed from the investigative method or information retrieval system.

In addition to the survey of our library teaching faculty's intuitive use of the ACRL ILC's, we looked at the statistics compiled from our instructor reports during this period. Our current instructional program consists primarily of one-shot sessions connected to specific classes and assignments. Eighty seven percent of our instruction in 1999/2000 related to a particular discipline (see Figure 2).

Our instruction statistics indicated that although 61% of our sessions are for upper division (300, 400 level) undergraduate and graduate courses (see Figure 3), 52% of the students we teach are in lower division undergraduate (100, 200 level) classes (see Figure 4).

DISCUSSIONS WITH LIBRARY FACULTY

Three primary issues were gleaned from the formal and informal discussions with library teaching faculty. First, we recognized that we lacked a clearly articulated mission and goals for our instructional program. We also realized that teaching librarians did not agree on the fundamental role or desirability of teaching to outcomes and/or to the ACRL ILC's. We also found that moving to a more programmatic approach to instruction, assuming all agreed it was desirable, requires a variety of types of support.

Without a clearly articulated mission statement, we cannot incorporate library instruction goals into the mission and goals of the library as a whole. In addition, without a clear conception of the impact of either meeting or not meeting library instruction goals, we cannot clearly express the needs we have for resources and administrative support. This lack of clarity and articulation also hampers fully engaging with faculty in constructive conversations related to the role of information literacy in the university's curriculum.

Library instructors did not all agree that a more programmatic approach to our library instruction would be beneficial. Our discussions highlighted the recognition that outcomes-based teaching and adopting the ACRL ILC's as the basis for an instruction program are fundamental changes in approach for many librarians. Change of this magnitude presents support issues in areas

FIGURE 2. Total Sessions by Discipline

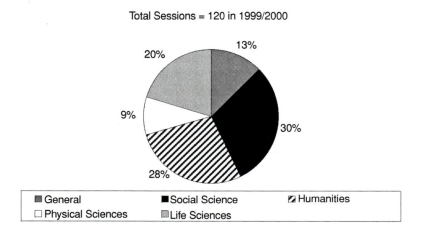

Total Sessions = 120 in 1999/2000

| General | Social Science | Humanities |
| Physical Sciences | Life Sciences | |

FIGURE 3. Number of Sessions by Academic Level

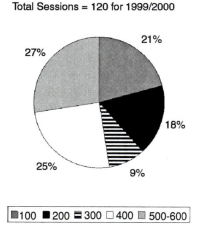

Total Sessions = 120 for 1999/2000

100 200 300 400 500-600

such as instructional design and assessment. In addition, librarians also need strategies for communicating library instructional goals and methods more clearly to university faculty.

Several librarians expressed the need for additional resources and training in instructional design, especially related to classroom activities and assign-

FIGURE 4. Number of Students by Academic Level

Total Students = 2816 for 1999/2000

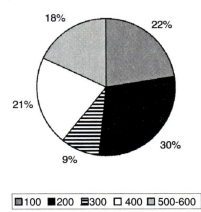

| ⊞100 | ■200 | ⊟300 | □400 | ▦500-600 |

ments. Most class sessions we do are designed in response to assignments designed by faculty members in the discipline areas. Librarians need to be able to negotiate with faculty about the information literacy goals for any given assignment. Then they must be able to help tailor the assignment to better support the mutually agreed upon outcomes.

Assessment of student learning is also an important area needing additional support. Librarians often think of assessment as a formal process, but informal strategies for assessing student learning can be easily incorporated as class session activities. Assessment, both formal and informal, can be very effective for engaging faculty in conversation about goals for library instruction.

Much work remains to be done in identifying the fundamental role of the ILC's in our instruction program. We all agreed with the essence of what they promote, and our survey of instructional practice demonstrated that we try to incorporate many of the major ideas into our instructional sessions. However, if we adopt them as the basis for our program, must we move to outcomes-based instruction? If so, what does that look like in terms of everyday teaching practice, specifically to our traditional "teaching to assignments"? Finally, are the ACRL ILC's the best articulation of the "outcomes" we want to address?

UNIVERSITY-WIDE DISCUSSIONS

This assessment of current practice also led to the identification of needs for university-wide participation. Having determined core competencies ideally

taught at the lower division undergraduate level, we identified two heavily enrolled first-year programs and the Writing Intensive Curriculum (WIC) program
as potential partners for collaboration. In addition, the importance of involving
faculty across campus in continuing discussions of ILC's led us to identify two
key committees for contact in the coming year: the university's Advancement of
Teaching Committee, and the Baccalaureate Core Committee.

Collaboration has already begun with the English composition program. We
asked to be involved with a recent curriculum revision of the required first year
composition course. Several of the library's instructors have been involved in
emphasizing and developing a library research component for the program. We
have also begun collaborating, albeit on a smaller scale, with Communications
111, another heavily enrolled course in the baccalaureate core. The coordinator
of the (WIC) program has long been an advocate for information literacy. She
regularly invites librarians to the seminars she holds for WIC faculty. We have
been invited to work with faculty on creating assignments that promote information literacy. She is also in favor of the idea of using juniors and seniors enrolled
in WIC program courses for a broad-based assessment of student information
literacy competence, which we anticipate conducting in the coming year.

The charge to the university's Advancement of Teaching Committee is to
provide professional development for faculty across the university focused on
teaching. We anticipate that this committee may be a key point of contact to
begin working with faculty on the design of assignments to address information literacy. The university Baccalaureate Core Committee is another important point for collaboration, because any university-wide information literacy
competency requirement must be approved by this committee.

BENEFITS AND CONCLUSIONS

The assessment itself served as a good introduction to the ACRL ILC's for
the library's teaching faculty. Many had not had the occasion to really look at
the competencies and grapple with how they fit within our teaching practices.
Many of the library faculty reiterated what we had already concluded in preparing the assessment: the standards, performance indicators and outcomes
were sometimes redundant and, in their totality, overwhelming.

The results of the assessment also highlighted the inefficiencies in our current program, such as teaching the same things at all levels of the curriculum.
This provided an additional impetus to identify areas within the university curriculum upon which to focus our efforts, especially at the lower division under-

graduate level. Comprehensive work with lower division students will hopefully provide a foundation upon which to base teaching higher level skills and concepts in upper division subject-based classes.

Following completion of the assessment, we discussed the ramifications of outcomes-based instruction and a more programmatic approach to library instruction. By increasing the awareness of everyone's current instructional activities and philosophies, these discussions created a venue in which library faculty could focus on instructional issues.

We recognized some important differences in the philosophy of, and approaches to, library instruction. Some of these differences can be alleviated with assistance and professional development. Although others remain, we were able to identify common ground upon which to build a shared understanding of our instructional mission. We can now communicate this mission and its goals more widely among library staff and administration, as well as when working with faculty outside the library. Finally, we have identified several major initiatives currently underway, and have taken the opportunity to participate.

NOTES

1. Carla Higgins and Mary Jane Cedar Face, "Integrating Information Literacy Skills into the University Colloquium: Innovation at Southern Oregon University," *Reference Services Review* 26, no. 3-4 (1998): 17-31; Carroll H. Varner, Vanette M. Schwartz, and Jessica George, "Library Instruction and Technology in a General Education 'Gateway' Course: The Student's View," *The Journal of Academic Librarianship* 22 (December 1996): 355-359; Rachel F. Fenske and Susan E. Clark, "Incorporating Library Instruction in a General Education Program for College Freshman," *Reference Services Review* 23 (fall 1995): 69-74.

2. Association of College and Research Libraries, *Information Literacy Competency Standards for Higher Education* (Chicago: Association of College and Research Libraries, American Library Association, 2000).

3. Nancy W. Colburn and Rosanne M. Cordell, "Moving from Subjective to Objective Assessments of Your Instruction Program," *Reference Services Review* 26, no. 3-4 (1998): 125-137.

4. Christopher Bober, Sonia Poulin, and Luigina Vileno, "Evaluating Library Instruction in Academic Libraries: A Critical Review of the Literature, 1980-1993," *The Reference Librarian* 51/52 (1995): 53-71.

5. Ibid.

6. Colburn and Cordell, p.125.

7. Diana D. Shonrock, ed., *Evaluating Library Instruction: Sample Questions, Forms, and Strategies for Practical Use* (Chicago: Research Committee, Library Instruction Round Table, American Library Association, 1996).

8. cf. Bober, Poulin, and Vileno.

BIBLIOGRAPHY

Association of College and Research Libraries. *Information Literacy Competency Standards for Higher Education.* Chicago: Association of College and Research Libraries, American Library Association, 2000.

Bober, Christopher, Sonia Poulin, and Luigina Vileno. "Evaluating Library Instruction in Academic Libraries: A Critical Review of the Literature, 1980-1993." *The Reference Librarian* 51/52 (1995): 53-71.

Colburn, Nancy W. and Rosanne M. Cordell. "Moving from Subjective to Objective Assessments of your Instruction Program." *Reference Services Review* 26 n. 3-4 (1998): 125-137.

Fenske, Rachel F. and Susan E. Clark. "Incorporating Library Instruction in a General Education Program for College Freshman." *Reference Services Review* 23 (1995): 69-74.

Higgins, Carla and Mary Jane Cedar Face. "Integrating Information Literacy Skills into the University Colloquium: Innovation at Southern Oregon University." *Reference Services Review* 26 n. 3-4 (1998): 17-31.

Shonrock, Diana D., ed. *Evaluating Library Instruction: Sample Questions, Forms, and Strategies for Practical Use.* Chicago: Research Committee, Library Instruction Round Table, American Library Association, 1996.

Varner, Carroll H., Vanette M Schwartz, and Jessica George. "Library Instruction and Technology in a General Education 'Gateway' Course: The Student's View." *The Journal of Academic Librarianship* 22 (1996): 355-359.

APPENDIX 1. SURVEY INSTRUMENT

Dear Colleague:

The RI Instruction Workgroup is making an assessment of the OSU Libraries' current practice of library instruction. We are using the ACRL "Information Literacy Competency Standards for Higher Education" (http://www.ala.org/acrl/ilstandardlo.html) as the basis for this survey. Other documents which have been consulted and incorporated as appropriate are the ACRL Instruction Section "Objectives for Information Literacy Instruction by Academic Libraries (Draft)" (http://www.libraries.rutgers.edu/is/projects/objectives/Objs.html)* and "Information Technology Literacy Competencies" (OSU Libraries, http://osulibrary.orst.edu/staff/davidsoj/competencies.htm). It is our intent to describe as accurately as possible those library instruction activities and practices which most reflect what we are actually doing in our library instruction program.

For **each department** (see the Valley Library Subject Librarian List at: http://osulibrary.orst.edu/staff/sublist.htm) for which you are subject librarian please describe the bibliographic instruction which you provide. Indicate which of the standards, indicators and outcomes you address in your instruction activities (e.g., general v. subject specific one shot, credit class, etc.) and at what level (e.g., lower division undergraduate, upper division undergraduate, graduate) you address them. We are primarily interested in the information for those departments for which you **provide instruction for students** (not research centers, institutes, etc.).

We have provided 2 survey sheets and encourage you to make photocopies for additional departments for which you are responsible. We would like you to provide a sheet for each department even though you may not provide instruction for that department at this time.

Standards, Performance Indicators, Outcomes and Objectives

The RI Instruction Workgroup of the OSU Libraries in its use of the ACRL "Information Literacy Competency Standards for Higher Education" (http://www.ala.org/acrl/ilstandardlo.html) has determined to use a two level approach. Our initial level (provided below) is considered as a basic level, and we have selected portions of the ACRL document for inclusion. We have retained the number/letter designations of the ACRL document in order to make comparisons with the original document and other documents based upon it

*Since our use of the draft "Objectives" in 2000, they have been approved by ACRL and are currently located at: http://www.ala.org/acrl/guides/objinfolit.html.

easier. In some cases we have reordered outcomes under the indicators to more accurately reflect the current OSU Libraries teaching approach. If we have chosen not to include an ACRL standard, performance indicator, or outcome we have omitted the number/letter for that item. We have also ensured that the information literacy competencies previously endorsed by the department (http://osulibrary.orst.edu/staff/davidsoj/competencies.htm) are all represented in this document as well.

Standard One
The information literate student determines the nature and extent of the information needed.

Performance Indicators:

1. The information literate student defines and articulates the need for information.

Outcomes Include:
1.1.b. Develops a list of questions or a thesis statement related to the topic.
1.1.e. Identifies key concepts and terms inherent in the thesis statement or question

- Can list terms that may be useful in locating information on a topic.
- Identifies and uses appropriate general or subject-specific sources to discover terminology related to an information need.
- Recognizes that a research topic may have multiple facets or may need to be put into a broader context.
- Can identify more specific concepts that comprise a research topic.

1.1.c. Explores general information sources to increase familiarity with the topic

- Knows that there are both general and subject-specific sources that can provide background information on a topic.
- Recognizes the difference between general and subject-specific information sources.
- Knows when it is appropriate to use a general and subject-specific information source (e.g., to provide an overview, to give ideas on terminology).

1.1.d. Refines and modifies the information need to achieve a manageable focus

- Understands that the initial question might be too broad or narrow.
- Narrows a broad topic and broadens a narrow one by modifying the scope or direction of the question.
- Understands that the desired end product will play a role in focusing the question.

- Understands that the search for background information will help provide an initial understanding of the topic that begins the process of focusing.
- Knows that the course instructor and librarians can assist in finding a manageable focus for the topic.

2. The information literate student identifies a variety of types and formats of potential sources for information.

Outcomes Include:

1.2.b. Recognizes that knowledge can be organized into disciplines that influence the way information is accessed

- Understands that there are three major disciplines of knowledge–humanities, social sciences, sciences-and that there are subject fields that comprise each discipline.
- Understands the importance of relevant subject field- and discipline-related terminology in the information research process.
- Understands how books and journals fit within a particular discipline or subject field and affect the researcher's access to information.

1.2.c. Identifies the value and differences of potential resources in a variety of formats (e.g.,multimedia, database, web site, data set, audio/visual, book)

- Recognizes that information is available in various formats.
- Understands that the format in which information appears may affect its usefulness for a particular information need.

1.2.d. Identifies the purpose and audience of potential resources (e.g., popular vs. scholarly, current vs. historical)

- Distinguishes characteristics of information provided for different audiences.
- Can identify the intent or purpose of an information source; this may require use of additional sources.

3. The information literate student considers the costs and benefits of acquiring the needed information.

Outcomes Include:

1.3.a. Determines the availability of needed information and makes decisions on broadening the information seeking process beyond local resources (e.g., interlibrary loan; using resources at other locations; obtaining images, videos, text, or sound)

- Can determine if material is available immediately.
- Knows how to use other services to obtain desired materials or alternative sources.

1.3.c. Defines a realistic overall plan and timeline to acquire the needed information

- Searches for and gathers information based on an informal, flexible plan.
- Acts appropriately to obtain information within the time frame required.

4. The information literate student reevaluates the nature and extent of the information need.

Outcomes Include:

1.4.a. Reviews the initial information need to clarify, revise, or refine the question

- Recognizes that a research topic may require revision, based on the amount of information found (or not found).
- Recognizes that a topic may need to be modified based on the content of information found.
- Understands that it is not always necessary to abandon a topic if an initial search for information was not successful.

1.4.b. Describes criteria used to make information decisions and choices

- Understands that the intended audience influences information choices.
- Understands that the desired end-product influences information choices (e.g., visual aids or audio/visual material may be needed for an oral presentation).
- Recognizes the need to consider various criteria, such as currency. (See also 2.4. and 3.2.)

Standard Two
The information literate student accesses needed information effectively and efficiently.

Performance Indicators:

1. The information literate student selects the most appropriate investigative methods or information retrieval systems for accessing the needed information.

Outcomes Include:

2.1.c. Investigates the scope, content, and organization of information retrieval systems

- Understands the structure and components of the system or tool being used, regardless of format.

- Can identify the source of help within a given information retrieval system and use it effectively.
- Can identify what types of information are contained in a particular system (e.g., not all databases are full text; content of catalogs, periodical databases, and Web sites).
- Demonstrates appropriate use of the library catalog (e.g., to identify book and journal holdings).
- Distinguishes among indexes, online databases, and collections of online databases, as well as gateways to different databases and collections.
- Selects appropriate tool(s)–indexes, online databases, etc.–for research on a particular topic.
- Recognizes the differences between Internet search tools and subscription or fee-based databases.
- Identifies and uses search language and protocols (e.g., adjacency) appropriate to the retrieval system.
- Determines the period of time covered by a particular source.
- Identifies the types of sources that are indexed in a particular database or index (e.g., an index that covers newspapers or popular periodicals and a more specialized index to find scholarly literature).
- Understands when it is appropriate to use a single tool (e.g., using only a periodical index when only periodical articles are required).
- Distinguishes between full-text and bibliographic databases.

2.1.d. Selects efficient and effective approaches for accessing the information needed from the investigative method or information retrieval system

- Selects appropriate information sources and determines their relevance for the current information need.
- Determines appropriate means for recording or saving the desired information (e.g., printing, saving to disc, photocopying, taking notes).
- Analyzes and interprets the information collected using a growing awareness of key terms and concepts to decide whether to search for additional information or to identify more accurately when the information need has been met.

2. The information literate student constructs and implements effectively-designed search strategies.

Outcomes Include:
2.2.a. Develops a research plan

- Understands that there is a process to searching for information.

- Recognizes that there are different types of information (e.g., background/specific), which may be suitable for different purposes.
- Gathers and evaluates information and appropriately modifies the research plan as new insights are gained.

2.2.b. Identifies keywords, synonyms and related terms for the information needed

- Identifies keywords or phrases that represent a topic.
- Understands that different terminology may be used in general sources and subject-specific sources.
- Identifies alternate terminology, including synonyms, broader or narrower terms, or phrases that describe a topic.

2.2.c. Selects controlled vocabulary specific to the discipline or information retrieval source

- Uses background sources (e.g., encyclopedias, handbooks, dictionaries, thesauri, textbooks) to identify discipline-specific terminology that describes a given topic.
- Can explain what controlled vocabulary is and why it is used.
- Identifies search terms likely to be useful for a research topic in relevant controlled vocabulary lists.
- Identifies when and where controlled vocabulary is used in a bibliographic record, and then successfully searches for additional information using that vocabulary.

2.2.d. Constructs a search strategy using appropriate commands for the information retrieval system selected (e.g., Boolean operators, truncation, and proximity for search engines; internal organizers such as indexes for books)

- Understands when it is appropriate to search a particular field, e.g., title, author, subject.
- Understands the concept of Boolean logic and can construct a search statement using Boolean operators.
- Understands the concept of proximity searching and can construct a search statement using proximity operators.
- Understands the concept of browsing and can use an index that allows it.
- Understands the concept of keyword searching and can use it appropriately and effectively.
- Understands the concept of truncation and can use it appropriately and effectively.

2.2.e. Implements the search strategy in various information retrieval systems using different user interfaces and search engines, with different command languages, protocols, and search parameters

- Uses help screens and other user aids to understand the particular search structures and commands of an information retrieval system.
- Is aware that there may be separate interfaces for basic and advanced searching in retrieval systems.
- Narrows or broadens questions and search terms to retrieve the appropriate quantity of information, using search techniques such as Boolean logic, limiting, and field searching.
- Identifies and selects keywords and phrases to use when searching each source, recognizing that different sources may use different terminology for similar concepts.
- Formulates search strategies to match information needs with available resources.
- Recognizes differences in searching for bibliographic records, abstracts, or full text in information sources.

2.2.f. Implements the search using research tools appropriate to the discipline

- Can locate major print bibliographic and reference sources appropriate to the discipline of a research topic.
- Can locate and use a specialized dictionary, encyclopedia, bibliography, or other common reference tool in print format for a given topic.
- Understands that items may be grouped together by subject in order to facilitate browsing.
- Understands a book's organizational structure (e.g., indexes, tables of contents, user's instructions, legends, cross-references) in order to locate pertinent information within the book.
- Understands and effectively uses the organizational structure of a typical book.

3. The information literate student retrieves information online or in person using a variety of methods.

Outcomes Include:

2.3.a. Uses various search systems to retrieve information in a variety of formats

- Recognizes that some material is not available online or in digitized formats and must be accessed in print or other formats (e.g., film, fiche, video, audio).

- Identifies research sources, regardless of format, that are appropriate to a particular discipline or research need.
- Recognizes the format of an information source (e.g., book, chapter in a book, periodical article) from its citation. (See also 2.3.b.)
- Understands that there are different research sources (e.g., catalogs and indexes) that are used to find different types of information (e.g., books and periodical articles).
- Recognizes search functionality common to most databases regardless of differences in the search interface (e.g., Boolean logic capability, field structure, keyword searching).
- Understands the organizational structure and access points of print research sources (e.g., indexes, bibliographies) and uses them effectively.

2.3.b. Uses various classification schemes and other systems (e.g., call number systems or indexes) to locate information resources within the library or to identify specific sites for physical exploration

- Understands how a call number assists in locating the corresponding item in the library.
- Uses call number systems effectively.
- Can explain the difference between the library catalog and a periodical index.
- Understands that different periodical indexes may have different scopes of coverage.
- Distinguishes among citations to various types of materials (e.g., books, periodical articles, essays in anthologies). (See also 2.3.a.)

2.3.c. Uses online or in person services available at the institution to retrieve information needed (e.g., interlibrary loan/document delivery)

- Can retrieve a document in print or electronic form.
- Understands that information not available locally can be retrieved through various methods.
- Identifies the appropriate service point or resource for the particular information need.
- Can initiate an interlibrary loan request by filling out and submitting a form either online or in person.
- Uses the Web site of an institution, library, organization or community to locate information about specific services, if appropriate.

4. The information literate student refines the search strategy if necessary.

Outcomes Include:
2.4.a. Assesses the quantity, quality, and relevance of the search results to determine whether alternative information retrieval systems or investigative methods should be utilized

- Determines if the quantity of citations retrieved is adequate, too extensive, or insufficient for the information need.
- Assesses the relevance of information found by examining elements of the citation such as title, abstract, subject headings, source, and date of publication.
- Evaluates the quality of the information retrieved using criteria such as authorship, point of view/bias, date written, citations, etc.
- Determines the relevance of an item to the information need in terms of its depth of information, language, and time frame.

2.4.b. Identifies gaps in the information retrieved and determines if the search strategy should be revised.
2.4.c. Repeats the search using the revised strategy as necessary.

5. The information literate student extracts, records, and manages the information and its sources.

Outcomes Include:
2.5.a Selects among various technologies the most appropriate one for the task of extracting the needed information (e.g., print, download, send files via e-mail, photocopier)

- Marks or records selected items or information relevant to the topic (e.g., uses mark functions in retrieval systems, records pertinent information from print resources).

2.5.c. Differentiates between the types of sources cited and understands the elements and correct syntax of a citation for a wide range of resources

- Identifies citation elements for information sources in different formats (e.g., book, article, television program, Web page, interview).
- Understands that the format of the source cited may dictate a certain citation style.
- Understands that different disciplines may use different citation styles.
- Understands that the appropriate documentation style may vary by discipline (e.g., MLA for English, University of Chicago for history, APA for psychology).

2.5.d. Records all pertinent citation information for future reference

- Explains necessity to cite all references (e.g., to avoid plagiarism; to give credit to the author(s); to provide readers with an access path to the resource).
- Understands how to use a documentation style to record bibliographic information from an item retrieved through research.
- Uses correctly and consistently the citation style appropriate to a specific discipline.
- Can locate information about documentation styles either in print or electronically, e.g., through the library's Web site.
- Recognizes that consistency of citation format is important, especially if a classroom instructor has not required a particular style.

Standard Three
The information literate student evaluates information and its sources critically and incorporates selected information into his or her knowledge base and value system.

Performance Indicators:

2. The information literate student articulates and applies initial criteria for evaluating both the information and its sources.

Outcomes Include:
3.2.a. Examines and compares information from various sources in order to evaluate reliability, validity, accuracy, authority, timeliness, and point of view or bias

- Locates and examines critical reviews of information sources using available resources and technologies.
- Investigates an author's qualifications and reputation through reviews or biographical sources.
- Investigates validity and accuracy by consulting sources identified through bibliographic references.
- Determines publisher or producer of information resources (e.g., sponsor of web site, journal publisher, etc.)
- Investigates qualifications and reputation of the publisher or issuing agency by consulting other information resources. (See also 3.4.e.)
- Determines when the information was published or where to look for that information.

- Recognizes the importance of timeliness or date of publication to the value of the source.
- Can determine if the information retrieved is sufficiently current for the information need.
- Understands that other sources may provide additional information to either confirm or question point of view or bias.

3.2.c. Recognizes potential sources of bias

- Understands that regardless of format, published and unpublished information reflects an author's, sponsor's, and/or publisher's point of view.
- Understands that, consciously or not, some information and sources may present a one-sided view and may express opinions rather than facts.
- Understands that some information and sources may be designed to trigger emotions, conjure stereotypes, or promote support for a particular viewpoint or group.
- Applies evaluative criteria to information and its source (e.g., author's expertise, currency, accuracy, point of view, type of publication or information, sponsorship).
- Searches for independent verification or corroboration of the accuracy and completeness of the data or representation of facts presented in an information source.

7. The information literate student determines whether the initial query should be revised.

Outcomes Include:
3.7.a. Determines if original information need has been satisfied or if additional information is needed.
3.7.b. Reviews search strategy and incorporates additional concepts as necessary
Understands that searches may be limited or expanded by modifying search terminology or logic.
3.7.c. Reviews information retrieval sources used and expands to include others as needed

- Examines footnotes and bibliographies from retrieved items to locate additional sources.
- Follows and evaluates relevant online links to additional sources. Uses new knowledge as elements of revised search strategy to gather additional information.

Survey Sheet. Standards, Performance Indicators, Outcomes, and Objectives

Name _____
Department/Discipline _____

G = Graduate (500-600)
U = Upper Division (300-400)
L = Lower Division (100-200)

	One Shot General			One Shot Subject Specific			Online Tutorial	Credit Class			One on One Ref Desk	(See Below)*			Comments
	L	U	G	L	U	G		L	U	G		L	U	G	
1.1.b															
1.1.e															
1.1.c															
1.1.d															
1.2.b															
1.2.c															
1.2.d															
1.3.a															
1.3.c															
1.4.a															
1.4.b															
2.1.c															
2.1.d															

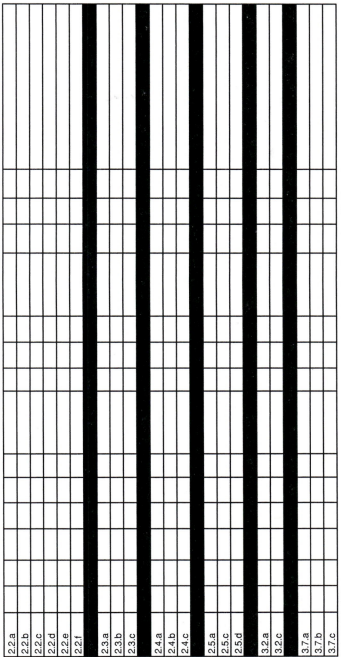

2.2.a																							
2.2.b																							
2.2.c																							
2.2.d																							
2.2.e																							
2.2.f																							
2.3.a																							
2.3.b																							
2.3.c																							
2.4.a																							
2.4.b																							
2.4.c																							
2.5.a																							
2.5.c																							
2.5.d																							
3.2.a																							
3.2.c																							
3.7.a																							
3.7.b																							
3.7.c																							

*Ideally, at what level would this outcome be introduced to students? L, U, or G

121

Collaborating to Advance Curriculum-Based Information Literacy Initiatives

Austin Booth
Carole Ann Fabian

SUMMARY. Partnerships with administrative and academic colleagues are needed for successful integration of ACRL information literacy standards into campus curricula. This article explores organizational structures, curriculum guidelines and standards for higher education, and suggests strategies to position ACRL IL standards within institutional planning documents and to initiate campus-wide adoption of IL standards. *[Article copies available for a fee from The Haworth Document Delivery Service: 1-800-HAWORTH. E-mail address: <getinfo@haworthpressinc.com> Website: <http://www.HaworthPress.com> © 2002 by The Haworth Press, Inc. All rights reserved.]*

KEYWORDS. Information literacy, faculty-librarian partnership, curriculum standards, academic administration/administrators

Austin Booth is Director of Collections & Research Services, General Libraries, University at Buffalo (E-mail: habooth@acsu.buffalo.edu).

Carole Ann Fabian is Applied Arts Librarian, General Libraries, University at Buffalo (E-mail: cafabian@buffalo.edu).

[Haworth co-indexing entry note]: "Collaborating to Advance Curriculum-Based Information Literacy Initiatives." Booth, Austin, and Carole Ann Fabian. Co-published simultaneously in *Journal of Library Administration* (The Haworth Information Press, an imprint of The Haworth Press, Inc.) Vol. 36, No. 1/2, 2002, pp. 123-142; and: *Information Literacy Programs: Successes and Challenges* (ed: Patricia Durisin) The Haworth Information Press, an imprint of The Haworth Press, Inc., 2002, pp. 123-142. Single or multiple copies of this article are available for a fee from The Haworth Document Delivery Service [1-800-HAWORTH, 9:00 a.m. - 5:00 p.m. (EST). E-mail address: getinfo@haworthpressinc.com].

DEFINING INFORMATION LITERACY

Academic librarians are actively exploring a variety of models to advance the integration of information literacy standards into academic programs, including credit-bearing "stand-alone" information literacy courses and curriculum-integrated models. Definitions of information literacy (IL) abound in the literatures of academic librarianship and higher education. Useful summaries of a variety of these definitions can be found on the Institute for Information Literacy Web pages.[1] In working with teaching faculty and academic administrators, we have found that broad, contextual statements that tie together both the concerns of libraries and other higher education constituencies are the most useful for initiating productive campus-wide dialogues. In "Information Literacy as a Liberal Art," Jeremy Shapiro and Shelley Hughes provide such a definition: "In its narrowest sense information literacy includes the practical skills involved in effective use of information technology and information resources, either print or electronic. Information literacy is a new liberal art which extends beyond technical skills and is conceived as the critical reflection on the nature of information itself, its technical infrastructure and its social, cultural and even philosophical context and impact."[2] Shapiro and Hughes go on to expand upon their definition of information literacy as a liberal art; they cite tool literacy, resource literacy, social-structural literacy, research literacy, and publishing literacy as critical goals of an information literacy program–five competencies that not only directly parallel the ACRL Information Literacy Standards,[3] but link the ACRL standards to typical higher-education goals.

REVIEW OF IL INTEGRATION LITERATURE

No one document or body of literature addresses all aspects of IL integration, nor the interconnectedness of ACRL standards and higher-education priorities for learning. It is incumbent, therefore, on the IL advocate to piece together frameworks, strategies and implementation plans from the research and experiences of others gathered in the professional literature of librarianship and higher education.

A large interdisciplinary body of work on various aspects of information literacy can be identified in academic library, higher education administration, and K-12 library and education publications. We have surveyed these distinct areas of investigation and have found interesting commonalties and useful resources for further study in support of academic IL integration. The academic-library literature tends to present in-depth analyses of specific aspects of IL; this complex discussion of the parts sometimes obscures the whole, interconnected picture. The K-12 literature often provides a more integrated view of the strategic, programmatic, and pedagogical aspects of IL integration. Both literatures stress the need for collaborative goal setting, planning, implementation, and assessment. Of particular interest here is the attention paid in these literatures to the concepts of collegial partnership and institutional readiness as they relate to the development of IL programs.

The literature of academic librarianship contains an extensive and growing body of work on partnering with faculty. Although this literature presents many useful models for the library practitioner, it tends to focus almost exclusively on work with faculty at the course level, as opposed to a strategic focus at the administrative or programmatic level.[4] Arguments which emphasize the importance of faculty-librarian collaboration are presented in Betsy Baker's seminal article "Bibliographic Instruction: Building the Librarian/Faculty Partnership."[5] Baker demonstrates and reinforces the necessity for integrating instruction into the research process, and for achieving a balance among faculty, students, and the library. She also discusses the attributes and strengths both faculty and librarians can bring to the research process to benefit students. Evan Ira Farber, in "College Libraries and the Teaching/Learning Process: A 25-year Reflection," provides an overview of the growing instructional role of academic librarians over the past twenty-five years, and the changing relationship between librarians and teaching faculty.[6] A fascinating recent collection of essays, *The Collaborative Imperative: Librarians and Faculty Working Together in the Information Universe*, contains both a range of examples of relationships with classroom faculty, practical tips, and case studies, as well as more theoretical discussions.[7] Within this collection, Doug Cook's chapter, "Creating Connections," provides a particularly useful overview of the literature on library-faculty collaboration.

Larry Hardesty has written several significant pieces on faculty culture, including an essay that tracks important trends in higher education for librarians to consider: a shifting emphasis on research content and specialization, and a de-emphasis of teaching process and undergraduate education.[8] These are critical trends that must be accommodated by librarians as they plan partnerships with faculty. Hardesty's work also implies that IL instruction planning groups need to focus on discipline-based program development, rather than solely course-specific development. Maureen Nimon also emphasizes the importance of disciplinary outcomes and assessment, but does so within the promotion of a highly individualized, course-integrated model of instruction.[9] She suggests that librarians need to partner not only in the development of IL instructional components but also in the measurement of student outcomes and program assessment. She outlines a three-fold partnership strategy: shared goals, shared teaching of techniques and tools, and an integrated "audit" tool. Nimon also points to some basic educational methods for effective IL instruction: context specificity, usefulness to learner, multiple opportunities for learning, rapid feedback, availability of remediation, incremental instruction, transferable skills, and modular design.

Although academic library literature pays considerable attention to relationships between librarians and teaching faculty, it pays less so to relationships between librarians and non-library campus leadership, including administrative, decanal and departmental officers. Hannelore B. Rader's, "A New Academic Library Model: Partnerships for Learning and Teaching," for instance, looks at partnerships with academic peers and external organizations, but does not discuss partnerships with institutional administrative personnel and bodies.[10] It is important, therefore, that IL program developers look beyond the academic library literature and study models described in both higher education administration and K-12 education publications for useful vocabulary, processes and structures that can be adapted to IL integration goals.

K-12 librarians have a history of working in a standards-based environment for teaching and learning. Their work on learning outcomes, or document-based teaching methods, for example, can provide useful strategies to academic librarians. In "Beyond the Frontline: Activating New Partnerships in Support of School Libraries," for instance, Ray Doiron demonstrates ways in which IL can be a unifying concept for institution-wide collaborative development of curricular programs.[11] The article points to the roles of a variety of players and their relationships to standard-setting bodies.

A review of literature of higher-education administration proves equally fruitful. Philip Glozbach's "Conditions of Collaboration: A Dean's List of Dos and Don'ts" recommends structures, roles, and decision-making processes for effective administrative-faculty shared governance and leadership.[12] He emphasizes a consultative approach, a focus on institutional mission development and the need for flexible, goal-oriented progress. Glozbach's approach provides useful structures and processes for librarians who wish to cultivate productive relationships with academic administrators. A related article, Guffey, Rampp and Masters' "Barriers and Issues for Shared-Governance Implementation in Academia," outlines critical factors in collaborative leadership and governance including: clear definition of roles, achievable goals, effective communication, mutual trust, experienced colleagues, consistent participation of all collaborators, commitment of time, advocacy of higher governing bodies, accountability, and acknowledging successes.[13] Articles that discuss faculty involvement in IT integration also frequently mention prototypes for library involvement in campus-wide policy setting conversations that can be applied to IL integration.[14]

Frank, Raschke, Wood and Yang, in "Information Consulting: The Key to Success in Academic Libraries," explore basic definitions of partnership and the integration of librarians into the mainstream of academic endeavors across the campus.[15] They draw an important distinction between cooperative and collaborative approaches. Collaborative partners bring their goals "to the table," and together construct plans and programs to achieve common goals; in cooperative alliances, partners respect and support parallel but independent goals, and do not, as a rule, work together to create merged programs. The collaborative mandate is effectively described and argued in Betsy Wilson's "The Lone Ranger Is Dead: Success Today Demands Collaboration," a keynote article to Wilson's ACRL presidential year.[16] She underscores the important contribution that librarians bring to collaborative actions by their natural proclivity towards and historical culture of communication, sharing and cooperation. The library community as a whole believes in the value of inclusive, cross-boundary, inter-disciplinary participation–values that need to be introduced into campus dialogues.

This article seeks to add to the IL literature by presenting strategies for the design of IL programs that mirror learning goals articulated in national, institutional, departmental accreditation and curricular guidelines. In addition, we examine institutional readiness, the cultivation of collegial relationships, and communication processes. Below, we discuss three baseline components for the initiation of campus-wide IL programming: development of collegial partnerships, evaluation of institutional readiness, and utilization of standard-setting resources.

CAMPUS-WIDE PARTNERSHIPS

In this overview, we describe a framework for collegial relationships that involves identifying key partners and supporting shared goals. Specific approaches to developing partner relationships within this framework will be discussed later in the article.

Initiation of campus-wide curriculum-based information literacy programs is a multi-layered, incremental, repetitive process whereby librarians undertake to educate not only student populations but also their administrative and academic colleagues about the goals articulated in the ACRL IL standards. Basic to the curricular integration of IL standards is the establishment of an inclusive foundational network throughout the institution involving administrators, faculty and librarians with student learning as the focus (see Figure 1).

This student-centered development model emphasizes the importance of interaction and collaboration among multiple stakeholders. The selection of

FIGURE 1

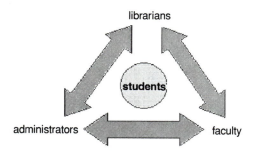

collegial partners among these stakeholders is critical to the success of an IL integration program. Development and maintenance of partnerships is fundamental to any IL program, and involves several significant components: recognition of peers, identification of common goals, interest in collaboration, time to nurture relationships, and establishment of an effective and appropriate communication model for all partners. Prioritization of IL standards must be achieved with each partnered constituency–library administration and library peers, institutional leaders, decanal and departmental unit leaders, and individual faculty members.

At the library administration level, leadership must be aware of and support the standards proposed by ACRL, and act to embed these standards in every activity of the library. Library leadership needs to emphasize that information literacy is *the* central and underlying priority of all library activities. Important initial steps are:

- the inclusion of IL standards in library mission/vision statements
- creation of dedicated IL position(s) or inclusion of IL responsibility in staff job descriptions and library committee charges
- clear guidelines for library staff indicating the extent of library commitment to IL as a goal
- articulation of IL goals as they relate to distinct library activities
- development of accountability/assessment tools to document activities contributing to IL goals
- emphasis on outreach and marketing of library resources, services and programs in support of IL integration into campus curricula
- regular reporting of progress in campus achievement of IL skills to library staff.

Once library administrators and practitioners align and subscribe to these IL priorities, they can begin initiating partnered relationships with peers in the wider campus community.

The first critical partnership, and the group with whom librarians have the most natural affinity, are the teaching faculty. The literature of academic librarianship is replete with examples of productive relationships between librarians and individual faculty members. Below, we summarize what librarians should look for in selecting faculty partners. Among the faculty, librarians find a diversity of both content areas and teaching styles. Librarians should consider the following criteria to help identify IL partners among the faculty:

- colleagues who share pedagogical goals
- colleagues who are interested in developing the information competencies of their students at the same time they present course content
- colleagues who are willing to adjust teaching goals to incorporate skill-building, transferable IL competencies
- colleagues who practice a learner-centered model
- colleagues whose courses demonstrate authentic content and purpose
- colleagues who regularly review and revise their teaching methods to improve student learning outcomes.

To secure a supportive environment for librarian-faculty partnerships, librarians must develop inroads to campus leadership. As the Institute for Information Literacy argues, "Information literacy depends on cooperation among classroom faculty, academic administrators, librarians and other information professionals. In order to effectively implement a program all parties must be involved. Information literacy programs require the leadership and support of academic administrators . . ."[17] Identifying goals we share with campus administrators is crucial to the success of IL programs. The importance of articulating shared goals cannot be overemphasized–campus administrators, after all, exert the greatest influence over the institution by defining priorities and controlling the budget. These priorities inform program initiation and provide the financial justification for the creation of campus-wide educational initiatives. Administrative influence directly controls the quantity, quality, and nature of institutional resources and programs, all of which figure prominently in IL development.

INSTITUTIONAL READINESS

Once collegial partnerships have been established among library peers, faculty, and administrators, the next challenge is to evaluate institutional readiness and to advocate for curricular IL integration. Fundamental to campus-wide

IL implementations are: first, a common understanding of IL standards and their relationship to the curricular goals of the university; and second, an evaluation of readiness in terms of institutional posture and climate for curricular development and re-design.

In order to create an effective IL program, it is essential to introduce the IL lexicon to campus administrators and faculty, and to do so in terms relevant to their goals. The Institute for Information Literacy's *Information Literacy in a Nutshell: Basic Information for Academic Administrators and Faculty* is an extremely useful document that includes vocabulary, guidelines and strategies for initiating conversations about IL. The concise definition of information literacy given in this document, ". . . the ability to locate, evaluate, and use information to become independent life-long learners . . ." includes language not unfamiliar to campus administrators and academics, language that is often articulated in statements concerned with learning goals for higher education.[18] A review of both external and institutional documents such as accreditation standards or mission/vision statements reveal commitments to student learning that can serve as a springboard for advancing the library IL agenda and as a backdrop for collaboration with key campus leaders. A frequent review of these documents provides informative sources for learning about national standards, institutional goals, and disciplinary criteria. As discussed below, examination of these and similar documents can help librarians develop language and articulate arguments crucial to gaining broad-based support for campus-wide IL integration.

Librarians need to keep abreast of the professional literature and trends monitored and echoed by campus administrators. Regular review of articles in the *Chronicle of Higher Education*, *EDUCAUSE Review* and *Syllabus*, for example, can give librarians insight into key trends in teaching and learning within institutes of higher education. Recurrent analysis of this literature together with review of key planning documents can help librarians anticipate responses to needs articulated outside of the institution. Librarians need to demonstrate the close alignment of IL goals and the goals of campus administrators in order to justify and gain support for IL instruction. We can often demonstrate this alignment in one of three ways: (1) through describing the parallels between specific administrative goals and specific information literacy standards; (2) through demonstrating the ways in which students will need to master information literacy skills in order to meet national and local teaching/learning goals; and (3) through revealing the alignment of instructional methods used to achieve national and local teaching/learning goals and the instructional methods used to achieve information literacy goals.

Attention to external and internal administrative documents will also help librarians to recognize and mirror changes in institutional goals as a result of changes in campus leadership. It is not uncommon, for example, for institutions to experience dramatic shifts from a teaching/learning emphasis to one that is more research oriented, or vice versa. Fortunately, the ACRL IL standards are flexible enough to accommodate and support both academic directives. It is incumbent upon librarians therefore, to adapt and re-shape their strategies for IL integration to keep apace both with sea changes in institutional priorities, as well as the management, interpretation and use of an ever-increasing information base. As noted above, both external and internal goal-setting documents provide guidance and opportunities for aligning the library goals with those of campus leaders. The following section gives examples of some key documents and suggestions for exploiting their content in order to advance the library IL agenda.

STANDARD-SETTING RESOURCES

Key Documents Beyond the Local Campus

There are three types of documents produced beyond the campus that can be useful in linking information literacy standards and goals to administrative agendas: (1) national statements on education by government and non-government agencies; (2) reports and recommendations by accreditation bodies; and (3) literature which reports on trends in higher education. Librarians need to be conversant in the language of higher education expressed in these three document types in order to demonstrate how information literacy standards are related to broader educational initiatives. It is up to librarians to make the links between information literacy and trends in higher education, and to convince campus leaders that information literacy programs are as vital to their success as to ours.

Important examples of such external documents include both governmental and non-governmental reports. The *GOALS 2000: Educate America Act*, for example, enacted in 1998 by the U.S. House of Representatives, charges America's educators with educational reform, with an emphasis on establishing learning standards, and demonstrable performance outcomes.[19] The Act seeks to improve learning and teaching by developing national standards for student achievement, citizenship, adult literacy, and lifelong learning. Most of the goals and objectives mentioned in *GOALS 2000* rely on information literacy skills for their fulfillment. Developing an informed citizenry (SEC. 102. National Education Goals), for example, relies on information literacy skills surrounding critical thinking, particularly evaluation skills. The notion of an informed citizenry, after all, rests on the ability to analyze and evaluate information in order to discriminate between facts and opinions. These analytical and evaluative skills are made explicit in ACRL standard 3: "The information literate student evaluates information and its sources critically and incorporates selected information into his or her knowledge base and value system." Another *GOALS 2000* objective quoted frequently in higher-education literature is to "increase substantially . . . the proportion of college students who demonstrate an advanced ability to think critically, communicate effectively, and solve problems." Thinking critically, communicating effectively, and solving problems are, of course, also fundamental information literacy skills.

   What Work Requires of Schools: A SCANS Report for America 2000, prepared for the U.S. Dept. of Labor, articulates fundamental competencies required for successful participation in America's workforce.[20] This report sets the stage for introducing "lifelong learning" skills as a uniform national goal, and introduces language for basic competencies in information and technology literacies. The *SCANS Report* identifies basic foundations and five competencies necessary for tomorrow's workforce, including information skills such as acquiring, analyzing, organizing, and maintaining information, as well as using computers to communicate and process information. Librarians can use documents like the *SCANS Report* to demonstrate that information literacy skills are already part of important national education and training program directives. As librarians, we must show our campus administrators and legislators that information literacy skills enable students, workers and others to adapt to new contexts through the ability to transfer knowledge into new situations. The talents of recognizing information needs, locating useful sources of information, and making bridges between new and previously gained information are all essential information literacy skills.

   Accreditation bodies also generate useful documents such as accreditation standards, reports and recommendations, programs for institutional self-study, and guidelines for evaluation teams. These documents are useful resources for librarians, and are easily linked to information literacy standards. Accreditation standards are, after all, goals that universities, colleges, schools, and programs are mandated to achieve. Many accrediting bodies are now calling for the demonstration of the teaching of information literacy skills, if not the measuring of them. The Southern Association of Colleges and Schools (SACS) Commission on Colleges, *Criteria for Accreditation: Educational Support Services,* for example (section 5.1.2) mandates library participation in preparing students for effective use of information resources.[21] Directly parallel to the ACRL IL Standards, the SACS criteria underscores the concept of "lifelong learning," and specifically calls for the development of campus partnerships in order to integrate lifelong learning skills into the curriculum.

   Librarians should look for statements that emphasize the teaching methods that librarians have found most effective in information literacy instruction.

The American Association of Higher Education's document, "Powerful Partnerships: A Shared Responsibility for Learning," for example, clearly articulates a partnered approach to developing an individualized, experiential and document-based teaching method.[22] Their report cites key pedagogical requirements such as deference to multiple learning styles and attention to transferable literacy skill development. These statements not only justify librarians' own teaching methods, but also foster an approach that, by their very reliance on problem solving and document-based research, involve information literacy skills.

In order to participate fully in conversations with campus administrators, and to shape new academic directions, it is vital that academic librarians be cognizant of trends in higher education. For the last decade, the literature of higher-education administration has focused on questions of assessment. The publication of *A Nation at Risk* in 1983 prompted an interrogation of American education at all levels.[23] The 1990s saw an exploration of the quality of teaching and learning, with a focus on two questions: how effectively are students learning, and how effectively are teachers teaching? Attempts to answer these questions have led to a great increase in assessment efforts. Universities and colleges are being forced not only to articulate their goals and methodologies, but also to demonstrate via visible measures their effectiveness in reaching those goals.

The majority of states mandate assessment of higher education in one form or another. Most institutions of higher education have assessment programs or at least are in the planning stages of developing an assessment program. The agenda-setting AAHE "Principles of Good Practice for Assessing Higher Education," states the case most succinctly: "[S]tudent learning is a campus-wide responsibility, and assessment is a way of enacting that responsibility. Faculty play an especially important role, but assessment questions can't be fully addressed without participation by student affairs educators, librarians, administrators, and students . . . assessment is not a task for a small group of experts but a collaborative activity; its aim is wider, better informed attention to student learning by all parties with a stake in its improvement."[24] The centrality of faculty in the design of academic assessment programs is described by Jean Mores and George Santiag in "Accreditation and Faculty Working Together."[25] Mores and Santiag's discussion of outcomes assessments as focal to institutional accreditation and successful achievement of institutional educational mission and goals, is relevant to library efforts for IL integration as well. It is essential that librarians be involved in the development of assessment programs, not only to ensure that information literacy goals themselves are included in campus-wide assessment programs, but also to demonstrate that information literacy instruction is necessary to meet other campus-wide goals as articulated in general education programs, educational technology initiatives, and disciplinary standards.

Many colleges and universities are concentrating planning efforts and financial resources on the assessment of learning, particularly on the recording and measurement of learning outcomes. The Middle States Commission on Higher Education's, *Characteristics of Excellence in Higher Education: Standards for Accreditation*, for example, emphasizes learning outcomes as a framework for assessment and accreditation and makes consistent reference to the integration of library skills into the curricular program of the institution.[26] Librarians can work with academics in defining learning outcomes by helping to frame institutional self-assessments within the context of approaches to teaching and learning rather than an inventory of inputs such as hours spent in the classroom and texts used. Learning outcomes go far beyond the particularities of subject matter covered by specific disciplines–they encompass a much broader range of skills that cross multiple disciplines, including critical thinking, collaborative reasoning, creative abilities, the management of technology, and communication skills.

Furthermore, librarians can use learning outcome data to demonstrate that many campus-wide or departmental learning outcomes are dependent on information literacy skills, and therefore, that the library is crucial to achieving these learning outcomes. Librarians need to participate in the campus-wide activity of developing student outcomes in order to articulate the extent to which their interests are aligned with the expectations of other campus constituents. As a recent Association for Research Libraries report on establishing a role for libraries in learning-outcomes assessment programs puts it, "The library can build on a shared view of what are important student learning outcomes. All the individual communities are being asked to prepare students in ways that go beyond their expertise in their fields. It is this shared need to go beyond our traditional focus on what students need to know that creates an opportunity for the library."[27]

Campus-wide discussion of national standards, accreditation documents and academic administrative literature present wonderful opportunities for librarians to suggest ways of achieving campus learning goals while furthering IL agendas. In order to take advantage of these opportunities, however, librarians must join the appropriate conversations through proactive involvement with campus accreditation teams, self-study groups, and sitting faculty committees with a teaching and learning charge. Librarians should not restrict themselves to committees that focus specifically on questions of library holdings and bibliographic access, but should extend their membership to groups that are concerned with broader campus-wide concerns. Librarians participating on committees that set goals for general education, for example, would find multiple opportunities to demonstrate that information literacy skills go well beyond the confines of the library buildings.

Key Documents at the Local Campus Level

Local campus documents are also strategically important for librarians seeking to advance IL initiatives. Documents as varied as institutional mission/vision statements, central campus administration long and short-term planning documents, reports of local assessment or accreditation teams, general education requirements, state or system-wide standards, and local campus documents on teaching and learning, frequently mirror the trends in higher education mentioned above. Campus documents translate national trends into more precise language and into specific plans to be implemented locally. Again, librarians need to be proactive in relating IL agendas to these expressed agendas, showing local campus administrators how furthering IL goals will advance their own goals and agendas as well.

What local documents should librarians be looking at to identify inroads for IL integration? Documented teaching/learning goals or school-wide requirements offer opportunities for librarians to integrate information literacy into curricular programs. Librarians should look for any skills required or targeted to programmatic groups or particular learning experiences–honors programs, residential colleges, EOP, at-risk students, or general education requirements, etc. Look for groups that have spelled out requirements, learning outcomes, and goals that are held in common with ACRL IL standards. Librarians will find that colleagues responsible for the general education program as well as those responsible for many of the academic degree programs are also interested in critical thinking, the effective use of information and technology, the research process, and collaborative reasoning. Librarians can hook information literacy programs to efforts to help at-risk students, for example, through demonstrating that information literacy skills are of benefit to students not only in their academic lives, but also in their future jobs. Current studies on effective intervention reveal that the academic success of at-risk students is highly linked to curricular-based higher-order thinking skills, authentic problem solving, and cooperative and active learning. A campus-wide at-risk program based on information literacy principles would emphasize all these skills and instructional practices.

Local campus reports on educational technology also provide fruitful opportunities to advance IL agendas via linking IL goals to information technology initiatives. Institutional administrators see access to information technologies as a powerful marketing and retention tool for incoming students. Librarians can help campus administrators realize that merely providing a technological infrastructure–that is, access to computer-based resources and productivity tools–does not insure student success in meeting institutional learning goals. Only in the blending of IT and IL initiatives through curricular integration can these resources be effective in advancing the goals of students, faculty, librarians and administrators alike.[28]

On many campuses, increased attention to the reformation of teaching methods has accompanied the growing emphasis on assessment described above. Information literacy movements as well have called for adapting the way we teach in order to account for what we know about how students learn. Both teaching-method reformation and IL movements call for increased resource-based learning, hands-on activities, and problem-solving methods. These techniques are not only what we use to teach information literacy, they are information literacy. In other words, information literacy is as much about teaching how to learn as about teaching a particular content. Research-based education, for instance, is an important pedagogical trend in colleges as well as undergraduate education programs within research institutions. The foundation of research-based learning is that students choose their own learning materials from information resources, which enables them to become active, independent learners, while teachers and librarians act as facilitators in this learning process. Research-based learning and critical thinking are fundamental to information literacy programs. In other words, research-based learning *is* information literacy instruction, so librarians should look for programs and colleagues who foster this approach.

Key Documents at the Decanal/Departmental Level

Decanal and departmental offices also develop content and skills criteria for their programs, including transferable skills, performance/proficiency criteria, and research-based learning opportunities. Librarians should look for curricular programs that are using a learning-outcomes approach to assess their efforts. Look for programs in which faculty have begun to define the goals of their courses, curriculums, and programs in terms of what students should be able to do at completion of a particular course or program. Inclusion of program-wide IL instruction can be achieved when the critical question being asked is: "what do students need to know and be able to do after they graduate from this course, this program, this university?" rather than "what does my discipline traditionally teach at this level?" When librarians are involved in posing these learning-outcomes questions to faculty, they have an opportunity to demonstrate forcefully how IL skills are either (1) identical to the learning outcomes faculty identify, or (2) necessary to achieve faculty-identified learning outcomes.

The library must take the initiative in determining what it has to offer that will help academic departments or programs achieve greater success in achieving departmental or programmatic learning outcomes. Frequently if a department has defined learning outcomes for their degree program and how they are achieved through the course requirements, the department has come to some sort of consensus about outcomes it believes are important to its graduate's future success. The next step is typically for the faculty responsible for each course to identify the extent to which each outcome is a focus of the course, and collectively across the curriculum to determine which outcomes are covered to what degree. The librarian may then be able to fill the gaps in the program, supplying instruction that will lead to learning outcomes the department wishes to achieve but which is not being taught in its courses or course sequences. The departments may then be receptive to including components developed by the library in the curriculum in order to increase the emphasis on a number of shared outcomes. The *Teaching Goals Inventory,* developed by Thomas A. Angelo and Patricia K. Cross, provides a useful analytic tool for librarians working with faculty to articulate outcome-based goals.[29] The *Inventory* reiterates national curriculum guidelines and higher-education teaching trends and describes critical questions about teaching methods while promoting emphasis on learning skills in addition to content retention.

Almost all disciplines include a focus on critical thinking and problem-solving skills. Our goal is to convince administrators that these same skills are reinforced via IL instruction programs. The chart in Figure 2 illustrates how well the ACRL IL standards align with selected disciplinary goals.

A chart such as this shows that information literacy is already part of disciplinary instructional goals, not something new that librarians want to add to the curriculum. It also demonstrates the way in which information literacy competencies support departmental goals for student learning. The ACRL Instruction Section provides a useful list of pedagogical journals in various subject areas that can be consulted for additional specific examples of disciplinary teaching goals.[30]

As facilitators of IL integration, librarians must pose the following questions when working with teaching faculty and/or departmental and decanal administrators:

- What is the relationship between disciplinary goals and the ACRL IL standards? Simply put: what does IL look like in a given discipline? What ACRL standards match given departmental teaching goals?
- What should students be able to do upon completion of a particular course or program? How can ACRL standards help students achieve these goals?
- What are the best teaching methods to use to achieve these goals? How can IL instruction become transparently embedded in this teaching method?

- How can I, as a library practitioner, team effectively with faculty and what do I need to learn in order to teach effectively to this goal?
- What assessment methods are appropriate, in terms of assessing both teaching and student learning, in this area?

FIGURE 2. ACRL IL Standards in Context

Information literacy competencies support departmental goals for student learning. While each discipline-specific goal can be shown to correlate to *many* IL standards, this chart demonstrates how selected specific ACRL IL standards (column 2) fulfill selected specific disciplinary teaching and learning goals (column 1). ACRL IL standards are cited using the following notation system:

Standard #. Performance Indicator #. Outcome #.

(Example: **ACRL# 1.4.2.**)

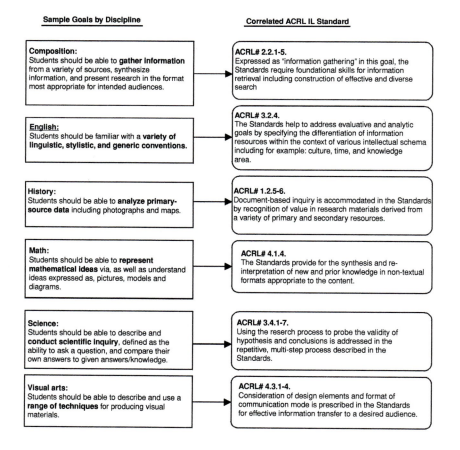

Sample Goals by Discipline

Correlated ACRL IL Standard

Composition:
Students should be able to **gather information** from a variety of sources, synthesize information, and present research in the format most appropriate for intended audiences.

ACRL# 2.2.1-5.
Expressed as "information gathering" in this goal, the Standards require foundational skills for information retrieval including construction of effective and diverse search

English:
Students should be familiar with a **variety of linguistic, stylistic, and generic conventions.**

ACRL# 3.2.4.
The Standards help to address evaluative and analytic goals by specifying the differentiation of information resources within the context of various intellectual schema including for example: culture, time, and knowledge area.

History:
Students should be able to **analyze primary-source data** including photographs and maps.

ACRL# 1.2.5-6.
Document-based inquiry is accommodated in the Standards by recognition of value in research materials derived from a variety of primary and secondary resources.

Math:
Students should be able to **represent mathematical ideas** via, as well as understand ideas expressed as, pictures, models and diagrams.

ACRL# 4.1.4.
The Standards provide for the synthesis and re-interpretation of new and prior knowledge in non-textual formats appropriate to the content.

Science:
Students should be able to describe and **conduct scientific inquiry**, defined as the ability to ask a question, and compare their own answers to given answers/knowledge.

ACRL# 3.4.1-7.
Using the reserch process to probe the validity of hypothesis and conclusions is addressed in the repetitive, multi-step process described in the Standards.

Visual arts:
Students should be able to describe and use a **range of techniques** for producing visual materials.

ACRL# 4.3.1-4.
Consideration of design elements and format of communication mode is prescribed in the Standards for effective information transfer to a desired audience.

CONCLUSION

Our discussion of keystone opportunities expressed in national, local and departmental documents brings us back to our model for student-centered programmatic development. The analytic and practical processes are circular in structure, each component being extremely referential to the others. It is easy to see, therefore, that one can most successfully achieve curricular IL integration through the concerted efforts of all campus constituencies. Librarians, individual faculty members, departmental leaders, and high-level campus administrators need to be committed to and engaged in the IL integration process. Librarians need to work simultaneously with colleagues from each of these areas to insure that IL agendas are advanced in both the most narrow and most broad planning at the course, departmental, and campus-wide levels.

Librarians need to adopt a strategic, forward-looking, entrepreneurial approach for integrating the library agenda into institutional documents and for making IL a centerpiece of university success measures. It is important to identify and underscore solutions to institutional goals that are already provided for in library IL standards. If IL can be represented as a vehicle to meet external criteria, for example, administrators may embrace integrating IL tenets into internal mission statements and program planning.

In an effort to learn about institutional and departmental needs, latitude must be given to librarians to adopt both passive and pro-active outreach approaches. Useful information can be gleaned from both active outreach and for more reflective, analytical activities. Librarians who have traditionally supported departmental needs primarily through collection development activities, for instance, may choose to market library acquisitions in terms of their suitability for integration into existing course syllabi. Others may choose more hands-on and direct relationships with faculty in co-developing assignments, assessments, and participation in classroom instruction for content and skill-building tasks.

Whatever outreach style an individual librarian chooses to adopt is less important than the activity of analyzing faculty needs and selecting opportunities for library collaboration. Librarians need to take a responsive and adaptive posture toward IL integration based on their assessment of faculty needs. Some methods for identifying faculty perceptions, needs, and preferred outreach/interactive methods include: focus groups of teaching faculty, surveys of teaching faculty, attendance at departmental meetings, individual faculty interviews, and analysis of course syllabi. Strategies described throughout this article require vigilant repetition for effective IL programming. Regular review of critical literature, identification of key partners, nurturing of partnered relationships, assessing program components and outcomes are critical activities to be continually reviewed, revised and repeated. Librarians should consider IL integration in terms of an ongoing process, as opposed to a task-based, end-product activity. By accepting the relationship-based evolutionary nature of collaborative program development, curriculum-integrated IL programs will continue to demonstrate their centrality, vitality, flexibility and worth in meeting the teaching, learning and research goals of higher education.

NOTES

1. Association of College and Research Libraries Institute for Information Literacy, "Institute for Information Literacy," [Web page]; available on the World Wide Web at http://www.ala.org/acrl/nili/nilihp.html.
2. Jeremy J. Shapiro and Shelley K. Hughes, "Information Literacy as a Liberal Art," [Web page]; available on the World Wide Web at http://www.educause.edu/pub/er/review/reviewarticles/31231.html.
3. Association of College and Research Libraries, "Information Literacy Competency Standards for Higher Education," [Web page]; available on the World Wide Web at http://www.ala.org/acrl/ilcomstan.html.
4. For excellent discussions of working with faculty on course-related IL instruction, see Ruth Dickstein and Kari Boyd McBride, "Listserv Lemmings and Fly-brarians on the Wall: A Librarian-Instructor Team Taming the Cyberbeast in the Large Classroom," *College and Research Libraries* 59 (1998): 10-17; Vaughan C. Judd and Betty J. Tims, "Integrating Bibliographic Instruction into a Marketing Curriculum: A Hands-on Workshop Approach Using Interactive Team-Teaching," *Reference Services Review* 24 (1996): 21-30; Linda L. Stein and Jane M. Lamb, "Not Just Another BI: Faculty-Librarian Collaboration to Guide Students Through the Research Process," *Research Strategies* 16 (1998): 29-39; and Scott Walter, "Engelond: A Model for Faculty-Librarian Collaboration in the Information Age," *Information Technology and Libraries* 19 (2000): 34-41.
5. Betsy Baker, "Bibliographic Instruction: Building the Librarian/Faculty Partnership" in *Integrating Library Use Skills into the General Education Curriculum*, eds. Maureen Pastine and Bill Katz (New York: The Haworth Press, Inc., 1989), 311-328.
6. Evan Ira Farber, "College Libraries and the Teaching/Learning Process: A 25-year Reflection," *Journal of Academic Librarianship* 25 (1999): 171-177.
7. Dick Raspa and Dane Ward, *The Collaborative Imperative: Librarians and Faculty Working Together in the Information Universe* (Chicago: Association of College and Research Libraries, 2000).
8. See Larry Hardesty, "Faculty Culture and Bibliographic Instruction: An Exploratory Analysis," *Library Trends* 44 (1995): 339-67.
9. Maureen Nimon, "The Role of Academic Libraries in the Development of the Information Literate Student: The Interface Between Librarian, Academic and Other Stakeholders," *Australian Academic & Research Libraries* 32 (March 2001): 43-52.
10. Hannelore B. Rader, "A New Academic Library Model: Partnerships for Learning and Teaching," *CRL News* 62 (2001): 393-96.

11. Ray Doiron, "Beyond the Frontline: Activating New Partnerships in Support of School Libraries," *Teacher Librarian* 26 (1999): 9-14.

12. Philip A. Glotzbach, "Conditions of Collaboration: A Dean's List of Dos and Don'ts," *Academe* 87 (2001): 16-21.

13. J. Stephen Guffey, Larry C. Rampp, and Mitchell M. Masters, "Barriers and Issues for Shared-Governance Implementation in Academia," *The Educational Forum* 64 (1999): 14-19.

14. See, for example, Margaret L. Rice, and Michael T. Miller, "Faculty Involvement in Planning for the Use and Integration of Instructional and Administrative Technologies," *Journal of Research on Computing in Education* 33 (2001): 328-36.

15. Donald G. Frank, Gregory K. Raschke, Julie Wood and Julie Z. Yang, "Information Consulting: The Key to Success in Academic Libraries," *The Journal of Academic Librarianship* 24 (2001): 90-6.

16. Betsy Wilson, "The Lone Ranger Is Dead: Success Today Demands Collaboration," *College & Research Libraries News* 61 (2000): 698-701.

17. Institute for Information Literacy, "Information Literacy in a Nutshell: Basic Information for Academic Administrators and Faculty," [Web page]; available on the World Wide Web at http://www.ala.org/acrl/nili/whatis.html.

18. "Information Literacy in a Nutshell."

19. "Goals 2000 Legislation and Related Items," [Web page]; available on the World Wide Web at http://www.ed.gov/G2K. For the text of the act, see: http://www.ed.gov/legislation/GOALS2000/TheAct/.

20. US Department of Labor, Secretary's Commission on Achieving Necessary Skills, "What Work Requires of Schools: A SCANS Report for America 2000," [Web page]; available on the World Wide Web at http://www.academicinnovations.com/report.html.

21. Southern Association of Colleges and Schools (SACS) Commission on Colleges, "Criteria for Accreditation: Educational Support Services," [Web page]; available on the World Wide Web at http://www.sacscoc.org/SectV.htm.

22. American Association of Higher Education, American College Personnel Association, and National Association of Student Personnel Administrators, "Powerful Partnerships: A Shared Responsibility for Learning," [Web page]; available on the World Wide Web at http://www.aahe.org/teaching/tsk_frce.htm.

23. National Commission on Excellence in Education, *A Nation at Risk: The Imperative for Educational Reform: A Report to the Nation and the Secretary of Education*, United States Department of Education (Washington, D.C.: U.S. G.P.O, 1983).

24. American Association for Higher Education, "Principles of Good Practice for Assessing Student Learning," [Web page]; available on the World Wide Web at http://www.aahe.org/principl.htm.

25. Jean Avnet Mores and George Santiag, Jr., "Accreditation and Faculty Working Together," *Academe* 86 (2000): 30-4.

26. Middle States Commission on Higher Education, "Characteristics of Excellence in Higher Education: Standards for Accreditation," [Web page]; available on the World Wide Web at http://www.msache.org/.

27. Kenneth R. Smith, "New Roles and Responsibilities for the University Library: Advancing Student Learning through Outcomes Assessment," [Web page]; available on the World Wide Web at http://www.arl.org/stats/newmeas/heo.html. Smith's piece also provides for background information about learning assessment efforts in higher education and libraries' involvement in such efforts.

28. See, for example, Lee Bollinger's (University of Michigan) recent report "President's Information Revolution Commission Report," which links teaching content and methods to academic information infrastructures and outreach. The Report presents a good model for an integrated IT/IL initiative including recommendations for creating a new institutional environment for learning, learning outcomes, undergraduate students and research, e-outreach, new upgraded campus infrastructure, experimental deployment and evaluation of emerging technologies. Lee Bollinger, "President's Information Revolution Commission Report," [Web page]; available on the World Wide Web at http://www.umich.edu/pres/inforev/.

29. Thomas A. Angelo and K. Patricia Cross, "Teaching Goals Inventory," in *Classroom Assessment Techniques: A Handbook for College Teachers* (San Francisco: Jossey-Bass, 1993), 20-21.

30. ACRL Instruction Section, Research and Scholarship Committee, "Pedagogical Journals," [Web page]; available on the World Wide Web at http://staff.lib.utexas.edu/~beth/is/journals.html.

Leading Information Literacy Programs: Immersion and Beyond

Elizabeth Blakesley Lindsay
Sara Baron

SUMMARY. Professional development opportunities for instruction librarians have been greatly improved by the Association of College and Research Libraries' Institute for Information Literacy Immersion program. An intensive information literacy program, Immersion participants return to their institutions with strengths, skills and possibilities to incorporate new ideas about information literacy into their programs. The experiences of the two authors and reactions from other participants will illustrate the benefits and importance of Immersion and other programs for professional development. *[Article copies available for a fee from The Haworth Document Delivery Service: 1-800-HAWORTH. E-mail address: <getinfo@haworthpressinc.com> Website: <http://www.HaworthPress.com> © 2002 by The Haworth Press, Inc. All rights reserved.]*

KEYWORDS. Library instruction, information literacy, professional development, library education, continuing education

Elizabeth Blakesley Lindsay is Literature, Languages and Cultural Studies Librarian, University of Massachusetts-Dartmouth, University Library, 285 Old Westport Road, North Dartmouth, MA 02747 (E-mail: elindsay@umassd.edu).

Sara Baron is Instruction Coordinator/Instructional Technology Center Director, University of Massachusetts-Boston, Healey Library, 100 Morrissey Boulevard, Boston, MA 02125 (E-mail: sara.baron@umb.edu).

[Haworth co-indexing entry note]: "Leading Information Literacy Programs: Immersion and Beyond." Lindsay, Elizabeth Blakesley, and Sara Baron. Co-published simultaneously in *Journal of Library Administration* (The Haworth Information Press, an imprint of The Haworth Press, Inc.) Vol. 36, No. 1/2, 2002, pp. 143-165; and: *Information Literacy Programs: Successes and Challenges* (ed: Patricia Durisin) The Haworth Information Press, an imprint of The Haworth Press, Inc., 2002, pp. 143-165. Single or multiple copies of this article are available for a fee from The Haworth Document Delivery Service [1-800-HAWORTH, 9:00 a.m. - 5:00 p.m. (EST). E-mail address: getinfo@haworthpressinc.com].

INTRODUCTION

Professional development for instruction librarians was greatly enhanced in 1999 with the launch of the Association of College and Research Libraries' Institute for Information Literacy Immersion program. Several hundred librarians have been selected to participate in this intensive program that combines national expertise in the fields of library instruction, assessment, and information literacy. Participants return to their institutions with different strengths, skills and possibilities to incorporate new ideas about information literacy into their programs.

Although librarians gain similar sets of skills from Immersion, the ways in which those new skills will be used at the home institution varies widely. The authors hold similar positions at two different campuses in the same state university system. They had very different experiences in implementing skills learned at Immersion. In addition, survey results of other Immersion participants illustrate a broad range of experiences following the program.

A SNAPSHOT OF IMMERSION

Immersion is a competitive, intensive learning experience for instruction librarians. Planned and implemented by the Institute for Information Literacy, part of ACRL, Immersion has two tracks, and has been held twice a year as a regional session and as a national session. Ninety participants are accepted for national Immersion programs, with sixty in Track I and thirty in Track II. Track I focuses on the librarian as an individual within a program and provides training in areas dealing with pedagogy, assessment, and learning styles. Track II is geared for those already managing a program. These participants receive extensive training in leadership and management while working on an action plan to solve a prepared case study they bring to the program. This article focuses primarily on Track I.

Immersion has three basic goals. The program aims to prepare librarians to become effective teachers in information literacy programs. A second goal is to support librarians and educators in playing a leadership role in the development and implementation of information literacy programs. The program also provides the skills to forge new relationships throughout the education community for information literacy-based curriculum development.

Learning outcomes for Immersion participants vary from year to year, as the program is enhanced. The extensive outcomes for the 2001 institute are available at the Institute for Information Literacy Web site. The Immersion faculty members have programmed outcomes in several different areas: from information literacy to teaching, from leadership and management to assessment. The Track I program includes an opening overview of information literacy and additional sessions on the psychology of learning and learning styles, presentation techniques and evaluation, assessment, teaching with technology, pedagogy, leadership and management.

In addition to formal class sessions, there are ample opportunities for networking. The program includes homework and reflective writing on the process. Networking is a significant component of the Institute. As the name Immersion implies, this program includes day sessions, evening meetings, and group discussions. A true sense of community is built among the participants. The fact that all the participants have similar interests in and share a level of dedication to information literacy and library instruction gives Immersion an energy and a sense of connection that is not always present at library conferences. The fact that many of us earned our library degrees before information literacy gained importance in our work makes Immersion quite valuable, as the institute provides a grounding in current trends and models in the field.

Participants leave Immersion with a set of skills and new knowledge, and return to their home institutions with plans for incorporating new ideas into their programs. Immersion and other opportunities for continuing education and professional development are crucial to the field, particularly in emerging areas such as information literacy.

LITERATURE REVIEW

The library profession takes continuing education and professional development seriously, as evidenced by the abundant research and professional literature, national and state association conferences and workshops, and offerings of graduate programs covering librarians' attempts to stay current with modern information practices. This literature review covers three areas of continuing education and professional development: training instruction librarians in graduate school; history and types of continuing education and professional development for instruction librarians; and the Immersion Institute for Information Literacy.

Since the emergence of library instruction in professional literature in the 70s and 80s, librarians have been bemoaning the fact that most graduate programs in library and information science (hereafter SLIS) neglect formal education in library instruction. A history going back to 1975 illustrates numerous findings of SLIS programs lacking in formal library instruction training (see Table 1). Mandernack discovered that "very often BI is treated only as a component of another course, and those schools that do offer full courses are relatively few in number."[1] Examinations of SLIS curricula today find library instruction in a slightly better place than 25 years ago. While there are more courses devoted to library instruction and information literacy, it is still extremely difficult to get a strong commitment from SLIS programs to address new pedagogies required of librarians.

Research finds that there are several reasons SLIS programs have continuously neglected significant training for instruction librarians. Brundin outlines several of these: (1) library schools do not want to teach "teaching," viewing this as the role of education departments; (2) the enormous scope of teaching and communication concepts needed by instruction librarians can't be covered in one semester; (3) there are not enough students with library instruction as a career goal to warrant offering the class; (4) the belief that instruction is a part

TABLE 1. History of Analysis of ALA Accredited Graduate Programs and Library Instruction Training

1975	Survey, "results showed that library instruction received only superficial attention . . . in the curricula" of ALA accredited program respondents. (Brundin, p. 179)
1977	A survey concluded that library instruction training was often folded into one or two class sessions of a reference course. (Brundin, p. 179)
1979	The Committee on Education of the Bibliographic Instruction Section of the Association of College and Research Libraries (ACRL) found several graduate programs offering special sessions in library instruction; however, none of those were part of the regular curriculum. (Brundin, p. 179)
1980	A survey of the extent of instructional design training in ALA accredited programs discovered that "many schools required no such competencies and that a few were requiring the mastery of very traditional ones (instructional design competencies)." (Brundin, p. 179)
1980	A report concludes "that the status of bibliographic instruction (in library schools) has not improved substantially." (Patterson, p. 6)
1983	The Education for Bibliographic Instruction Committee of ACRL reported ". . . a growing support, not only among practicing librarians, but also among library educators of the importance of bibliographic instruction." (Brundin, p. 180) However, the support manifest in graduate training was not discovered.
1984	50% of ALA accredited programs surveyed responded to questions about course offerings in BI. 32% offered a BI course. 91% (including those with a separate course) integrate BI concepts into regular courses. (Larson, p. 13)
1985	49% of ALA accredited programs surveyed provided syllabi for analysis. 26% offered a BI course. 53% integrated BI concepts into regular courses. (Larson, p. 14)
1986	A survey of 180 academic librarians in the Wisconsin Association of Academic Librarians revealed "only sixteen individuals received it (LI training) as part of their library science master's degree program." (Mandernack, p. 197)
1994	The ACRL Bibliographic Instruction Task Force on Strategic Options for Professional Education reported "There is a great need to convince library schools and employers of the importance of offering a BI course in library school or including it as a component in an existing course." (Instruction Section).
1997	Cerise Oberman describes the need for a national information literacy institute at LOEX. IIL begins work later in the year, and the first national and regional Immersions are held in 1999, both at SUNY-Plattsburgh.

of reference rather than a separate skill; (5) an assertion that theory and research (not practice) should be the focus; and (6) the belief that most instruction librarians have some type of teaching experience already.[2] In spite of these excuses, scholars and practitioners have continued to argue that "it is clearly the responsibility of our schools of library and information science to prepare librarians adequately to teach patrons to use the library."[3] More recently, a 1994 report of the ACRL Bibliographic Instruction Section Task Force in Strategic Options for Professional Education recommended that SLIS programs must be "convinced" to teach regular classes devoted to library instruction.[4]

While she condemns SLIS programs for continuing to neglect courses in instruction, Bril argues that many SLIS students themselves are not aware of the teaching skills they must learn, noting that "the value of learning something new is not fully appreciated until one has failed or anticipates failure by relying solely upon intuition."[5] Almost twenty years after Bril made this comment, there are still many librarians teaching on "intuition." Though speaking of public library employees, Glen Holt remarks that new graduates of SLIS programs enter the library profession with "prior training (that) reflects all the weaknesses and strengths of public and private K-12 education, myriad collegiate experiences and the vagaries of MLIS professional instruction."[6] With academic librarians in the same boat, so to speak, it is ironic that many entry level librarian positions thrust these new graduates, with limited teaching skills, in front of millions of students to teach them research skills.

It is disheartening that Hogan's 1980 comment that "practitioners do not expect library schools to graduate students who are fully qualified to design and implement an instruction program during the first year of employment" still carries truth for some employers and many SLIS programs.[7] Even a cursory glance through job advertisements will reveal an inordinately high number of jobs which require librarians to teach, meaning many employers do expect certain skills from SLIS graduates. Judith Peacock argues that information literacy requires more pedagogical skills than have ever been expected of librarians. She states "many reference librarians enter the workforce unprepared for their teaching role. Few graduate librarianship courses provide the requisite basics and, frequently, the new librarian has little or no prior theoretical or practical training to inform their own practice."[8] With today's demands on instruction librarians even greater than they were twenty-five years ago, we rely heavily on continuing education to supplement and expand upon our graduate education. As L. Hunter Kevil stated in 1996, "since library schools cannot supply what we need, we simply get it elsewhere or do without."[9]

The American Library Association defines continuing education as "a learning process which builds on and updates previously acquired knowledge, skills, and attitudes of the individual . . . (it) comes after the preparatory education necessary for involvement in or with information, library, media services."[10] With "the burden for workshops and conferences on bibliographic instruction (being) carried primarily by the associations,"[11] we are incumbent on national associations such as the American Library Association, Association of College and Research Libraries, and LOEX to advocate for training in library instruction pedagogies. There are also numerous state library organizations that support the continuing education of instruction librarians.

In addition to new expectations for library instruction and information literacy training skills, the simple fact is that we must maintain proficiency in an ever-changing information environment. If librarians do happen to gain skills in instruction during their graduate programs, they still face a knowledge shelf-life of less than five years.[12] As Weingrad notes, "the librarian who relies on the pre-service degree to carry through the working lifetime cannot hope to negotiate the perpetual whitewater of today's changing society. Continuing professional education is no longer an option; it is vital to professional health"[13] and "the keystone of successful performance is the maintenance of a high level of competence—and that involves a deliberate and routine program of engaging in appropriate continuing education."[14] The notion of having a deliberate program or plan for continuing education is echoed by other authors who also argue that continuing education should be an integral part of annual evaluations.[15] As a major indicator of job performance, another contingent of researchers pleads with library administrators to provide adequate funding for the professional development of staff.[16] Another major discussion thread in the literature on professional development needs of librarians examines certification for our profession.[17]

Regardless of the debates over certification, funding, annual evaluations and SLIS program offerings, librarians must be able to meet and maintain the competencies required to perform their jobs. Weingrad offers several reasons why this is essential, including the concept of "occupational obsolescence, the danger that one's expertise will become outdated due to changing conditions."[18] Obsolescence is a "clear and present danger" in a profession where information and retrieval options are growing exponentially. With new information literacy competency standards, we have guidelines for helping people learn to overcome information obstacles. Second, Weingrad mentions "the need of all reference staff . . . to engage in continuing education."[19] The scope of this training effort should include all library staff, as the profession is changing dramatically at all levels. Furthermore, traditional public/technical services divisions are blurring with shared responsibilities and collapsed hierarchies. Third, Weingrad argues, we have a professional and ethical responsibility to maintain competence in our skills.[20]

There are many options and opportunities for continuing education. The traditional workshop or lecture remains popular. However, Mandernack notes that "self-study and workshops, the methods most frequently employed both to learn about BI initially and to keep abreast of new trends, are often insufficient, depending upon chance and availability."[21] Varlejs studied librarians who use self-directed learning for continuing education. Her study of ALA personal members found that 77% of respondents had participated in self-directed learning at some time. In addition, respondents indicated that they spent three times as many hours on self-directed learning as other continuing education events.[22]

Weingrad lists eight continuing education activities: formal group activities; formal individual activities; informal group activities; self-directed learning; publications; presentations; teaching; and participation in association activities.[23] DeZelar-Tiedman discusses cross-training as a viable continuing education option. She states that "cross-training may allow librarians to pursue areas of interest that don't fit with their current job description."[24] Similar to cross-training, peer coaching is another option for continuing education. Huling defines peer coaching as "a collaborative process in which two or more people at the same level observe, provide feedback, and coach one another on specific and agreed upon performance issues."[25] Related to these ideas, Brundin found that library science students who completed a field experience "indicated that the most valuable aspects (were opportunities) to observe how reference librarians handle library instruction . . . having a chance to see how library instruction is organized and managed . . . and learning how one personally performs under pressure and relates to those being instructed."[26] It is important to note that this SLIS experience was part of a field study, not a standard class. For instruction librarians, continuing education has been the primary means of learning pedagogical skills needed to teach information literacy. In the early nineties, a new movement began that has resulted in the most comprehensive continuing education for instruction librarians to date.

Since library instruction is largely absent from most SLIS programs, continuing education has been a primary means for gaining expertise in teaching library users research skills. However, instructional demands have become greater with the advent of information literacy standards and new pedagogical expectations. Peacock argues that "the new information literacy model represents a more sophisticated conceptualization of the librarian's role and relationship to the client, as well as to that of content design and delivery."[27] Training that once informed bibliographic instruction librarians how to best direct students to sources must be transformed into an experience in which "the librarian attains a high level of educational credibility by demonstrating sound pedagogical knowledge and reflective practice."[28] Sound pedagogy and skilled practice are two of the objectives for the Immersion Institute on Information Literacy.

The notion of a national continuing education program focused on information literacy and library instruction began in 1997 with a presentation by Cerise Oberman at LOEX. Her subsequent letter to Bill Miller, then president of ACRL, explained the need for a national information literacy institute and offered a plan of action based on the overwhelming responses she had received in the month after LOEX.[29] Oberman laid the groundwork for the IIL's work in designing and implementing a national institute. Her subsequent article in *College & Research Libraries News* outlined the progress made by ACRL and the IIL in making Immersion a reality.[30] In addition to the Immersion Institute, the IIL set three other goals, which are ongoing projects: best practices programs, K-12 community partnership programs and the IIL Web page.

Participants of Immersion 1999 and 2000 shared stories of their experiences in *College & Research Libraries News*. Chris Grugel, an Immersion 1999 participant, stated that "this was an effective 'hands-on' working conference . . . As each session progressed, I felt that I had a better understanding of how to develop an encompassing information literacy program."[31] In addition to developing his ideas, Grugel developed a network of peers. His closing comments state "this conference has given the participants a learning community to bounce and trade ideas with over the next year. A very active discussion list continues to ask questions and explore ideas in shaping information literacy programs."[32] Rosemary McAndrew, a participant in the Immersion 2000 program, provides a cogent summary of the curriculum and also captures the essence of Immersion: "An immersion program is not a conference, not a meeting, nor a workshop . . . it is an active process in which you, as participants, share responsibility with each other and the faculty to make learning happen."[33] More importantly, McAndrew sums up the Immersion learning experience by defining it as "the setting for some impressive risk-taking."[34]

INFORMATION LITERACY AT THE UNIVERSITY OF MASSACHUSETTS, BOSTON FOLLOWING IMMERSION 1999

As the Coordinator of Library Instruction, I am responsible for everything related to Library Instruction (LI) on our campus, including scheduling classes, marketing the program, training librarians, managing LI opportunities on-site and online, and planning for the future of the program. UMass Boston is an urban, commuter, public university serving 13,000 students from the greater Boston area. Our student body is largely international and above traditional college age, with the average student being 32. LI on the campus historically included general orientations and walk-in sessions, course-related instruction, and written handouts.

I attended Immersion in 1999 one month after beginning work at UMass Boston. The program appealed to me as a learning and networking opportunity. Being a professional librarian for less than two years, I applied for Track I, which "focused on individual development for new instruction librarians who are interested in enhancing, refreshing, or extending their individual instruction skills." I found the institute an intensive, enlightening, and energizing experience. The Institute has three basic goals: (1) to prepare librarians to become effective teachers in information literacy programs; (2) to support librarians, other educators and administrators in playing a leadership role in the development and implementation of information literacy programs; and (3) to forge new relationships throughout the educational community to work towards information literacy curriculum development. Two years later, there are several significant ways my Immersion experience has influenced information literacy at UMass Boston.

Information literacy training has increased and improved over the last two years. My own classes are much more about critical evaluation of information than library research. Teaching the process of effectively locating, evaluating and using information is quite different than teaching about specific sources or search strategies. I have varied my teaching to accommodate more learning styles of students. I now offer more hands-on training, group processes, and experiential learning opportunities. In addition to my own teaching styles, I have shared teaching strategies with other library instruction staff. We have two training events a year covering some aspect of pedagogy and library instruction. Past sessions have included creativity in instruction, incorporating technology into library instruction, incorporating information literacy concepts into library instruction classes, and assessing student learning with information literacy objectives.

Technology and information literacy training have advanced dramatically over the last two years at our library. We designed and built a hands-on learning environment with the latest technologies. The facility offers a wireless network with 24 computers, Smartboard, ceiling mounted projector, document camera, VCR, DVD, microphone and speakers, and an instructor's console with touch-pad control of all the equipment. In addition to all of the equipment, classroom furniture is easily movable into rows, small groups, or one large group. Two other technology-related events have been the development of an information literacy tutorial and a library instruction Web site. The tutorial is an interactive training tool with 8 modules covering the major goals expressed in the ACRL Information Literacy Competency Standards. The tutorial will be completed in Fall 2001. A library instruction Web site is also being created.

This site will offer students access to library instruction and information literacy information 24/7/365. Furthermore, we offer faculty information about library instruction and information literacy and how to incorporate both into their classes.

One final way information literacy has increased in the teaching at UMass Boston is through General Education. All freshmen and sophomores are required to take freshman and intermediate general education seminars. One of the core competencies in both seminars is information literacy. We work with 70% of the general education classes directly through library instruction and information literacy training. Information literacy is also integrated into one of the first year seminars catering to a special group of students. Accepted for their academic promise, this class is provided much more support than the regular seminar. A designated librarian works with these students throughout the semester, providing information literacy instruction in a detailed and methodical fashion.

Immersion prompted a formal redefinition of bibliographic instruction on our campus. Library instruction and information literacy training was discussed and planned through several venues. Just a month after Immersion, I formed the Information Literacy Group, consisting of several instruction librarians and staff from other library departments. Our mission was to assess current library instruction activities, develop an information literacy definition for our library and campus, and write recommendations for future instructional activities. The group worked over a year and accomplished the three objectives.

We have also developed a mission statement for library instruction. All instruction librarians were involved in the process of approving a mission statement to guide the instruction program in the future. We also agreed upon programmatic goals to guide our instructional activities. This was significant for our staff, who had heretofore thought of instruction as an extension of reference–a means of getting students to the correct books or databases. Thinking about the program in terms of information literacy training and skill development helped us redefine what we do. We are currently writing objectives to help us meet our instructional goals.

The other major management change following Immersion involved assessment. Following much discussion and debate with instruction librarians, we began assessing our classes. The first year we assessed classes, we measured faculty satisfaction with library instruction. The following semester, we also assessed student satisfaction with library instruction. We are currently developing an instrument to assess student learning of information literacy concepts.

Huge strides in an information literacy dialogue on campus have been made over the last two years. As mentioned, the library has developed a close relationship with the General Education program. Through our discussions about incorporating information literacy into classes, we have emerged as information literacy leaders on campus. General Education faculty know they can contact us for information, guidance, and if needed, classes on fulfilling the information literacy competency in their courses. In addition, the library formalized the relationship with General Education faculty by developing the GenEd Faculty/Librarian Buddy Program. In this program, we provide each General Education faculty member a librarian to work with over the semester. The librarians contact the faculty and offer to assist in the following ways: assistance with developing library assignments; training with library resources; distribution of library handouts; and coordination of library instruction.

Librarians have also worked with other faculty and departments on campus to spread the word about information literacy. Several of us are on campus committees, where we have opportunities to share information and expertise about not only library services (which may be the reason we were invited), but also information literacy concepts. Several examples include the New Student Orientation Planning Committee. A librarian was able to secure an information literacy training session, to accompany the more traditional financial aid, disabled students, and fitness facilities sessions. I served on the Faculty Joint Discipline and Grievance Committee, which focused on Internet plagiarism. I was able to share ideas about ethical uses of information, one of the competencies in the ACRL Standards on Information Literacy. The Retention Committee was another opportunity to highlight how library instruction reduces students' anxiety of libraries and research and how information literacy training helps them become independent seekers and evaluators of information. Campus involvement through committees has been instrumental for the library to emerge as an expert on not just books, but on information in general.

One final way the information literacy dialogue on campus has increased is through the library forums we have with faculty. The Library has hosted two events for faculty to keep them informed about library issues. The first dealt with costs of information, but I was able to finagle one session on information literacy. A librarian from a sister campus spoke eloquently about information literacy and the challenge libraries face in being information literacy leaders on campus. Her presentation was so popular that faculty requested a follow-up session specifically on information literacy. About 30 faculty attended the follow-up session, and a number of recommendations came out of the meeting.

While we have made great strides over the last two years in incorporating information literacy into library services and the campus dialogue, there are still many challenges. One challenge involves staff attitudes about information literacy. There are some librarians who resist the idea that information literacy is integral to what we do. Having the traditional "bibliographic instruction" background, they focus on teaching students about specific sources and Boolean searching rather than information in general. With 50-minute classes, they may be right, but I argue that you can teach the same concepts from an information literacy perspective. There are also differing staff perceptions about the actual role of librarians. Are we teachers or "keepers of the knowledge/information?" I had a debate with one librarian about whether or not we should even be teaching information literacy skills. She argued that this was the faculty's job, not librarians. I am happy to say that there is more staff support for information literacy, but it is a slow process and there are still areas of contention.

Another challenge is with the role of information literacy within the library milieu. With multiple tasks and few staff, information literacy is often pushed aside. Being the Coordinator of Library Instruction, I must continuously champion the cause. While information literacy concepts are prominent in our Library Strategic Plan and I have administration support for my endeavors, there are still hurdles within the library. The campus environment is another hurdle. While supporters of the library and information literacy are growing, there is a large contingent of faculty who have no idea what we are doing. It is my job to market our program and our expertise to people within and without the library. Immersion gave me many skills to do this.

INFORMATION LITERACY AT THE UNIVERSITY OF MASSACHUSETTS, DARTMOUTH FOLLOWING IMMERSION 2000

My position title is Literature, Languages and Cultural Studies Librarian at the University of Massachusetts, Dartmouth. UMass Dartmouth has a student body of approximately 6,000 and is one of five campuses of the UMass state system. Mainly an undergraduate institution, a handful of graduate programs also exist. The campus includes colleges of arts and sciences, business, engineering, nursing, and performing and visual arts.

There are seven reference/instruction librarians, and as my job title indicates, we are responsible for specific programs. In addition to the typical collection development liaison relationships, we also serve as the primary contact for faculty and students and handle all library instruction within our liaison departments.

I moved into this position a year before I went to Immersion. Given that my duties include the English department, I was initially given primary responsibility for all English (ENL) 101-102 instruction. The goals for information and computer literacy had already been passed into the general education curriculum and were to be delivered in ENL 101-102, as they are the only classes required of all students. While I came in with the goals already in place, there was no intact program. I was able to design sessions to meet the research needs of the different ENL 101 and 102 sections, including the basic use of newspaper and magazine databases, the differences between popular magazines and scholarly journals, and the effective use of advanced databases in social sciences and humanities. I also created an instructional session for selecting and using search engines and evaluating information found on the Internet.

While I have not made major changes to the content of this program, the Immersion experience has impacted my delivery in several ways. One effect of Immersion is that I attempt to include a wider array of instructional activities based on different learning styles. I remain very resistant to lecture/demonstration as the only experience in a session, but Immersion led me to consider alternatives. When possible, I have shifted from having individuals working at a computer alone to having pairs or small groups collaborate. I have also felt freer to experiment with the pacing, order, and balance of the amount and the material being presented with the hands-on time allowed for individuals to work. I have begun producing handouts that are more visually oriented, including screen shots of various resources and placing some explanatory materials into text boxes. Integrating more concrete critical thinking exercises, if nothing more than a brief focus on actually thinking and talking about topics before hitting the keyboard also has positively impacted the students' learning. Immersion also augmented my self-confidence to be even more persistent with instructors, to keep asking questions, offering expertise and services, and above all, to continually reinforce that the students are not coming for a library tour or a computer workshop, but rather to a research session that they need to be prepared for in advance.

After a busy academic year, my Immersion experiences have re-emerged to guide me during a summer of involvement with planning for the implementation of a pilot program for English 101 and 102. The program is moving away from traditional rhetorical training into a true writing program, which will focus on process and growth as writers, will incorporate the use of portfolios, and will use creative non-fiction rather than traditional essays or literature. With the nine instructors who are involved with the pilot, I have worked to create critical thinking exercises which will include some library research and other types of primary research, moving away from the general overview session into a more focused library instruction program for English 101. These exercises also allow for better assessment measures. The new English 102 will incorporate more traditional patterns of library research, but we are working to increase the faculty's knowledge and participation in this area. This has also become an opportunity to incorporate more tenets of information literacy into the planning for these tailored, more specific sessions.

In the spring semester of 2000, a colleague and I wrote an assessment tool for use with ENL 101-102 to be used during the 2000-2001 academic year. After attending Immersion, I knew for certain that the assessment tool really wasn't one, but with school starting within weeks, I went ahead and used it. There are currently plans to update and expand the assessment efforts for ENL 101-102 and for all library instruction across the disciplines. This is the one area in which I have been asked to give workshops to colleagues. The day spent on assessment at Immersion 2000 with Debra Gilchrist made Immersion worth the trip.

Except for assessment, what I have not accomplished since Immersion is to widely disseminate the knowledge among my colleagues. Due to institutional politics and culture, I have not been used as, or encouraged to be, a major change agent or even a source of information as other Immersion participants have been. Immersion has the potential to be professionally rewarding on various levels, although for some participants, the rewards will be on an individual, personal level. Given that Track I is geared toward the individual teaching librarian, this is quite acceptable, and perhaps even a better outcome. Being sent to Immersion with an institutional mandate and expectation for overhauling programs and affecting colleagues may be uncomfortable and daunting for some librarians. If the librarian manages or coordinates various programs, she or he should attend Track II in order to hone managerial skills and work towards solutions for program-level issues. Immersion can and has equipped librarians to become heavy-duty problem solvers, but it has also produced a number of quietly effective information literacy librarians.

DISCUSSION OF SURVEY

In writing this article, we discovered how the content of the 1999 and 2000 Immersion sessions differed, in addition to our own range of reactions and experiences. The survey we conducted of fellow Immersion "graduates" shows that others also had a wide range of experiences with Immersion and with their work afterwards. The survey questions were sent by e-mail to the lists maintained by the ACRL for Immersion participants (see Appendix 1). The questionnaire went to four lists: 1999 Immersion (SUNY-Plattsburgh), 2000 Immersion (University of Washington, Seattle), 1999 regional Immersion (SUNY-Plattsburgh) and the 2001 regional Immersion held in Wisconsin. A total of forty-three responses were received. Questions 1, 2 and 4 reflect ACRL's stated goals for the Immersion program. The remaining questions were designed to measure participation in the profession, specific changes to programs post-Immersion, career choices, and continued awareness and interest in information literacy.

Twenty-nine of the forty-three respondents (67%) found Immersion effective or extremely effective in improving their skills in teaching. Twenty-six (60%) felt Immersion was effective or extremely effective in its impact on their leadership skills in regard to developing programs, while twenty-three (53%) felt that Immersion had the same level of impact on their leadership qualities in terms of implementing programs. See Figures 1, 2 and 3 below for complete responses.

While some unique programs have been developed and implemented, a number of similar projects have been accomplished at multiple campuses. Ten respondents indicated that they had developed a new major program, making substantial changes in pre-existing programs. Six have incorporated active learning into various teaching situations, while five had developed outcomes-based learning sessions. Eight people designed new sessions for either a new or existing class. Three developed Web-based tutorials, while two have developed new credit courses. One person modified an existing credit course, one developed a program for assessing the library instructors, and one devel-

FIGURE 1. Immersion's Impact on Improvement in Teaching Information Literacy

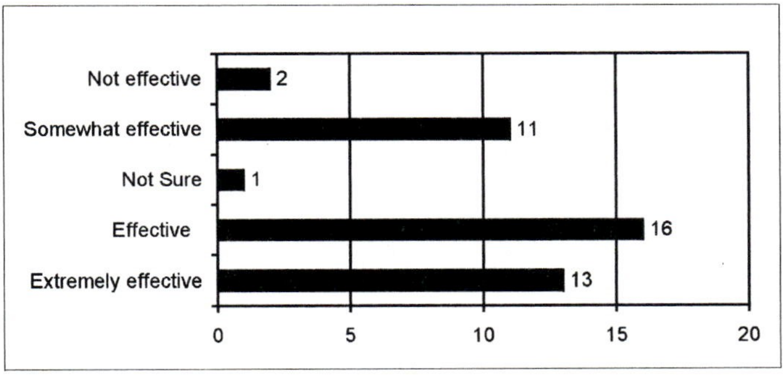

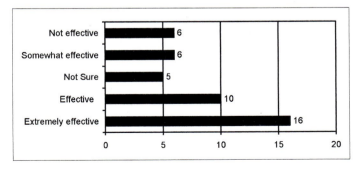

FIGURE 2. Immersion's Impact on Leadership in Developing Information Literacy Programs

FIGURE 3. Immersion's Impact on Leadership in Implementing Information Literacy Programs

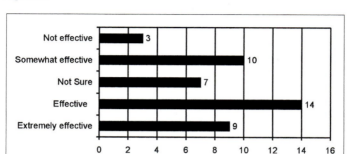

oped a new program for student worker training based on Immersion. Four people have developed new mission statements and/or successfully increased campus awareness of information literacy. Pre-tests for specific classes have been developed, and one campus has developed a pre-test given to all first year students. A post-test will be given when the students finish their sophomore year.

There was some overlap with replies regarding implementation. Among the responses: three have had information literacy concepts included in college-level statements or programs, two have implemented credit courses, and two have implemented Web tutorials, while others have made inroads with faculty, written successful grant applications, and designed new workshops for students and faculty. Six people mentioned making major changes in their overall teaching approach.

As for professional involvement in research and publication, seventeen of the forty-three have made accomplishments in this area since Immersion. These projects range from presentations given on campus to regional library conferences and newsletters to publication in national journals. Several people noted, though, that their projects were in progress before Immersion and that the Immersion experience had no impact on the content, completion or publication of the material. Others noted that they had published and presented before attending Immersion.

Thirty-one of the forty-three respondents have recognized information literacy-related issues since Immersion that need further study. Assessment topped the list of these responses, with eleven replies. Other items mentioned several times included ethical use of information, faculty relationships and campus politics, active learning, learning styles and theory, and designing programs beyond the first year experience for the entire curriculum. Other items mentioned include project management, expectations of employers for college graduates, information seeking behavior and theory, avoiding redundancy in instruction programs, statewide information literacy programs, information literacy and distance learners, technology, working with disabled learners, and course design. Two respondents felt that Immersion did not adequately cover information literacy well enough as a whole concept.

Only five people reported changing jobs, but a couple of others noted that Immersion made them consider a change. Several respondents have moved internally, either into another area of library services or upward into a managing or coordinating role in instruction and reference.

The most important outcome of Immersion for nine people was the networking and resultant ongoing friendships and relationships with like-minded colleagues. As one Immersion 1999 graduate stated, becoming "linked to a national network of kindred spirits and outstanding, like-minded professionals" was the most important outcome. Another three noted that seeing what other people were doing and realizing we face similar issues was crucial. Five people noted that gaining confidence in themselves and realizing their skills in teaching and leadership was the most important outcome. As one Immersion 2000 participant noted, "Immersion really gave me the confidence to bring new projects to faculty members." A member of the Wisconsin 2001 group mentioned that she "used to feel like the 'great pretender'" in the classroom, but that Immersion gave her a background in pedagogical basics and a renewed confidence in her knowledge and skills. Another five felt they emerged with a clear sense of what information literacy is and what instruction involves. Gaining knowledge about assessment was most important for eight people. Others noted gaining fresh enthusiasm for library instruction and energy for making changes and trying new teaching methods. One person came to view him/herself as an integral part of the university's educational mission, while another felt s/he had become an informed leader. Three Track II participants noted the most important part of Immersion was the action plan and what they've accomplished with those projects since Immersion.

FUTURE DIRECTIONS

It should be made clear that this article and the survey were not done on behalf of or for the benefit of ACRL. However, some of the comments received in regard to how the program could be improved are notable. Several stated the need for better definition of the two tracks, with suggestions ranging from making the tracks more distinctly different to bringing the tracks closer together. Others argued for adding an intermediate track and making Track II for upper level management personnel. One person requested more regional Immersions so that more people can get access to the program.

While Immersion covers a great deal of ground, there are a few areas that Immersion could better address. As a Wisconsin 2001 participant said, "the most difficult moment of the week is when you return to your library, look around and realize the enormity of what needs to be done." In addition to completing Immersion with an overwhelming amount of information and ideas for new programs and directions, returning to the home library as the only person who has undergone the experience of becoming energized and renewed can be frustrating. The leadership and management component of Track I might be more valuable if geared more specifically toward methods of achieving institutional support. Generally, while at Immersion, people feel energized, get new ideas, and make contact with others who think the same way and are interested in the same programs and issues. Given the competitive nature of the application process, Immersion participants also find themselves among the "cream of the crop," working with some of the best, most energetic librarians from a wide range of libraries. Immersion needs to be more focused on the reality of the post-Immersion experience back at the home institution. Many Immersion participants return to libraries where they may be the only ones, either in terms of personnel or philosophical outlook, who are available for, and committed to, information literacy (as a different process than bibliographic instruction or library instruction), and who are interested in and prepared for making major changes to programs.

In addition to Immersion, numerous opportunities for professional development and networking with like-minded colleagues exist. The Center for Teaching and Learning at your home institution may be an interested partner and also a source for continued training and discussions about pedagogical issues. National and state organizations are an obvious source, particularly the round tables, special interest groups, and committees which provide programming at conferences and pre-conferences. These groups are also responsible for newsletters, e-mail discussion groups and other committee documents, such as best practices statements. Programming of regional consortia may be another source of professional development opportunity. For Track I participants, applying for Track II may be another option. Of the people surveyed, twelve indicated they definitely planned to apply in the near future, while another six respondents showed possible interest in Track II.

Some graduate programs of library and information science may also be a source for more formal continuing education, even if the sessions are not part of the regular curriculum. Seeing more universities and colleges increase course offerings in library instruction and information literacy related areas could only be beneficial for librarians in training and for librarians already in practice.

The need for continuing education opportunities and networking opportunities is indeed significant, particularly related to information literacy, and Immersion certainly fills a large gap. As a professional development activity, Immersion can be many things to many people, including the chance to meet other librarians working on similar issues, gaining knowledge and skill in teaching and managing, creating new ideas for programs, and renewing one's enthusiasm for the field.

NOTES

1. Scott B. Mandernack, "An Assessment of Education and Training Needs for Bibliographic Instruction Librarians," *Journal of Education for Library and Information Science* 30 (1990): 194.
2. Robert E. Brundin, "Education for Instructional Librarians: Development and Overview," *Journal of Education for Library and Information Science* 25 (1984-1985): 180.
3. Mary Ellen Larson and Ellen Meltzer, "Education for Bibliographic Instruction," *Journal of Education for Library and Information Science* 28, no. 1 (1987): 9-25.
4. Instruction Section, Association of College and Research Libraries, "ACRL BIS Task Force on Strategic Options for Professional Education (SOPE)" [Web page], January 1994 [cited August 28, 2001]; available from the World Wide Web at http://www.ala.org/acrl/is/publications/sope.html.
5. Patricia L. Bril, "Should Library Schools Teach Library Instruction?" *Journal of Academic Librarianship* 8, no. 1 (1982): 35.
6. Glen E. Holt, "Training, a Library Imperative," *Journal of Library Administration* 29, no. 1 (1999): 81.
7. Sharon Anne Hogan, "Training and Education of Library Instruction Librarians," *Library Trends* 29, no. 116 (1980): 122.
8. Judith Peacock, "Teaching Skills for Teaching Librarians: Postcards from the Edge of the Educational Paradigm," *Australian Academic and Research Libraries* 32, no. 1 (2001): 28.
9. L. Hunter Kevil, "Continuing Education and the Reinvention of the Library School," *Journal of Education for Library and Information Science* 37 (1996): 185.
10. Jana Varlejs, "On Their Own: Librarians' Self-Directed, Work-Related Learning," *Library Quarterly* 69, no. 2 (1999): 175.
11. Larson and Meltzer, "Education for Bibliographic Instruction," 10.
12. See Huckle and Albritton.
13. Darlene Weingrad, "Competence and the New Paradigm: Continuing Education of the Reference Staff," *The Reference Librarian* 45 (1994): 194.
14. Darlene Weingrad, "Continuing Education," *Journal of Education for Library and Information Science* 31, no. 4 (1991): 369.
15. See Mannon; Kreszock; and Durey.
16. See Cetwinski; Holt; Peacock; Weingrad.

17. See Kevil and Huckle.
18. Weingrad, "Competence and the New Paradigm," 175.
19. Weingrad, "Competence and the New Paradigm," 175.
20. Weingrad, "Competence and the New Paradigm," 175.
21. Mandernack, "An Assessment of Education and Training Needs," 199.
22. Varlejs, "On Their Own," 173.
23. Weingrad, "Continuing Education," 370.
24. Christine DeZelar-Tiedman, "A Perfect Fit: Tailoring Library Positions to Match Individual Skills," *Journal of Library Administration* 29, no. 2 (1999): 34.
25. Nancy Huling, "Peer Reflection: Collegial Coaching and Reference Effectiveness," *The Reference Librarian* 66 (1999): 65.
26. Brundin, "Education for Instructional Librarians," 188.
27. Peacock, "Teaching Skills," 27.
28. Peacock, "Teaching Skills," 28.
29. Cerise Oberman, "A Vision for I.I.L" [Web page], July 17, 1997 [cited August 28, 2001]; available from the World Wide Web at http://www.ala.org/acrl/nili/vision.html.
30. Cerise Oberman, "The Institute for Information Literacy: Formal Training is a Critical Need," *College & Research Libraries News* 59, no. 9 (1998): 703-705.
31. Chris Grugel and Madeline A. Copp, "Immersion '99: Reports from the Institute for Information Literacy Program," *College & Research Libraries News* 60, no. 9 (1999): 724.
32. Grugel and Copp, "Immersion '99," 725.
33. Rosemary McAndrew, "Immersion 2000: Making Learning Happen," *College & Research Libraries News* 61, no. 10 (November 2000): 909.
34. McAndrew, "Immersion 2000," 912.

BIBLIOGRAPHY

Albritton, Rosie L. "Continuing Professional Education: A Management Development Approach." *The Reference Librarian* 30 (1990): 237-255.

Bril, Patricia L. "Should Library Schools Teach Library Instruction?" *Journal of Academic Librarianship* 8, no. 1 (1982): 34-35.

Brundin, Robert E. "Education for Instructional Librarians: Development and Overview." *Journal of Education for Library and Information Science* 25 (1984-1985): 177-189.

Cetwinski, Tom. "Using Training for Recruitment and Retention." *Georgia Library Quarterly* 37, no. 1 (2000): 5-10.

DeZelar-Tiedman, Christine. "A Perfect Fit: Tailoring Library Positions to Match Individual Skills." *Journal of Library Administration* 29, no. 2 (1999): 29-39.

Durey, Peter. "The Appraisal and Professional Development of Staff in Academic Libraries." New Zealand Libraries 46 (1991): 7-9.

Grugel, Chris, and Madeline A. Copp. "Immersion '99: Reports from the Institute for Information Literacy Program." *College & Research Libraries News* 60, no. 9 (1999): 723-726.

Hogan, Sharon Anne. "Training and Education of Library Instruction Librarians." *Library Trends* 29, no. 116 (1980): 105-126.

Holt, Glen E. "Training, a Library Imperative." *Journal of Library Administration* 29, no. 1 (1999): 79-93.

Huckle, Marion. "The Library Association, Continuing Professional Development and Chartering Workshop." *The Law Librarian* 30, no. 3 (1999): 183-185.

Huling, Nancy. "Peer Reflection: Collegial Coaching and Reference Effectiveness." *The Reference Librarian* 66 (1999): 61-74.

Instruction Section, Association of College and Research Libraries. "ACRL BIS Task Force on Strategic Options for Professional Education (SOPE)." [Web page], January 1994 [cited August 28, 2001]; available from the World Wide Web at http://www.ala.org/acrl/is/publications/sope.html.

Kevil, L. Hunter. "Continuing Education and the Reinvention of the Library School." *Journal of Education for Library and Information Science* 37 (1996): 184-190.

Kreszock, Martha. "A Holistic Look at Professional Development." *North Carolina Libraries* 55 (1997): 7-11.

Larson, Mary Ellen, and Ellen Meltzer. "Education for Bibliographic Instruction." *Journal of Education for Library and Information Science* 28, no. 1 (1987): 9-25.

Mandernack, Scott B. "An Assessment of Education and Training Needs for Bibliographic Instruction Librarians." *Journal of Education for Library and Information Science* 30 (1990): 193-205.

Mannan, Susan. "Continuing Education: How to Pursue It." *Indiana Libraries* 9, no. 1 (1990): 38-43.

McAndrew, Rosemary. "Immersion 2000: Making Learning Happen." *C&RL News* 61, no. 10 (November 2000): 909-912.

Oberman, Cerise. "A Vision for I.I.L." [Web page] July 17, 1997 [cited August 28, 2001]; available from the World Wide Web at http://www.ala.org/acrl/nili/vision.html.

_____. "The Institute for Information Literacy: Formal Training is a Critical Need." *College & Research Libraries News* 59, no. 9 (1998): 703-705.

Patterson, Charles D. "Librarians as Teachers: A Component of the Educational Process." *Journal of Education for Library and Information Science* 28, no. 1 (1987): 3-8.

Peacock, Judith. "Teaching Skills for Teaching Librarians: Postcards from the Edge of the Educational Paradigm." *Australian Academic and Research Libraries* 32, no. 1 (2001): 26-42.

Varlejs, Jana. "On Their Own: Librarians' Self-Directed, Work-Related Learning." *Library Quarterly* 69, no. 2 (1999): 173-201.

Weingrad, Darlene. "Competence and the New Paradigm: Continuing Education of the Reference Staff." *The Reference Librarian* 45 (1994): 173-182.

_____. "Continuing Education." *Journal of Education for Library and Information Science* 31, no. 4 (1991): 369-370.

APPENDIX 1. TEXT OF SURVEY

We are writing an article for a special information literacy issue of the *Journal of Library Administration*. The article will focus on our experiences at Immersion and the effects of Immersion on our programs. We would like to include some data on how other participants have been influenced by Immersion, and we would appreciate your input on the following questions. We may use your comments in the article, but anonymity is guaranteed. If you do not want to be quoted, just let us know when you reply.

For the questions that ask for your ratings, please delete the choices other than your answer. Thank you.

1. How effectively did Immersion improve your capabilities for teaching information literacy?

Extremely effective
Effective
Not Sure
Somewhat effective
Not effective

2. How effectively did Immersion impact your leadership role in the development of information literacy programs/curriculum?

Extremely effective
Effective
Not Sure
Somewhat effective
Not effective

3. Describe an information literacy program you have developed or improved since Immersion.

4. How effectively did Immersion impact your leadership role in the implementation of information literacy programs/curriculum?

Extremely effective
Effective
Not Sure
Somewhat effective
Not effective

5. Describe how you have implemented a new information literacy program component since Immersion.

6. Have you made professional presentations or published articles on information literacy issues since Immersion?

Yes
No
If so, please give citation(s).

7. What was the single most important outcome of your participation in Immersion?

8. Since Immersion, have you recognized information literacy issues you'd like to learn more about?

Yes
No
If so, please list:

9. Have you changed jobs since Immersion?

Yes
No

10. For Track I participants, do you plan to apply for Track II within the next few years?

Yes
No

Comments are welcome.

Please respond to elindsay@umassd.edu by Friday, July 27.

Thank you very much for your time.

Sara Baron (Immersion '99)
UMass Boston

Elizabeth Lindsay (Immersion '00)
UMass Dartmouth

The Radical Syllabus:
A Participatory Approach
to Bibliographic Instruction

Sherri B. Saines

SUMMARY. Students in the one-credit College Information Seeking Skills class complained about the workload, groaned over assignments, and declined to participate in class. How could the class be redesigned to enable students to enjoy the work, participate, and get excited about libraries? The author tried a new approach, based on informal education theories, which engages students in the creation of the syllabus. The participatory syllabus has its own challenges, yet is more rewarding for the instructor. Students in the participatory classes were more engaged in the classroom activities and discussions. Their final projects showed an increased level of interest and creativity. Perhaps fewer topics get covered in the participatory classroom, but "the less we teach the more they learn." *[Article copies available for a fee from The Haworth Document Delivery Service: 1-800-HAWORTH. E-mail address: <getinfo@haworthpressinc.com> Website: <http://www.HaworthPress.com> © 2002 by The Haworth Press, Inc. All rights reserved.]*

KEYWORDS. Bibliographic instruction, syllabus, participatory syllabus, information seeking skills

Sherri B. Saines is Reference and Instruction Librarian, Ohio University Libraries, Athens, OH. Much of her pedagogy arises from training and experiences in village development work in Burkina Faso.

[Haworth co-indexing entry note]: "The Radical Syllabus: A Participatory Approach to Bibliographic Instruction." Saines, Sherri B. Co-published simultaneously in *Journal of Library Administration* (The Haworth Information Press, an imprint of The Haworth Press, Inc.) Vol. 36, No. 1/2, 2002, pp. 167-175; and: *Information Literacy Programs: Successes and Challenges* (ed: Patricia Durisin) The Haworth Information Press, an imprint of The Haworth Press, Inc., 2002, pp. 167-175. Single or multiple copies of this article are available for a fee from The Haworth Document Delivery Service [1-800-HAWORTH, 9:00 a.m. - 5:00 p.m. (EST). E-mail address: getinfo@haworthpressinc.com].

STATEMENT OF THE PROBLEM

I have this dream of an Information Competency class that is so absorbing that students rush to register, that extra sections must be opened, that student evaluations read, "I worked hard, and I learned to love the library."

The reality is, of course, far from that dream. Students in the elective one-credit College Information Seeking Skills class complain about the workload, groan over assignments, and decline to participate in class. The drop rate for this class is as high as 50%. Students uniformly write on their evaluations, "this is too much work." Or, "you mean there is homework?" Classroom "discussions" often fall flat. Students leave still believing, on the whole, that research is boring and difficult. How could the class be redesigned to enable students to enjoy the work, participate, and get excited about libraries?

PROJECT OBJECTIVES

Drawing on experiences in village development in Africa, the author opted to radicalize at least one aspect of the class: producing the syllabus. This paper describes the process by which students create the syllabus, and the successes and problems that process creates. The new approach engages students right from the beginning in their learning. The hope is that they will come to own the syllabus, the class, and the homework. Hopefully, they will also learn more.

METHODOLOGY

Participatory pedagogy is used to involve students in creating the syllabus for a one-credit Bibliographic Instruction class. Librarians began the class by presenting a skit that portrays students who cannot navigate the library. Using Participatory Education's "Seven Questions," the instructor leads the class in discussion about problems students encounter in research. Next, students write down their questions about research, one question per Post-It. They place these Post-Its on the wall, and then work together to organize them into categories logical to the group. Using these categories, the group dictates the order in which topics are covered throughout the term. Class sessions are planned week to week from a store of tested activities.

In more detail, this is how it works: students arrive at the classroom lab on the first day of class to find the computers are all turned off. Each seat has the librarian's business card, the "business card" for the class with pertinent Web addresses, and a stack of Post-Its.

The skit begins almost immediately. Librarians playing the parts of students meeting in the library express their frustration over trying to find sources for an assignment. One advises, "It's all on the Internet anyway." The other opines, "The stacks are like a dungeon." A third student in the background, however, approaches a librarian and asks how to find what she needs. After a quiet consultation, she leaves, happy. Applause follows.

The instructor then asks the "Seven Questions" (below), allowing time for answers and silences, taking notes on an easel, encouraging students to interact. The crux of this series of questions is the seven-fold repetition of the question, "Why?" to get students to think about the real reasons for their need to learn.

Seven Questions for Discussion a la Freire

1. What did you see?
2. What problems does this represent?
3. Are these problems real?
4. Give examples of your experience with these problems.
5. Which is the most important problem?
6. Why does this problem exist? Why? Why? Why? Why? Why? Why?
7. What are possible solutions?

And then . . .

How do we get from confusion to competency?

From the repetition of this exercise over several terms, it is clear that the students are aware of the inadequacy of their library skills. (They are, however, increasingly confident of their Internet searching skills.) They believe they "should" know these things, that probably they were taught and never paid attention. Groups usually agree that library skills are necessary for college and useful for life (but never fun, interesting, exciting, fascinating . . .).

Next the discussion leader tapes up a large sign reading, "From Confusion to Competency" and asks students to write on the Post-Its which questions they will need to have answered if they are to master the skills of gathering information. Any and all questions count. Students write one question per Post-It, the more, the merrier. In fact, the leader encourages as many as possible. The leader suggests areas that might arouse curiosity: what do you want to know about databases? the library building? librarians? Internet searching?

When nearly everyone has stopped writing, students may begin sticking the questions randomly on the wall under the "Confusion–Competency" sign.

Then they are asked to group these into eight to ten categories that make sense to them, and to prioritize the categories.

These categories are the topics to cover, and the individual Post-Its are the details about what the students want to know. This is the syllabus, with its topics and the order in which they will be tackled. During the term, the last few minutes of each class period are devoted to checking what has been covered and asking whether students are ready to move on, or if new questions have arisen.[1]

Several limitations of this technique are obvious from the beginning. First, this will not work with large classes–fifteen students is an optimal size. Six or fewer students generate too few questions and more than twenty cannot reach consensus, or do so by excluding many classmates. Secondly, this takes extra time. This session takes the entire first 50-minute class, and nothing else gets "covered." This will be discussed later.

TIMELINE

The UC 105: College Information Seeking Skills course was inaugurated in the winter term of January 1999, and taught each term since (three times per year). Beginning with spring term 2000, this method of producing the syllabus has been used (4 times) with varying results. At the end of the first iteration, students' final projects were much more creative and interesting than those from previous terms. Students complained less and were more engaged in the class as it unfolded. Subsequent classes were less obviously enthusiastic, but the quality of the final project continues to rise, and pre-test/post-test scores verify that learning is increasing slowly but significantly over time. The reason for the improvement is unclear; the statistics do not show that the radical syllabus makes the difference.

Why has student enthusiasm fallen over time? Too many variables between classes mean this will not be answered definitively, but suggested reasons include: differences in the make-up of the student group; differences in enthusiasm or methods of the instructor; and larger size of the group.

INSTRUCTOR'S ROLE

The most important role of the instructor in creating the radical syllabus is to believe in the process over the content, thereby ceding control of the content to the students. The most frequently asked question about this approach is: what if students don't ask for topics they need? In many cases, skills can be introduced as a piece of the topic students have requested, and it does not seem an intrusion. One example is that students always ask to learn how to search the Internet more effectively. This takes two class periods because one must first understand the mechanics of Boolean searching and how indexes are structured.

The opposite is also true: students may ask for topics which are not normally on the syllabus. Every class, for example, has asked for a tour and demo of the microfilm area, which was not on the original syllabus at all. The first time this topic appeared, it was a scramble to learn the ins and outs of the very large microfilm floor and its various machinery in time for the class. The only exception to this "give 'em what they want" rule so far has been a refusal to use class time to do a walking tour of the library, opting instead for various versions of a self-guided tour.

In between these opposites, the instructor hopes to be wise enough to know when to push ahead or insist on covering a point anyway. Like all leadership roles, teaching is also art and intuition.

The real deciding factor is, of course, philosophical. The Participatory Instructor believes that the less we teach the more they learn. Part of giving up control of the classroom is accepting that some "important" things will not get covered. If teachers teach to the students' expressed needs, the students are more likely to care. If teachers teach to the students' pace, they are more likely to absorb the information. An instructor may find that students ask for more time to master a skill, or they may leave no entrée into some topic usually considered important, like citation style.

One class in particular illustrates this concept. It was a difficult term with this group in many ways. They complained that the assignments were unclear; I restated them, wrote them on handouts, posted them on the Web forum. They complained that I graded too hard; I eased up (just a little). They complained that the assignments were too long; I cut back some. They asked me to please "just take over and stop asking them what they wanted"; I refused. They asked for another and another explanation of the thesis statement. For one assignment, almost no one turned in the work, and we stopped and backtracked for an entire class period to erase the profound confusion. Near the end of the class, a student commented that she didn't really believe I would listen to their ideas. We covered fewer topics than ever, and I was very frustrated. And then–their final projects were the best batch I have ever seen.

Another, more important question is never asked: Do you then use Participatory Education techniques to present the topics requested? How could this method be used in the day-to-day classroom? This is the obvious next step, and a harder ideal to fulfill. After this active, respectful, creative exercise on the first day, the second day usually begins with twenty minutes of lecture/demonstration about the structure of our library home page or how to write a decent topic sentence. It is almost worse to have raised students' expectations for something new and different than never to have begun this way.

It is important to distinguish between Active Learning and Participatory Education (see Table 1). Day to day, this class does integrate "Active Learning" techniques such as are often cited in journal articles about good bibliographic instruction practice. But Participatory Education is more radical. In "Active Learning" the teacher still designs input, and has points to get across. In Participatory Education the teacher only guides the students' discovery process, ideally never actually "giving" any fact. The role of the teacher is to help structure situations in which students can learn what they desire to learn. In its purest form, Participatory Education goes on to restructure the larger society around it; the lessons of the classroom cannot help but spill out into real-life problem solving.

A PARTICIPATORY APPROACH WON'T . . .

Participatory Education has much to offer, but it is not, obviously, a panacea. Good teaching is still an incredibly difficult challenge; however, Participatory Education changes the challenges! Nor will this approach be of any use if an instructor is not meticulous about learning objectives and class plans, as always. No "method" will take up the slack for poor preparation.

The necessity to accept the students as co-creators of structure and content is also basic to the success of this approach. Any condescension will be seen as inconsistent practice, and students will not develop the rapport necessary for fair exchange. "Ya gotta believe 'cause you can't fake it" would be a fitting motto for Participatory Education leaders.

BARRIERS TO IMPLEMENTATION

The first barrier to implementing true Participatory Education is that it takes so much more time than we have. To "guide" and "allow" and "facilitate" the students to "discover" the way to create a good ERIC search would take . . . how long?

TABLE 1

PARTICIPATORY EDUCATION	vs.	ACTIVE LEARNING
• Students set goals	• Instructor sets goals	
• Instructor creates environment which allows discovery	• Instructor demonstrates or lectures briefly; hands-on	
• Instructor as co-learner	• Instructor as knowledge keeper	
• Discussion and experience teach	• Instructor teaches	

The second real barrier to Participatory Education is that most teachers do not believe it can work in their discipline. "My field" is too detailed and complicated to allow such meandering. Here the Participatory Instructor disagrees, believing that all–ALL!–real learning is discovery, the rest is just rote learned to please a teacher. If we believe this theory, our teaching must change.

The third barrier is that Participatory Education is harder. The use of discussion out of which ideas are drawn means the instructor must be very good at leading discussion. Excellent facilitator skills are germane to any success. Like teaching itself, this seems to be a skill that takes a lifetime to build. Discussion can be frightening because it can get out of control, head off in the wrong direction, not arrive at the conclusions we hoped for, or fall dead.

TIPS FOR LEADING DISCUSSIONS

Instructors can learn how to be effective facilitators. Experience is the most valuable tool, but here, at least, are a few pointers:

- Ask and wait. Really wait. Wait longer. Restate the question and wait some more. Many students need to gather their thoughts or hear others get an idea started before they are ready to contribute.
- Stay out of the discussion. Ask a question and "leave the circle." Come back with a provocative idea, but "step out" again. Insist that students talk to each other, not just to you.
- Write ideas on a flip chart to emphasize your role as facilitator (i.e., only on the periphery of the real work). Be careful not to restate everybody's ideas as if you were allowing them in. Write them down the way they are stated without "clarifying" or hesitating.
- Remember that real discussion has no preconceived answer. Make it plain in word and action that the ideas are the most important thing.
- Be ready to lead wherever the discussion goes. Plan ahead for many contingencies. For example, the final project for this class is derived from ideas generated by students. If it is announced that the final can be anything within certain parameters, then that promise must be kept.

REACTIONS

Student response to the whole idea of a student-led classroom varies. The Teacher-as-Facilitator confuses, even angers, some students, but invigorates others. Each term at least one student asks in exasperation if the instructor would "just take over." Many times they cannot express what they need and really have no guidance to offer about whether to move on or delve deeper. The homework still reveals that many students feel lost during the classroom activities but never ask for clarification, or that they felt they understood when they did not. Frustration can run high at times. The rewards must outweigh the frustrations; in my experience, they do.

ROOTS OF PARTICIPATORY APPROACH

I encountered the pedagogy of Paulo Freire in the context of village consciousness-raising work in West Africa in the 1980s. After a week-long training seminar of this method, I had immediate occasion to apply it to working with village women's groups to write a grant for a gas-powered grain mill. Experience taught me, in sometimes painful ways, that the student on the front line knows what she needs to know. Close adherents to Freire's work will argue that in adapting those experiences to the American classroom, I have committed the common sin of leaving out the social transformation elements of his theories. But I can imagine liberation happening if one could perfect this teaching style. Classes might involve challenging discussions about equal access to information, societal effects on the creation of information, or feminist critiques of the process of research.

Although *Pedagogy of the Oppressed* [2] is Freire's seminal work, it is difficult reading. It might be easier to understand his theories by reading an introductory article in an education encyclopedia, such as the interesting summary from infed.org (www.infed.org/thinkers/et-freir.htm).[3] Nor is Participatory Education a thesaurus term in ERIC. Other terms used to refer to Freirian thought include participatory research, critical pedagogy, feminist pedagogy, and a host of nonstandard others. The easiest way to get at Freire, in the end, is to use his name in a keyword or cited reference search.

Parenting is also high on my "bibliography." Parenting has taught me to really listen even when I am the boss. Faber and Mazlish's [4] work on talking to kids is true for dealing well with anyone. Listening to students teaches us to teach better. In this class, students are asked to give one-minute responses to prompts such as, "If I were teaching this class, I would . . ." Students are usually surprised to discover changes in the next class in response to their ideas. Often students' breakthroughs come right after some ego-busting critique is implemented.

Experience in facilitating strategic planning sessions and leading Internet instruction classes with public library patrons have only solidified my convictions throughout the intervening years. People come to educational opportunities with wildly varying abilities and questions. Allowing them to express what they already know, and be explicit about what else they want to learn, sets a tone for the experience that nothing else I have tried accomplishes.

CONCLUSION

Both pleasure and challenge result from allowing students to guide the content of a library skills class. While it may be frightening to give up control, many students respond positively by engaging more completely in the class. The next step will be to allow students to lead the day-to-day activities of the classroom and to delve into the social issues of information equity. Time limitations, however, make those more difficult goals.

NOTES

1. For an example syllabus and photographs, see Ohio University Libraries, "UC 105: College Information Seeking Skills Syllabus," [Web page], Fall 2001; available on the World Wide Web at http://www.library.ohiou.edu/libinfo/depts/refdept/ciss/syllabus.htm.
2. Paulo Freire, *Pedagogy of the Oppressed* (New York: Herder and Herder, 1970).
3. "Paulo Freire," in "Infed: The Encyclopedia of Informal Education," [Web page], 2001; available on the World Wide Web at http://www.infed.org/thinkers/et-freir.htm.
4. Adele Faber and Elaine Mazlish, *How to Talk so Kids will Listen and Listen so Kids will Talk* (New York: Rawson Wade Publishers, 1980).

Something Old, Something New, Something Borrowed, Something Blue: Active Learning in the Classroom

Patricia R. Krajewski
Vivienne B. Piroli

SUMMARY. This article deals with the experience of the librarians at the Simmons College Libraries as they integrated active learning strategies into the library instruction program for first year students. Occurring over two semesters, students took self-guided tours of the library and played a game of library jeopardy in the fall, and participated in the research process during workshops in the spring. Research indicates that students who are active partners in the learning process increase their chances of retaining material. The librarians attempted to measure the success of the program through anecdotal evidence and reviews of students' research paper bibliographies. *[Article copies available for a fee from The Haworth Document Delivery Service: 1-800-HAWORTH. E-mail address: <getinfo@haworthpressinc.com> Website: <http://www.HaworthPress.com> © 2002 by The Haworth Press, Inc. All rights reserved.]*

KEYWORDS. Active learning, collaboration, first year programs, games, learning styles, library instruction, workshops

Patricia R. Krajewski is Reference Librarian, Simmons College Libraries, 300 The Fenway, Boston, MA 02115 (E-mail: krajewsk@simmons.edu).

Vivienne B. Piroli is Reference and Instruction Librarian, Simmons College Libraries, 300 The Fenway, Boston, MA 02115 (E-mail: vivienne.piroli@simmons.edu).

[Haworth co-indexing entry note]: "Something Old, Something New, Something Borrowed, Something Blue: Active Learning in the Classroom." Krajewski, Patricia R., and Vivienne B. Piroli. Co-published simultaneously in *Journal of Library Administration* (The Haworth Information Press, an imprint of The Haworth Press, Inc.) Vol. 36, No. 1/2, 2002, pp. 177-194; and: *Information Literacy Programs: Successes and Challenges* (ed: Patricia Durisin) The Haworth Information Press, an imprint of The Haworth Press, Inc., 2002, pp. 177-194. Single or multiple copies of this article are available for a fee from The Haworth Document Delivery Service [1-800-HAWORTH, 9:00 a.m. - 5:00 p.m. (EST). E-mail address: getinfo@haworthpressinc.com].

INTRODUCTION

Active learning has existed in one form or another since time began. Memories of favorite teachers exist often because of that teacher's ability to capture students' attention and impart lessons in a fun and seemingly effortless way. Why is it that some teachers manage to captivate their students and others seem to lecture their students into disinterest and intense dislike of the subject matter? It is possible to suggest the presence of active learning in the classroom made the difference between lessons that were drudgery and those that were exciting and engaging. It is these latter qualities that exist in active learning classrooms. The point of this teaching strategy is to infuse students with enough enthusiasm to encourage them to become active partners in the learning process.

Many students initially perceive library research as a dull but necessary evil. Combined with the misconception that the answer to every research question can be found on the Internet, instruction librarians have a daunting task, attempting to reverse those ideas. With each passing year it has become more essential that instruction librarians rise to this challenge. Five years ago many incoming freshmen were intimidated by some of the technology the college library offered; indeed many had never used e-mail or surfed the Internet. Today that profile is rare and students arrive in college with sophisticated technology skills. The difficulty here is to convince them of the difference between being proficient with technology and being good researchers. Those students who spend the instruction session Web surfing, checking e-mail, and instant messaging are those for whom this distinction has greatest relevance. However, recent research indicates that this type of simultaneous multi-tasking is typical behavior of Generation Y.[1] Therein lies the challenge for librarians, making information literate beings from technology savvy students.

SIMMONS COLLEGE FIRST YEAR PROGRAM

The realization that this was the task facing librarians fueled the drive to introduce a more integrated, active learning approach to library instruction sessions for first year students. Approaching the 2000-2001 academic year, the Simmons College library instruction team faced the challenge of developing an instruction program for the first year seminar that would engage students and teach them the skills they needed to perform college research. The first year program at Simmons College is a full year (two-semester) program where rotating faculty from several undergraduate departments teach classes of about 17 students writing, research, and critical thinking skills. Called the Multidisciplinary Core Course: Culture Matters (MCC), its content includes multidisciplinary topics designed to help students investigate issues of multiculturalism in their societies. All first year students at Simmons College are required to take the MCC course, which has been in place for approximately five years.

Initially the libraries' involvement in the MCC course was limited to a one-shot instruction session in the second semester as the students were preparing for their final research paper. In 1999, the library instruction team designed a Web-based course guide to reinforce the library instruction sessions. In subsequent years the guide was expanded and enhanced. Faculty received it in a positive way and encouraged students to use it in the preparation of their research. Despite this, faculty still saw areas in the research process where students were lacking. The original format for library instruction was a single, eighty-minute class, using a combined lecture and demonstration method. Librarians lectured on resources and demonstrated searches on topics suggested by faculty. Students were given time to experiment with those resources using their own topics. Based on questions received at the reference desk, and faculty feedback, it was clear that learning and retention from the library instruction sessions was not optimal. While some students were engaged and found the library instruction sessions helpful, others were not as interested in the lecture portion as they spent much of the session looking at their e-mail or surfing the Internet.

BACKGROUND

Many students had never checked out a book from the library, did not know where the periodicals were located, or did not understand the difference between the library catalog and a database. The literature is full of accounts of librarians facing similar problems, needing a jolt in their library instruction programs, and coming up with similar solutions, infusing them with active learning techniques. Most librarians who write about using active learning techniques admit that the lecture format of teaching works well in some situations; however, studies show they are not conducive to retention and are disliked by students.[2,3] Those who reported their experiences universally cited the shortcomings of the lecture format:

- students' attention reduces as lectures go on,
- lecture format is best suited for one learning style, auditory learners,
- lectures are best suited for learning factual information, and
- students are bored by lectures.4

Those who tried active learning methods found that they engage students longer, are suited for students of different learning styles, are effective in teaching processes, and can be fun for students. Karen Williams and Jennifer Cox reported their experiences with integrating active learning techniques into the library instruction program at the University of Arizona. They decided that active learning strategies were necessary because the goals they set for the library instruction program went beyond just imparting factual information: "The lecture method, used exclusively in the old presentation, is effective when the goal is to have students learn factual information."[5] Although their goals included imparting some factual information about the facilities and resources at the library, they also included teaching skills for life-long learning. They decided that active learning was most effective for teaching these processes.

Cox and Williams believe that their risks paid off, as both library instructors and students responded favorably to the new program. They did, however, note that if students complained about the lecture format before, they now voiced concern over transferring active learning exercises into their own specific searches.[6]

Katherine Strober Dabbour reports on using active learning successfully for Library Instruction for the Freshman Seminar at California State University, San Bernardino. Her study indicates that students found active learning activities valuable to their library learning.[7] Her experience shows that active learning techniques are "a welcome enhancement to the traditional lecture format," and she highly recommends its integration into library instruction programs.[8]

Randle Gedeon wrote about his experiences using active learning techniques under special circumstances at Western Michigan University. Understanding that the teaching methodology worked well for many library instructors, he wondered if it could translate well into a larger, lecture-hall setting. Like instructors in the other examples, Gedeon identified a need for teaching a process—performing searches on the college's OPAC and ERIC database—rather than teaching factual-type information. Unlike in the other example, Gedeon's special circumstance was that he had to teach this to a very large group. Gedeon used an enhanced lecture format wherein he broke up short lectures with active learning activities. He found this format to be successful.[9]

Jeanette Drueke recounts her experiences at the University of Nebraska, using active learning techniques in a library instruction class. Drueke found the active learning technique called the "jig-saw method" to be successful: "anecdotal evidence from the students, the professor, and the librarian was strongly positive."[10]

At Montana State University, Bozeman used variations of Drueke's active learning methodology. Student evaluations from the initial round of the new library instruction format indicated that students preferred active learning techniques in the sessions over lectures. Faculty feedback did not change significantly from when the sessions were lectures, but the library did receive thank you notes that often praised the libraries for an improvement in the format.

These instruction librarians point out that there was an element of risk in implementing active learning techniques. Students, teachers, and library instructors all must buy into a new way of presenting library instruction. One element Cox and Williams stressed as essential to the program's development, though, is the willingness to take risks.[11]

Time is also a necessary commitment for successful integration of active learning into a library instruction program. Among the steps the University of Arizona team listed as essential to integrating active learning into a program are taking time for developing a program, and training instructors.[12] Gedeon also discussed the time and effort needed for proper planning in a successful active learning program.[13]

LIBRARY JEOPARDY

Aware of the difficulties in trying to teach library literacy during a single eighty-minute class session, the director of the MCC program at Simmons College agreed with librarians that a second library instruction session in the fall semester was necessary. The Simmons instruction librarians decided to develop a new fall instruction program and to revamp the instruction sessions taught in the spring. Curious to know what the library would do in an additional fall semester session, the director was met with the response, "Play library jeopardy."

The idea to play a game based on the popular television show came from a listserv. Thanks to the contribution of a librarian at Creighton University, Nebraska and a site visit there by a Simmons instruction librarian, the basis for developing a library jeopardy game was born. This concept satisfied the goals discussed by the librarians and the MCC director. Goals included getting students into the library early in the fall semester; introducing them to the librarians and library services in a non-intimidating, fun manner; helping students find pertinent library service points and collections; introducing students to the library catalog, and the process of checking out books.

Library jeopardy involved not only a quiz game, but also a self-guided tour of the library. The entire team of three instruction librarians set to work to take this concept to a practical reality. Identifying the areas to include on a self-guided tour became the first priority. This activity forced librarians to confront the areas, signage, and other aspects of the library that were confusing to students, and to devise ways to make them more accessible and friendly. It became necessary to list and prioritize the areas, collections, and services that students needed to know about. These areas (such as the circulation desk, computer workstations, and periodicals room) were highlighted on a series of thirteen posters displayed throughout the library.

The content of the posters focused on topics ranging from printing to database use to the Web, to getting around the periodicals stacks. The wording of the posters was done in a question and answer format using very colloquial language and a familiar tone. A simple font and colorful graphics helped to highlight the content. In some instances, digital photographs of the circulation desk, reference desk, and stacks were included to prompt visual recognition when students saw these actual locations. It was important that the poster content could stand on its own as it was not intended that students would take the tour in any sequential order. Yet it was important that the relationship between all the posters was recognized.

A graphic of an "information pyramid" was designed and used to tie the elements of the posters together. The three levels of the pyramid were books, articles, and the Web in ascending order. The pyramid graphic also had the advantage of weighting the role of each of these elements. Books at the foundation level are where students begin the research process, current supporting material can be found in articles, and the Web forms the final component. It helped to indicate in a visual way that the research process involves looking at a variety of resources to create a balanced and inclusive research paper. The presence of the information pyramid became a unifying force as it appeared on many of the posters.

Taking ideas for poster content to finished products presented unforeseen challenges. It was a simple enough procedure to draw mockups and later create the overall look in an MS Word document with inserted images. Difficulties arose in making those initial documents into posters. Many articles document the initiatives of teachers when preparing active learning lessons. Recycled paper, buttons who have lost their garments, and pasta pieces feature regularly in lesson plans in school systems where there are budgetary constraints. Anticipated as an in-house production, the scale of the posters proved to be greater than the equipment available, particularly as these posters were to be made in color. The resolution to this problem was outsourcing the project to a commercial copy shop, which resulted in a much higher cost than had originally been budgeted for. Dry mounting the posters onto poster board was done in-house. The overall look was very professional and added to the visual impact on the students and other library patrons. Despite the familiar tone and quirky graphics, it was important that the posters have the power to make students stop and pay attention–hence the decision to have them produced professionally.

With one part of the project complete, it was time to create the content of the library jeopardy game. Some modifications were made on the format of the television version. There were four categories in each round and four answers in each category in the first round and five answers per category in the double library jeopardy round. The categories were given names such as "Information Pyramid," "What's Where," "Beatley Basics," "Looking up Stuff," and "Techno-How." Designing answers to questions on the poster content was a challenge. With only thirteen posters in total, getting enough variety of information on which to base the questions and answers required ingenuity. It was also important to make sure questions and answers contained no ambiguities. As a means of testing the questions and answers, the instruction team ran a trial version of library jeopardy with members of the library staff. At this point final alterations to the contents of the questions and answers were made. The Web/Electronic Resources librarian created a Web-based game board, complete with dollar amounts for each category, daily doubles, and final library jeopardy. It was important to create as authentic a game board as possible to ensure buy-in from the students. Today's first year students are not beyond being cynical or aloof from something they perceive to be hokey.

MCC faculty members were supportive of this approach to library instruction, as some of their requests were incorporated into the design of the tours and content of the game. A key part of the tours was the process of checking out a book on an MCC-related topic. One poster was dedicated to the library catalog. This poster had index cards attached to it, each with a unique topic written on it. There were enough index cards to equal the number of students in each class. The goal was for students to search the library catalog to find a book on the topic, retrieve the book from the stacks, and check it out at the circulation desk using their ID card. This extra active learning exercise was included at the behest of the faculty as they admitted to being shocked every year when they discovered that students had yet to check out a book mid-way through their second semester. The index cards served the dual purpose of providing a topic to search, and soliciting feedback from students. At the end of each library jeopardy session, librarians asked the students to respond to the two questions listed on the card, "Please tell us one thing you learned today; and what else would you like to know?" Student feedback was both interesting and useful. The library instruction team looked to it to assess the students' perception of library jeopardy. The librarians would also use the feedback in the redesign of the spring semester workshops.

Partnerships for Success

The logistics of setting up the library for the self-guided tour and library jeopardy game required a lot of planning and organization, as well as reliance on cooperation with fellow librarians, faculty, and other colleagues throughout the college. The self-guided tours and library jeopardy game were done in the same eighty-minute class period, with two classes of approximately 20 students each. To facilitate the smooth running of library operations and to direct and assist students during the self-guided tours, other library staff members volunteered to participate and help out during library jeopardy sessions. Another area where collaboration occurred was in the setting up of the posters, which were arranged on easels throughout the library. The goodwill of many departments was called upon to lend a dozen easels to the library for almost two months. The advantage of these various collaborations meant that there was a heightened interest in this activity and many faculty and staff on campus came to see the posters and watch a game of library jeopardy.

Collaboration was only one aspect of creating buy-in for this active learning exercise. Another tool used was marketing. The posters acted as a marketing device because they were colorful, attractive and located in many parts of the library. Faculty and students unrelated to the MCC course commented to members of the library staff about what a great and useful addition they made to the library. The posters were helpful to all new students whether they were first years or not. Some of the other initiatives involved partnering with other groups on campus such as the food service company and the bookstore. In conjunction with the food service company, library staff members designed and ordered travel, spill-proof mugs, which bore the symbols of both the library and the food service company. They advertised the libraries' Web page with the slogan, "The Libraries' Web site is open 24/7: www.simmons.edu/resources/libraries," and were filled with some sweet treats and a coupon for discounted refills on drinks at the cafeteria. The mugs were handed to students as door prizes when they completed the session. The College's bookstore generously donated grand prizes for the class with the highest overall library jeopardy score.

FROM LIBRARY JEOPARDY TO LIBRARY WORKSHOPS

Library jeopardy certainly garnered attention as a new and flashy tool for delivering library instruction to first-year students at Simmons College; however, it was not the only new strategy implemented in the MCC library instruction program. The academic year 2000-2001 saw the introduction of a new kind of library workshop during the spring semester for MCC students. Utilizing active learning techniques aimed at equipping students with basic information literacy skills, the MCC spring library workshops incorporated strategies that were at least old, new and borrowed, if not blue.

Workshop Purpose and Planning

As the spring semester began, only one of the three librarians responsible for developing library jeopardy was available to develop the workshop component of MCC's library experience. One of the original planners moved to a branch library and another was on maternity leave for much of the semester. The two new planners were former student assistants in the reference department, and thus, were familiar with MCC and the library jeopardy program. The two held the unique position of both having the institutional knowledge to build on the existing program, and having the outside perspective to add fresh and innovative ideas to it. As the instruction team began developing the library workshops, they talked to the MCC director about her goals and ideas. She indicated her support of teaching library skills and information literacy by including *The Curious Researcher* by Bruce Ballenger as part of her required texts. The book includes sections on library infrastructure and library research. Clearly, the director of the MCC program saw the importance of teaching information literacy to all first year students.

The next step was to assess feedback from MCC students to help determine which library competencies to focus on. Librarians analyzed and kept track of index card responses, looking for trends in the types of things students wanted to know. Similarly, the library obtained copies of bibliographies with paper titles and grades from some MCC final research papers of the previous year, looking for the amount and quality of sources cited.

After consulting with the MCC director, analyzing feedback, and considering current information literacy trends and standards, the library instruction team brainstormed strategies for developing an effective library workshop. Librarians wanted to teach students with a variety of learning styles. They also wanted to focus on the process of research and critical thinking through active learning methods.

The Simmons librarians believed that using active learning strategies to teach the library workshops would engage students, allow them to control their own learning, and give them an opportunity to have hands-on practice at information literacy before they even left the workshop. As Snavely says in *Designs for Active Learning*, "This active engagement helps students integrate new material with what they already know. It helps them formulate new ideas in their own words and it helps students with a variety of learning styles understand the material in ways they would not if it was delivered in a lecture format. In short, it increases student's learning."[14] The Simmons librarians hoped that active learning and participation from students would be the key to success in the library workshops.

Once a pedagogy was decided on, the specific content of the workshops needed to be developed. The librarians consulted several places before deciding what to include. As Simmons subscribes to over 100 electronic databases, interfaces are consistently changing, and MCC by its very definition requires multidisciplinary research, the librarians decided the workshop must teach students more than just to how to navigate a canned search in a particular database. As Lise M. Dyckman writes, " . . . no instruction program can possibly keep up with the number of individual resources being added daily–searchers need the skills to navigate among these resources, to manipulate them, and to critically evaluate which would serve their current needs."[15] It was more important to help students become more information literate–to be able to articulate their information need, find it, and evaluate it. The Simmons librarians established that they should design the workshops to walk students through the research process.

Workshops

Before meeting for the workshops, each faculty member informed the librarians about what specific topic their class was researching or discussing. The librarians would frame the workshop around this topic to make it more relevant to the students. Beyond the custom topics, all the workshops followed the same format. The design of the workshops was laid out in a Web-based course guide. (See Figure 1.)

The MCC Library Research Course Guide both guided the actual workshop and remained available as a resource for students to refer to later. The course guide was designed with consideration to student feedback from the library jeopardy response cards, and the skills librarians knew were necessary for basic information literacy competency. As such, the course guide included sections on evaluating information and creating a bibliography, two skills students needed to complete the research process, and sections on contacting a librarian, using Simmons and other libraries, and frequently asked questions. The bulk of the workshop, though, followed the format outlined in the "Research Your Topic" section of the course guide.

FIGURE 1

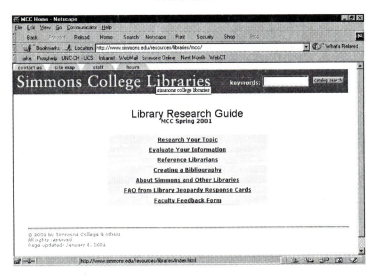

The workshops were structured so that students worked in small groups (approximately four students per group) through various concepts and activities, such as brainstorming topics, creating keyword search strings, and identifying sources to start searching for information. Two librarians alternated between leading the workshops and facilitating the small groups; the faculty member also participated as a small group facilitator. In this way, librarians talked less about how particular databases work, and more about the process of approaching research; students worked together, talking and thinking about topics, and spent less time focusing solely on the computer.

Each workshop began by reviewing the contents of the course guide and showing students how to access it. Then the librarians explained the importance of having a specific topic to research. The librarians broke the students into their small groups, and asked them to choose a general topic to brainstorm. The groups engaged in ten minutes of a process called concept mapping. (See Figure 2.)

Concept mapping allows students to narrow their general topics to more manageable, specific topics. It also allows them to flush out synonyms and related terms that they can use in keyword searching. After the students present the results of their concept maps, the librarians segue into a discussion of keyword searching. After explaining the basic Boolean search operators "and"

FIGURE 2. Concept Mapping Example

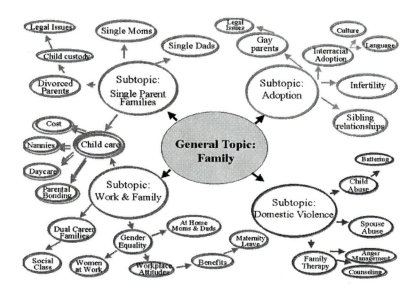

and "or," the librarians demonstrate how the operators connect concepts by searching the "database" of students. Librarians hold up signs with the words such as "jeans" and "glasses" written on them connected with a sign that reads "or." The librarians ask that all those students wearing "jeans or glasses" stand. Inevitably, most of the group stands. Next, the librarians replace the "or" sign with "and," and ask that all those students who are wearing "jeans and glasses" stand. Usually, the number of students standing is reduced significantly. This exercise actively demonstrates how Boolean operators work.

Following this exercise, the students are shown a sample matrix connecting keywords with Boolean operators. The librarians explain how the grid works, and then students rejoin their small groups and create a keyword grid to connect their main topic keywords, which were generated during the concept mapping process, with Boolean operators. (See Figure 3.)

After this activity, the librarians discuss some advanced keyword techniques such as proximity searching, phrase searching, grouping, and truncation. After demonstrating these techniques with the search words derived from the sample concept map and keyword grid, the librarians show the class how to use keyword searches to find relevant subject headings. First, the librarian explains the difference between keyword searching and subject searching, and the benefits and drawbacks of both (illustrated by a table on the course guide).

FIGURE 3

immigrant	**AND**	ethnicity	**AND**	education
OR		**OR**		**OR**
migrant	**AND**	race	**AND**	knowledge
OR		**OR**		**OR**
refugee	**AND**	nationality	**AND**	literacy

Next, while the students follow along on their desktops, the librarian conducts a keyword search incorporating Boolean operators, truncation, and grouping in the Simmons online catalog. Because the search yields several hundred results, the librarian explains it would be impossible to investigate all the hits. The class scans the first ten results and chooses a title from the list that looks relevant to the search. The librarian explains the various parts of the record, such as location, availability, publication date, and author. The librarian also points out the subject field, and shows the class how relevant results in a keyword search can yield good subject headings to search by for a more focused list of results.

After going through this process and discussing many search techniques with the class, the librarian reintroduces the Information Pyramid from library jeopardy. The librarian explains the foundational role in research of books, supplemented by articles, and including Web pages. Some recommended reference books are displayed on a cart, and students are reminded to use the library catalog to find books. Infotrac's Expanded Academic ASAP was demonstrated as a database for finding journal articles. Finally, the Librarians' Index to the Internet and Google were demonstrated as tools for searching the Web.

The final exercise the students performed in their groups was to search one of the four resources–the reference book cart, the online catalog, Expanded Academic ASAP, and the Librarians' Index to the Internet–to find a good resource for their group's topic. The librarians rove while the students search and help them find what they need. If the groups move quickly, they are encouraged to use another resource to find information. At this point, the class period is over. The librarians reiterate that the course guide will be available on the Web for the entire semester, and that the students should feel free to contact a librarian for help at any time. The librarians pass out candy as the class leaves–a reward for the hard work and energy the students displayed.

LEARNING FROM LIBRARY JEOPARDY AND WORKSHOPS

Certainly active learning is a good thing, but why is it so? It is fair to suggest that its appeal lies in its ability to adapt to a variety of learning styles. While the four main styles are those of Diverger, Assimilator, Converger, and Accomodator there are also combinations of these styles within individuals. It would be rare to find an individual who learned in only one way. Hence the need to design courses that appeal to the different styles. The game of library jeopardy, along with the self-guided tour and the research workshops, was designed to accommodate each of the learning styles and their various combinations.

The tour and game held considerable appeal for those members of the group who were Divergers. The posters on the tour could be approached in any order and contained discrete information. In terms of the library jeopardy questions, each team was allowed to collaborate to come up with the answer. While the answers to the questions were designed to eliminate instances of ambiguity, the instance of multiple questions within each category allowed this group to look at a particular topic from a variety of angles. The concept mapping activity also supported the Divergers' need for teamwork and brainstorming. The cooperative effort involved in bringing people and ideas together in order to problem solve is a preferred behavior of individuals with this dominant style.

Convergers also had an opportunity to benefit from this experience. Generally individuals with this learning style prefer to learn by thinking and by doing. Taking a physical tour of the library satisfied their need to see this library, and relating the information on the poster to the physical layout of the library and the presence of its resources allowed them to make connections. The activity of taking a card with a general topic printed on it, searching the catalog to find a book on the stated subject, going to the stacks, retrieving it and then checking it out at the circulation desk satisfied their desire to see a practical use of information. The process of concept mapping, creating keyword search strings, and applying the results to database searches further reinforced the conceptual being brought to a practical reality.

Accomodators, like Convergers, enjoy the active approach to learning. Less likely to think things through to logical conclusions, they prefer a trial and error method. Active experimentation helps them to learn best. The entire tour, library jeopardy, and workshops were experiences in active experimentation. The catalog search and book retrieval was again an opportunity for this group to try different ways of using the library catalog to find a book. Students could use keyword or subject searches to try and find a title. The content of one poster explained the different ways to search the catalog but students were not bound to any convention when searching for their book. Students were provided with a handout which explained the Library of Congress Classification scheme and detailed which letter classifications related to particular subject areas. Students were not required to take this handout, but its aim was to assist students as they attempted to find their book in the stacks. Similarly, the process of brainstorming and mapping concepts allowed for trial and error approaches to database searching. This whole process was a challenge and action oriented, two things that help Accommodators to succeed at learning.

Assimilators, unlike the last two categories, prefer to learn through observation and thinking. They like to gather their information and then synthesize it. Each process needs to make sense in theory to them. While this active learning did not aim to teach theory and was based more in practicality, it did have relevance for this learning style. As much of this activity was based on voluntary participation, students could be as active or as reserved as they chose to be. During library jeopardy, the success of any particular class depended as much on teamwork and some luck as it did on intelligence or the domination of one particular learning style. Even if the assimilators were not highly active in library jeopardy, the experience of the self-guided tour, checking out a book, and brainstorming in the workshops helped them to formulate a picture of how the library and its resources operate. The Web-based course guide provided this group with the chance to revisit the process they experienced in the workshops. They could assimilate the information on their own and direct any further queries to the librarians whose contact details were included on the course guide. The experience benefited them in terms of their future use of the library and its resources.

EVALUATION AND ASSESSMENT

Evaluating the success and benefits of an active learning experience such as this can be difficult. The novelty and visual attractiveness of the posters and the library jeopardy game brought a lot of praise. The lasting effects of the activity are harder to notice. While faculty did collaborate with librarians about including experiences on various skills and information on library services and resources, there was no concrete assessment of how students incorporated the experience into their classroom activities, research habits and skills in the future. Members of the MCC faculty were surveyed for their opinions on how they thought library jeopardy was developed and presented as well as how it benefited their students. Those who responded were very positive and commented that it was an excellent introduction to the library. After all the MCC sections participated in library workshops during the spring semester, the librarians added a faculty feedback form to the MCC course guide. Feedback for the workshops was also positive. Also, faculty enthusiastically praised the libraries for the entire year of MCC presentations.

Evaluating bibliographies from MCC students who went through the revised library instruction program, however, did not indicate any marked improvement, either in form or content from student bibliographies of the previous year.

The bibliographies were still inconsistently following style guides, and the resources were still overwhelmingly chosen from Web pages and popular magazines. To analyze the bibliographies, the librarians computed how many of each–Web pages, books, and periodicals–were cited by students. Within these counts, the library determined how many times individual sources were cited, how many print sources cited were held in the Simmons collection, and by best estimates because of poor bibliographical formats, how many articles were taken full-text from Simmons-owned databases. (See Figure 4.)

Comparing bibliographies from year to year may help in the assessment process. This type of assessment is a cumulative process and is not helpful in determining the immediate impact of the active learning features presented during library instruction sessions. One of the other indicators used for student assessment was feedback from the index cards. Some were left blank, but most students wrote comments. The latter question on finding out what else these students were curious about was most useful. The answers to these questions formed the basis of the FAQs section on the MCC course guide. These answers also let us know the ways in which the content of the posters or the organization of the tour and game could be improved. A future goal for this program is to develop criteria for measuring the outcomes of using our new model.

CONCLUSIONS

The librarians discussed the program and decided that active learning techniques certainly got and kept students attention. Questions at the reference desk from MCC students seemed to reflect a basic understanding of the library and research tools. However, the librarians decided that the rhythm of the workshops needed to be more consistent. Though the focus of the workshops changed, eighty minutes is still not enough time to adequately cover even the basics. The librarians were pleased with the new program overall, and given the risk involved in implementing such a different program, librarians were en-

FIGURE 4

Books	35%
Magazines/ Journals	35%
Newspapers	10%
Web sites	18%
Other	2%

couraged at the amount of participation displayed by the students during both the library jeopardy sessions and the workshops.

In many ways, the experience of the Simmons College libraries instruction team in integrating a new format for its first year program was like that of a bride on her wedding day. There was something old–the concepts of library use and research; something new–the use of enhanced active learning techniques to get these concepts across; something borrowed–the library jeopardy game idea from Creighton University Libraries, and something blue–the library jeopardy game board. In addition to following this adage, like a bride, the Simmons library instruction team also found itself having to take risks and accept a new way of being. Even after accepting the risks, the team found it had to adjust and change to continue its success. And like a happy bride, this new way of being and constant adaptability also brought joy and success. The Simmons College Libraries will continue to develop its first-year library instruction program and adapt it accordingly to ensure continued success.

NOTES

1. Karen Thomas, "Online Teens Are Instantly in Touch," *USA Today*, June 21 2001, 1D.
2. Katherine Strober Dabbour, "Applying Active Learning Methods to the Design of Library Instruction for Freshman Seminar," *College and Research Libraries* 58 (1997): 302.
3. Patrick Ragains, "Four Variations on Drueke's Active Learning Paradigm," *Research Strategies* 13 (1995): 41.
4. Ibid., 41.
5. Jennifer Cox and Karen Williams, "Active Learning in Action," *RQ* 31 (1992): 326.
6. Ibid., 330.
7. Dabbour, 304.
8. Ibid., 307.
9. Randle Gedeon, "Enhancing a Large Lecture with Active Learning," *Research Strategies* 15, no. 4 (1997): 301-9.
10. Jeanetta Drueke, "Active Learning in the University Classroom," *Research Strategies* 10 (1992): 81.
11. Cox, 326.
12. Ibid., 329.
13. Gedeon, 303.
14. Loanne Snavely, "Active Learning in the Library Instruction Classroom," in *Designs for Active Learning: A Sourcebook of Classroom Strategies for Information Education*, ed. Gail Gradowski, Loanne Snavely, and Paula Dempsey (Chicago: Association of College & Research Libraries, 1998), vii.
15. Lisa M. Dyckman, "Beyond 'First You Push This Button, Then . . . ': A Process-Oriented Approach to Teaching Searching Skills," *The Reference Librarian* 51/52 (1995): 264.

BIBLIOGRAPHY

Allen, Eileen E. "Active Learning and Teaching: Improving Postsecondary Library Instruction." *The Reference Librarian* 51/52 (1992): 89-103.

Ballenger, Bruce. *The Curious Researcher*. Boston: Allyn and Bacon, 2001.

Cox, Jennifer, and Karen Williams. "Active Learning in Action." *RQ* 31 (1992): 326-31.

Dabbour, Katherine Strober. "Applying Active Learning Methods to the Design of Library Instruction for a Freshman Seminar." *College and Research Libraries* 58
(1997): 299-308.

Drueke, Jeanetta. "Active Learning in the University Library Instruction Classroom."
Research Strategies 10 (1992): 77-83.

Dyckman, Lisa M. "Beyond 'First You Push This Button, Then . . . ': A Process-Oriented Approach to Teaching Searching Skills." *The Reference Librarian* 51/52
(1995): 249-65.

Gedeon, Randle. "Enhancing a Large Lecture with Active Learning." *Research Strategies* 15, no. 4 (1997): 301-9.

Jacobson, Trudi E., and Beth L. Mark. "Teaching in the Information Age: Active Learning
Techniques to Empower Students." *The Reference Librarian* 51/52 (1995): 105-20.

Keyser, Marcia W. "Active Learning and Cooperative Learning: Understanding the
Difference and Using Both Styles Effectively." *Research Strategies* 17, no. 1
(2000): 35-44.

Ragains, Patrick. "Four Variations on Drueke's Active Learning Paradigm." *Research
Strategies* 13 (1995): 40-50.

Snavely, Loanne. "Active Learning in the Library Instruction Classroom." In *Designs
for Active Learning: A Sourcebook of Classroom Strategies for Information Education*, edited by Gail Gradowski, Loanne Snavely, and Paula Dempsey, vii-ix. Chicago: Association of College & Research Libraries, 1998.

Teaching Information Literacy
to Generation Y

Kate Manuel

SUMMARY. Whether they are called the Nintendo Generation, Millennials, or Generation Y, contemporary 17- to 19-year-olds bring unique learning style preferences and worldviews with them when they come to libraries' information literacy classes. Prominent among their preferences are visual and kinesthetic learning styles. They have incredibly positive views of technologies' potentialities and their own abilities with technologies. Like all students, they learn more effectively when taught in accordance with their learning style preferences and when their worldviews are acknowledged. Changing teaching methods and materials for an information literacy course at California State University, Hayward, to accommodate better Generation Y learners correlated with improvements in students' attitudes and performances. *[Article copies available for a fee from The Haworth Document Delivery Service: 1-800-HAWORTH. E-mail address: <getinfo@haworthpressinc.com> Website: <http://www.HaworthPress.com> © 2002 by The Haworth Press, Inc. All rights reserved.]*

KEYWORDS. Generation Y, first-year students, learning styles, student attitudes, teaching methods, assessment of teaching methods

Kate Manuel is Instruction Coordinator, New Mexico State University, University Library, MSC 3475, New Mexico State University, P.O. Box 30006, Las Cruces, NM 88003-8006 (E-mail: kmanuel@lib.nmsu.edu).

The author would like to thank Judith Faust, Elizabeth Ginno, and Jennifer Laherty, former co-workers at California State University, Hayward, who collaborated in presenting some of the ideas discussed herein in a poster session at the 2001 national conference of the Association of College and Research Libraries.

[Haworth co-indexing entry note]: "Teaching Information Literacy to Generation Y." Manuel, Kate. Co-published simultaneously in *Journal of Library Administration* (The Haworth Information Press, an imprint of The Haworth Press, Inc.) Vol. 36, No. 1/2, 2002, pp. 195-217; and: *Information Literacy Programs: Successes and Challenges* (ed: Patricia Durisin) The Haworth Information Press, an imprint of The Haworth Press, Inc., 2002, pp. 195-217. Single or multiple copies of this article are available for a fee from The Haworth Document Delivery Service [1-800-HAWORTH, 9:00 a.m. - 5:00 p.m. (EST). E-mail address: getinfo@haworthpressinc.com].

195

INTRODUCTION

In an often-cited 1996 article, Catherine Lee discussed the learning style preferences of Generation X (born 1961-1981) and their implications for academic librarians. Lee's helpful article, though, appeared near the end of Generation X's matriculation as traditional first-year students at colleges and universities, and by 2001, articles offered administrators advice on managing Gen Xers as professional librarians.[1] Today's eighteen-year-olds are members of Generation Y (born after 1981),[2] and it behooves librarianship to acknowledge and accommodate Generation Y's learning style preferences, as well as their worldviews, earlier rather than later. While some Gen X characteristics are shared by Gen Y, especially its older members, Gen Y already displays some unique characteristics that have been extensively profiled by marketers eager to sell to a Gen Y population that is one third larger than the Baby Boom generation (born 1946-1964), and over three times the size of Gen X.[3] Savvy educators have also begun noting differences between Gen Yers' worldviews and those of their Gen X or older professors. Beloit College's annual *Mindset List* reminds instructors that for today's first-year students, John Lennon has always been dead and a woman has always been on the Supreme Court.[4]

This article compiles key demographics about Generation Y and discusses emergent literature on Gen Yers' major learning style preferences and predominant worldviews. It also begins elucidation of their implications for academic librarians by describing some improvements in students' attitudes and performance that correlated with shifting teaching methods and materials for a required information literacy course at California State University, Hayward, to match more closely Gen Y learning style preferences and worldviews. The correlations between changed teaching methods and student learning outcomes described herein should be considered only as suggestive of the power of teaching to the learners' styles rather than to the teachers', as findings reflect the performance of only the author's classes and there was no formal control group. Librarians should also be mindful that Generation Y displays the variation characteristic of any demographic group,[5] that their learning style preferences may fluctuate during their lifetimes, and that lifelong learning means that librarians may see everyone from Gen X to G.I. Generation (born 1901-1924) students in classrooms along with Gen Yers. Librarians' challenge is to match instructional styles to their student populations because students not intrinsically motivated learn better when taught in accordance with their learning style preferences.[6]

INFORMATION LITERACY
AT CALIFORNIA STATE UNIVERSITY, HAYWARD

Since 1998, librarians at California State University, Hayward (CSUH), have been teaching a one-credit course, LIBY 1010: Fundamentals of Information Literacy, that is one of two curricular offerings fulfilling a General Education information literacy requirement for incoming first-year students. Transfer students, who outnumber first-time first-year students by a nearly two to one ratio,[7] are exempt from this information literacy requirement, and matriculating first-year students can also meet it by taking Computer Science 1020: Introduction to Computers. Librarians, nevertheless, teach approximately ten sections of LIBY 1010, drawing anywhere from a minimum of twelve to over thirty students, during Fall, Winter, and Spring Quarters. LIBY 1010's initial syllabus and teaching methods were largely adapted from an elective, two-credit course, LIBY 1551: Information Skills in the Electronic Age.[8] Much instruction was provided by lecture or demonstration, and text was the predominant mode of communicating instructions when the author began teaching LIBY 1010 in Winter Quarter 2000. Concerned about poor student performances in mastering learning outcomes and negative student attitudes toward a required course that they commonly viewed as no more significant or beneficial than a one-credit General Education "support" or "activity" course that was also required, the author began investigating what was known about Gen Y learners. Over Spring and Fall Quarters 2000, instructional methods and materials were modified, in hopes of better meeting the needs of Gen Y learners, with the positive results discussed below. Pre- and post-tests administered at the beginning and end of each quarter, student performance on learning outcomes to be manifested in homework assignments and a final project, and student attitudes expressed on formal course evaluations constituted the basis for assessing the impact of more learner-oriented teaching methods and materials.

CSUH students are in many ways representative of Gen Y students, especially in their ethnic diversity and their participation in the workforce and the consumer economy. Gen Y is the most ethnically diverse generation yet in the United States: one in three is not Caucasian, one in five has an immigrant parent, one in ten has at least one parent who is not a U.S. citizen, and ninety percent of children under the age of twelve have friends of different ethnicities than their own.[9] Sixty-seven percent of CSUH students identify themselves as belonging to a "minority" group, with thirty-two percent of these Asian American, fourteen percent African American, and twelve percent Hispanic.[10] It is worth noting, though, that in California no ethnic group now constitutes a majority,[11] and that CSUH statistics do not adequately represent the multi-ethnic heritages of many students. Gen Yers have grown up as workers and consumers in a largely expanding economy. Forty percent of teens hold at least a part-time job, and one third of them work sixteen to thirty hours per week.[12] Teenagers as a group spend $140 billion per year and are individually credited with spending anywhere from $4,500 per teen per year to $100 per teen per week.[13] One out of nine high schoolers has a credit card, and a recent vote against credit card limits for minors in the U.S. Senate gives some indication of the importance that the banking, credit card, and retail credit lobbies attach to teenage consumers.[14] Among CSUH undergraduates, twenty-six percent are officially listed as part-time students, working the rest of their time; most full-time students, though, work, some as many as forty hours per week.[15]

GEN Y LEARNING STYLE PREFERENCES AND WORLDVIEWS

Positive Outlooks, Especially Toward Technology

Gen Y students generally express optimistic worldviews, reflective of the fact that for Gen Yers, "the Dow Jones only goes up, people only get wealthier, and America only fights effortless wars."[16] Nine in ten Gen Yers describe themselves as "happy," "competent," or "positive,"[17] a clear difference between Gen Yers and Gen Xers. New technologies, particularly computers, figure quite positively in Gen Yers' worldviews; indeed, some Gen Yers identify so strongly with their gadgets that "a key part of who they are is technology."[18] A poll of teenagers during National Science and Technology week in 1997 found that ninety-eight percent say computers have positively impacted their lives and ninety-two percent think computers will improve education, jobs, and lifestyles.[19] In one sense, Gen Yers' affinity for computers can facilitate their mastery of information literacy skills, as many respond more favorably to instruction delivered in hands-on computer laboratories than in traditional classrooms, and as they take to searching computerized catalogs, databases, and the Internet more readily than to using print tools.

More problematically, though, Gen Yers' positive attitudes toward computers can hinder their mastery of information literacy skills. Because they have essentially grown up with computers, they often overestimate their abilities to search for and evaluate computerized information.[20] In one study of Gen Y-aged students, one hundred percent of them said that the "huge increase in information sources that has come with the development of the Web" has made no difference in their "ability to sift out false information"; ninety-three percent said that "the wider potential readership on the Web makes it likely that misinformation and outright fraud will be detected"; and most claimed they were "expert at searching the Web."[21] Surveying of 109 students in

CSUH's LIBY 1010 classes in 2000 revealed that ninety percent of them claimed to be expert Web searchers, sixty-three percent thought the "most efficient way to begin research is to get on the Web and see what [they] find," and twenty-eight percent agreed that a "Central Internet Authority review[ed] all Web information for its accuracy." Gen Y students have been raised on claims that technologies have, or will soon, solve many problems–including those raised by the technologies themselves. Mere toddlers, or not even born in 1984, the temporal setting for George Orwell's technological dystopia, these students have particular trouble appreciating those information literacy standards that relate to economic, legal, and social aspects of information use.

The general positivity of the Gen Y worldview renders them an unresponsive audience for lectures on the downsides, the negatives, of anything, and their faith in technologies and their own abilities vis-à-vis technologies make them particularly unreceptive to discourses on the "evils" of the Internet, information on it, or the digital divide. In Winter 2000, two of the ten weeks of LIBY 1010 were devoted specifically to the Internet. The first week's instruction consisted of a lecture on the Internet's development, posting and accessing of information on the Internet, and social and ethical implications of the Internet. Following the lecture, a homework assignment asked students to classify URLs by their domain (e.g., .edu is educational); to use a subject directory to find information; and to use a search engine to find information. In the second week, students were given a lecture on the need and criteria for evaluating Internet information, as well as some in-class, active learning, group activities on evaluating Internet information. The Internet sessions were taught in the eighth and ninth weeks of a ten-week-long quarter, effectively positioning the Internet as an afterthought and addition to the print resources taught in the first through seventh weeks. Students' comments on the course evaluations for Winter 2000 centered upon their unhappiness with how the Internet was taught. First, the progression from print to electronic–essentially mirroring the chronological order in which Gen X and older librarians encountered these media–seemed artificial to the students, who often learned to value print books and articles after their initial familiarity with the Internet. Teaching the Internet as separate from books and articles also belied the fact that although the Internet can be thought of as a resource, Gen Yers generally view it as an access tool, a distribution mechanism for books, articles, and music. Instruction by lecturing was problematic in its own right, as is discussed below, but lecturing upon the drawbacks of the Internet was especially inappropriate for these students. They interpreted the words of caution said by the instructor about the Internet as "trashing" of a technology whose limitations they had not yet personally experienced by someone professionally threatened by the Internet.

Beginning in Spring Quarter 2000, modifications in how the Internet was presented to students were made that resulted in more positive student evaluations of the Internet portions of the course and in increased student mastery of learning outcomes. In Spring 2000, there were no separate classes on the Internet or evaluating Internet information. Rather, the Internet was incorporated into other classes on finding various types of information sources and evaluating information. This addressed the problem that students had with positioning the Internet as an afterthought to print sources. Lectures on using the Internet and evaluating Internet information were also replaced with active, discovery-learning opportunities. Students were, for example, asked to use Web search engines to find information on the performance of George W. Bush and John McCain in a debate the morning after the debate occurred. Students, who had previously rated themselves skilled Web searchers, were surprised to discover that they could find no pages with the information sought–only older pages on the debate's likely structure, topics, and outcomes. Students were next directed to URLs of particular pages, like CNN's, that provided the information. They then became a highly receptive audience for the lesson that search engines do not search pages live or in real time; rather, they rely upon indexing of Web pages done days or even weeks before. Similarly, after being given a brief list of criteria relating to authority and credibility; scope, coverage, and relevance; quality; bias and accuracy; currency and timeliness; and commercialism, students were given URLs of spurious Web pages, such as "Feline Reactions to Bearded Men" (http://www.improbable.com/airchives/classical/cat/cat.html) and "California's Velcro Crop under Challenge" (http://home.inreach.com/kumbach/velcro.html), and were asked to evaluate them. Every student in Spring 2000 accepted these spurious sites as genuine and scholarly, and could cite evaluative criteria to back up their categorizations, thereby proving to themselves not only the importance of evaluating but also the need to think while evaluating, rather than simply applying criteria uncritically.[22] Students learned more and viewed their instruction more favorably once instruction shifted from lecturing about the problems with Internet information to enabling students to experience the Internet's limitations themselves.

Oriented Toward Images, Not Linear Text

Even before the appearance of Gen Y, educators recognized that reading text is the primary and preferred mode of learning for only a small percentage of the population–and those chiefly the people who become teachers, librarians, etc.[23] In general, the average student retains only ten percent of what s/he reads but twenty to thirty percent of what s/he sees.[24] Visual modes of learning are especially important for Gen Yers, who grew up on television, video games, computers, the Web, and other increasingly sophisticated multimedia presentations.[25] Today's first-year college students have watched, on average, over 15,000 hours of television before coming to campus, and "text alone or text with only minimal pictures does not reflect the normal experiences of most students today, who spend far more time watching television than reading."[26] Much of their reading has actually been done on the Web, where people could more accurately be said to scan rather than to read.[27] Indeed, some speculate that the Web with its hyperlinks has already begun to transform the way in which humans process textual information: "What happens when you follow these links? You react with an itchy mouse finger, but not with your mind. Instead of finishing the paragraph you are reading, you're already off to another server to get more information. Your eyes are attracted by underlined text because it stands out–it's different, and must somehow be more important than the plain text that surrounds it . . . Our minds are becoming more and more dispersed by these reflexes . . . "[28]

With LIBY 1010, it was found that significant numbers of students simply would not process extensive written directions of the sort needed to tell them what databases to access and what do in these databases for homework. Students would either try to infer the directions from the substance of the homework questions, or they would turn up with incomplete assignments, claiming that they did not understand them. Extensive written directions were, in fact, accompanied by a fairly high number of student refusals to do particular assignments or portions of them. These refusals were by students who otherwise did the coursework but opted not to do a particular assignment, or portion of it, with the resultant loss of points, and were interpreted by this instructor as a form of the "not learning" described by Herbert Kohl. That is, students' unwillingness to follow these directions was not dismissed as simple laziness, disobedience, or lack of knowledge, but rather was viewed as an assertion of personal values and determination: "Not learning tends to take place when someone has to deal with unavoidable challenges to her or his personal and family loyalties, integrity, and identity. In such situations, there are forced choices and no apparent middle ground. To agree to learn from a stranger who does not respect your integrity causes a major loss of self."[29] Refusals were a particular problem in Winter 2000, when students were given directions telling them, for example, to:

- Go to HAYSTAC, the CSUH library catalog, at http://134.154.30.10.
- Click on the box labeled word search. It's the top box in the middle column.
- Enter some word(s) related to the topic of your final project and then press the Enter key or click on the Submit button.

- Look through the title list to find a book on your topic.
- Click on the record for this title to view the entire record.
- Etc. . . .

Librarians found these detailed, step-by-step, written directions congenial. Not so for the students in Winter and Spring 2000. Six out of thirty-three students (eighteen percent) in Winter quarter refused to do the assignment, as did three out of twenty-two students (fourteen percent) in Spring quarter. Scores on the completed assignments were themselves low–sixty-eight percent in Winter and sixty-two percent in Spring–as was the percentage of increase in students' post-test scores compared to their pre-test scores on questions relating to catalogs and databases (seventeen percent in Winter and twelve percent in Spring), the topics of this homework assignment. In Fall 2000, the catalog and database homework was first presented to students with pictures rather than words illustrating the directions. Reductions in students' refusals to do the assignment followed, as did increases in students' scores on the assignments and in the percentage of increase in post-test scores compared to pre-test scores on questions relating to catalogs and databases. Only one student out of twenty-five failed to do this assignment, a drop of between ten and fourteen percent in the refusal rate; the average grade was seventy-nine percent, an increase of eleven to sixteen percent; and the percent of improvement on post-test scores compared to pre-test scores rose to twenty-one percent, a gain of four to nine percent. These gains held true in Winter and Spring 2001, when visual rather than textual directions were also used.[30]

Related to Gen Y's orientation toward images is a preference for holistic processing and "nonlinear, nonsequential modes of learning."[31] Gen Yers generally need to see the big picture, in every sense of the word, when being introduced to concepts and procedures. "Modem kids don't learn by taking little logical bits and then stringing or weaving these bits into a picture. . . . They use whole pictures . . . to convey a technique or idea. They have to see a picture first; then a teacher can tear apart the picture into components and test students on their ability to rebuild the picture."[32] Many librarians and teachers, in contrast, are quite comfortable being told to do step X, then step Y, then step Z without first being told the outcome or purpose of these steps. In Winter 2000, LIBY 1010 students were introduced to focusing research topics by a worksheet featuring, in addition to a lot of text, a step-by-step approach that gave them little sense of how their focused topics related to the steps taken. The steps essentially asked students to narrow the range of information potentially relevant to their topics, but the relationship of their topic to this totality of information was obscured by the process. Students were asked to take their proposed final project topics–generally subjects of enormous scope such as crime or children–and ask themselves who, what, where, when, why, and how to reach a final, focused topic. The approach was sound but was initially inappropriately packaged for Gen Yers. Students worked through this list of questions and ended up with a written expression of a topic that they had trouble re-contextualizing within a broader information universe.

Beginning in Spring 2000, students were asked to focus topics using the same questions, but the questions were presented to them in a visual way, drawing upon a common graphic organizer layout.[33] Students more easily focused topics using this approach because they could first address whichever question (who, what, etc.) seemed most appropriate to them and could easily see where their focused topic fit with a broader information universe. Examination of students' final projects, which were to assemble resources on appropriately focused topics, revealed that students in Spring 2000 and subsequent quarters were better able than students in Winter 2000 to produce focused topics. This change in presentation was accompanied by a twenty-two percent decrease in the number of totally non-focused topics, a seven percent increase in the number of somewhat focused topics, and a thirty-five to forty-four percent increase in the number of fully focused topics. In Winter 2000, only fifty-six percent of topics were fully focused (e.g., types of bilingual education offered in California), while eighty-three percent of the topics were somewhat focused (e.g., history of cartoons) and twenty-two percent were non-focused (e.g., breast cancer). In Spring 2000, all of the topics were fully focused and included such questions as how the move to the United States has impacted the celebration of traditional Mexican holidays by Mexican Americans and whether wearing hard contacts stabilizes eyesight. In Fall 2000, while only ninety-one percent of topics were fully focused (e.g., effects of footware on track and field performance), one hundred percent were somewhat focused (e.g., recent innovations in roller coaster design or the chemistry of fireworks).

Desire for Customized Experiences and Choices

Gen Yers grew up with experiences of being the "absolute ruler[s] of [their] own digital universe[s]," creating virtual worlds where they can be whom they choose, control their settings, and determine courses of action, and because "the way you interact with your present software shapes your future needs,"[34] they expect future educational offerings to match current entertainment products. They have also come of age during a "mass customization" movement,[35] which touts technologies, such as personal digital assistants and intelligent agents, that (could someday) do their users' bidding. "Mass customization" has been promoted to Gen Yers as consumers of goods–offering them what they want for what they pay, offering them choices[36]–but it has also been offered to them by educational systems that increasingly allow, if not encourage, students to view themselves as consumers of learning, who can select the courses they need to get the degree they need to get the job they want to support the lifestyle to which they aspire. Articles in general interest periodicals like *US News & World Report*, for example, praise the potentialities of education at one's "own pace, and in places and at times of [one's] own choosing,"[37] while *Maclean's* asks "Why can't professors spend more time ensuring that courses are professionally relevant? Why is the focus on expanding the intellect rather than expanding marketable skills? Why don't four years of hard work and high bills lead more directly to a good career?"[38]

Required courses like LIBY 1010 inherently conflict with students' desires to be consumers of curricular offerings. Instead of being able to pick courses they think will most help them reach their desired ends, they are told they must take this course, whose purpose they are loathe to concede, particularly insofar as they view the Web as a universal information repository and themselves as master searchers. As one student aptly put it when describing LIBY 1010, a course he had not yet taken, to a peer, "LIBY 1010–I heard that don't do nothin' for you." In Winter and Spring 2000, though, students' desires to be consumers of their educations were thwarted not just in the taking of LIBY 1010 in itself but also within LIBY 1010's coursework. Beyond the choice of final project topic, which was left to students' choosing, all students were taught the same things, presumed to know–and want to know–the same things, and assessed using the same homework assignments. Students understandably resented this. During these two quarters, all students were given the same Internet assignment, an assignment that essentially assumed students had no prior knowledge of Web searching and great interest in learning the mechanics of searching. Everyone was asked to browse Yahoo! (http://www.yahoo.com) by subject categories to find a site with good information on her/his topic and then use two search engines from a listing of major search engines (e.g., Google, AltaVista) and compare their search results. Some students were adept Web-searchers and felt that subject directories and major search engines were old hat. These students saw this assignment as busywork, something anathema to Gen Yers.

In Fall 2000, recognizing students' desire for customizable learning experiences, three different versions of an Internet assignment were made available; students chose which version they did based upon their prior knowledge and personal interests. One version of the assignment focused on search basics (subject directories and syntax for using search engines) and was designed for those students who had had minimal exposure to computers or Web searching. Another version focused on specialty search engines such as SciCentral (http://www.scicentral.com) and Social Work Search (http://www.socialwork

search.com), which were often unknown to users of general search engines and enhanced their abilities to find relevant materials. Finally, there was an assignment focusing on the digital divide for students who either were more interested in the social impact of the Web than the mechanics of searching or who had the mechanics down but had never considered their societal implications. Students distributed themselves evenly among the three assignments–especially after being assured that one version really was not any "harder" than another. Fewer students refused to do these customized assignments: refusals dropped from seven out of thirty-three students in Winter 2000 and four out of twenty-two students in Spring 2000 to two out of twenty-five students in Fall 2000. Average scores on the assignment increased from sixty-nine percent in Winter 2000 and sixty-three percent in Spring 2000 to seventy-seven percent in Fall 2000, a gain of seven to fourteen percent. Simultaneously, students' post-test scores on questions having to do with the Web increased compared to pre-test scores by three to thirteen percent between Winter/Spring 2000 and Fall 2000. Other successful applications of customization included allowing students to choose the format of their final project's presentation (paper, oral report, Web page, poster, etc.) and giving them a choice of readings throughout the course.[39]

Low Thresholds for Boredom, Unwillingness to Memorize

Gen Yers are commonly characterized as having low thresholds for boredom[40] and short attention spans.[41] Indeed, some three million Gen Yers, roughly eighty percent of them boys, take Ritalin regularly to treat attention deficit disorders.[42] Gen Yers are also generally described as unwilling to memorize information and said to prefer that education come in entertaining packages.[43] None of these typically pejorative descriptions of Gen Y are all that surprising when one considers the environment in which they have been raised. Video games, music videos, television, and other entertainment media take much of the blame for the short attention spans, low thresholds for boredom, and preference for being entertained characteristic of today's youth: for example, Neil Howe and William Strauss write that Gen Yers "have grown up with video games in the same way that Boomers grew up with board games–but where the slow speed and little action of the 50's board game prompted imagination and conversation, the hyperspeed and furious action of the '90s video games controlled one and stifled the other."[44] Beyond the screens of entertainment products, though, theirs is a fast-paced world that actively celebrates rapid change:[45] certain Japanese electronic products now boast of having a three-month life cycle.[46] This fast-paced world also valorizes multi-tasking, doing several things at once, and "[t]eens are typically on the phone, with the computer on, surfing the Web, instant messaging or chatting and either listening to music or watching television at the same time. That's just the standard operating procedure for them."[47] After multi-tasking (e.g., working on the computer and listening to music), single-tasking (e.g., "just" reading a book or writing an essay) probably does seem somewhat "boring" in that it lacks stimuli normally present.

In reality, many of Gen Y's traits simply heighten traits previously characteristic of typical learners. The upper extent of the average attention span was twenty to thirty minutes before MTV or video games originated.[48] Lengthy or poorly delivered presentations were seen as "boring" long before the 1990s, and most people would rather not be bored than be bored, would rather be entertained than work. Good teaching has thus long recognized that the tempo and pacing of instruction, as well as the instructional strategies used, need to vary to keep students' interest.[49] Gen Yers are, however, more vocal about being bored, more willing to speak out against "pointless" memorization and busywork, than earlier generations of students.[50] They are also more likely to hold instructors accountable for making learning boring or interesting to them.[51] One assignment that LIBY 1010 students most resented as boring and pointless was an initial assignment introducing them to library locations, library services, and the basics of Library of Congress classification. Short answer questions asking students to write in names of places and services; checklists on which to mark the locations of places or services; and questions about materials to be found at given call numbers were hallmarks of the assignment and subsequent quiz. Students were asked to memorize which call numbers corresponded to which subject materials, not just the basic principles for reading LC call numbers. Memorization of call numbers and corresponding subjects was simply stripped from the syllabus in subsequent quarters. Instead, the assumption was made that sending students to find reference materials, books, and articles on their topic would, in itself, be conducive to getting the basic points across: after visiting astronomy materials in the QB section three or four times, most students understood that materials on a subject shared a location and had a sense of what that location was for their topic. Thus, repeated exposure to a concept substituted for memorization in adding to students' knowledge.

More fundamentally, though, in Spring 2000 the notion that "the more students enjoy their work, the more learning occurs"[52] was used to transform this assignment on library services, locations, and call numbers into a more ludic, a more playful, experience for students. The "boring" fill-in-the-blank and checklist assignment was replaced with a crossword puzzle. The clues corresponded to the questions of the old assignment, with the words to be written into the puzzle being what students had previously filled into the blanks or checked on lists. Student evaluations strongly indicated that they found this revised assignment more fun. Their post-test scores also increased by an additional ten percent compared to their pre-test scores on questions having to do with topics addressed on this assignment. While students in Winter 2000 did fourteen percent better on post-test questions on these topics than on pre-test questions, students in Spring and Fall 2000, who got the revised assignment, did twenty-four and twenty-five percent better, respectively, on the post-test questions than they had done on pre-test questions.

Active Learning Is Even Better When It Is Also Peer-Learning

Giving Gen Yers opportunities for active learning not only lessens their likelihood of boredom by increasing opportunities for engagement, but also increases their mastery of learning materials.[53] Lecture has long been recognized as a teaching method best suited to the learning styles and preferences of only a few students: "Very little of a lecture can be recalled except in the case of listeners with above-average education and intelligence."[54] The average retention rate for materials presented in lectures is five percent, compared to fifty percent for group discussion, seventy-five percent for practice by doing, and ninety percent for teaching others.[55] Lecture is an especially ineffective instructional technique for Gen Y students. Not only does "[t]he old, stand-and-deliver, you-will-listen-to-me, I-am-the-teacher-you-are-the-student approach . . . not work"[56] for Gen Yers, but Gen Yers are also more likely to tell teachers, in evaluations and elsewhere, that this is the case.[57] LIBY 1010 students were taught the types and uses of reference sources in Winter 2000 by lecture and demonstration. They were told what the types of reference sources were and what kinds of information each type provides, as well as shown examples of each type. Students did not retain much of this information, despite the fact that an entire class meeting and a homework assignment focused on reference sources.

Beginning in Spring 2000 students were introduced to reference sources by a kinesthetic learning activity that also drew upon their desire for customized learning experiences. Every student was given a set of four cards, each of which asked a question and gave the title of a reference book that would answer the question. Students looked up the book's title in the catalog, noted the call number, went into the reference stacks, found the item, and used it to answer the question. While doing so, they noted what type of reference source each item was. Every student was directed to four different reference sources relating to her/his topic. After each student had found the answers to her/his questions–effectively learning what types of sources gave what types of information–students shared their findings with each other. This enabled each student to learn about types of reference sources to which s/he was not directed and to learn from each other, a most effective way for Gen Yers to learn.[58] Evaluations expressed students' happiness to be up and moving about, as well as to be directed to information relevant to their topics. They also retained more information about the types of reference sources and their uses. While students who were lectured about reference sources did twenty-nine percent better on post-test questions than on pre-test questions, students who learned reference sources using kinesthetic methods did forty-one percent better on post-test questions than on pre-test questions, a gain of twelve percent.

Opportunities for peer learning are incredibly important for Gen Yers. Gen Yers identify strongly with others of their age group,[59] a phenomenon made explicable by the fact that Gen Yers have grown up in a society characterized by age segregation "to an extent unparalleled in the past."[60] Over one half of children born in the late 1970s will live in single-parent households for some period of time before turning eighteen;[61] one in four currently lives in a single-parent household; three out of four have working mothers; and the average teen spends less than thirty minutes per week alone with her/his father.[62] There simply have not been all that many members of earlier generations around to influence Gen Yers, forcing them to rely on their peers. Rely upon peers, they have: "Teachers report that compared with Gen Xers of a decade ago, today's kids get along less well with teachers, but better with one another."[63]

Promoting opportunities for peer-learning is a wise strategy because Gen Yers usually find peers more credible than teachers, than persons of earlier generations, when it comes to determining what is worth paying attention to, what is fun, and what is work.[64] Gen Yers' trust in peers can thus help to mitigate two other characteristics of Gen Yers that can work against their benefiting from active learning opportunities. First, Gen Yers tend to view education negatively, as like work, "important for one's future" but "depressing and dull."[65] Active learning seems particularly like work because it "requires personal effort . . . it's hard,"[66] and many Gen Yers "expect they will gain knowledge simply by listening to what an expert has to say, just as they simply expect to receive a product in the store simply by paying the price."[67] Indeed, Gen Yers have largely gotten good grades in school without doing much work, and without developing an appropriate sense of workloads.[68] By 1998, one third of eighth-graders and one fourth of tenth-graders had A or A– averages,[69] yet sixty-five percent of high school students said they are not trying very hard and seventy-five percent indicated they would try harder if pushed.[70] The 2000

National Survey of Student Engagement similarly found that while seventy-nine percent of first-year college students said their high schools expected them to study a "significant amount," fifty-five percent of them reported spending only one hour or less studying outside of class for every hour spent in class.[71] Gen Yers are also very attuned to what they view as "marketing" by members of earlier generations: "Teens readily reject false images. If a marketer is being dishonest, it will ring false to them. They have highly sensitive B.S. detectors that just go off the charts if they're lied to."[72] What this essentially means is that Gen Yers may be skeptical about their teachers' valuations of anything, especially their teachers' valuations of work as worth doing. When their peers can be made to see something as "fun," or as work worth the effort, though, Gen Yers are significantly more receptive to it.

CONCLUSIONS

All of the changes described above were in the style of presenting materials, not in the substance of materials presented. Students were asked to do and learn the same things; they were just asked to do so in ways that corresponded more closely to their learning style preferences and worldviews. Far from pandering to learners' supposed academic deficiencies or personal laziness, this approach sought to improve teaching by focusing upon learners' skills, attitudes, and needs. "The aim of teaching any subject should be to enable the learner to acquire an understanding of the structure of the subject being taught,"[73] but this cannot be done until material is made meaningful to learners by being approached from and integrated into learners' schemata, their frameworks of background knowledge and experience.[74] Because materials must be made meaningful to learners in order to be comprehensible by them, the "crucial element in all good teaching/learning experiences" becomes the learners themselves[75]–what they know, what their interests are, how they learn. The real focus of the changes to teaching methods and materials described herein is structuring the learning experience to (attempt to) guarantee the success of the learners.[76] Of course, correlation does not necessarily mean causation, and the improvements in student performance that accompanied the changes in teaching methods and materials described herein may be the result of chance. Or perhaps consciously trying to be a good, effective teacher for Gen Y students was in itself enough to prompt improvements in performance, whether by focusing the instructor more on teaching or by persuading the students that the instructor really was trying to reach them. Changing one aspect of teaching methods or materials (for example, incorporating more active learning) often in itself brought other changes (for example, a greater focus on peer-learning).

This makes it virtually impossible to single out one of these changes as most related to improvements in Gen Y's learning. Despite these uncertainties, though, the author remains convinced that changing teaching methods did result in improvements in student performance in her classes, and that much can be gained from teaching to learners' strengths and worldviews.

NOTES

1. Mary Ellen Beck, "The ABC's of Gen X for Librarians," *Information Outlook* 5, no. 2 (2001): 16-20.

2. Other terms used to denote this group include the Digital Generation, Net Generation, Nintendo Generation, Generation 2000, Generation Next, Y2Kids, Millenials, and Generation Y2K. One study suggests that today's teens find the Generation Y label problematic because it implies an extension of Generation X, a group they view, by a two to one margin, as having a "negative reputation." This study reveals that they prefer "millennials," a name they see as acknowledging "their technological superiority without defining them too explicitly in those terms," Neil Howe and William Strauss, *Millennials Rising: The Next Great Generation* (New York: Vintage Books, 2000), 10-12. Nevertheless, the "Generation Y" label is here applied to those currently living in the United States born between 1980 and 2000 because it is the term most commonly used.

3. Currently, over 70.4 million people, approximately twenty-six percent of the total U.S. population, are school-aged Gen Yers. Howe and Strauss, 74.

4. Beloit College, *Beloit College's Class of 2003 Mindset List* (2000).

5. "Like any social category (race, class, religion, or nationality), a generation can allow plenty of individual exceptions and be fuzzy at the edges. . . . Not every member will share it, of course, but every member will have to deal with it, willingly or not, over a lifetime." Howe and Strauss, 41.

6. Many students, unfortunately, do not find information literacy courses and skills, especially those fulfilling university requirements, motivating in their own right. While some thirty percent of libraries now offer basic or discipline-specific information literacy skills courses for academic credit, one study has found that students rank credit courses as their least preferred means of getting library instruction. Jeanne R. Davidson, "Faculty and Student Attitudes toward Credit Courses for Library Skills," *College and Research Libraries* 62, no. 2 (2001): 155-163. "Because they may see no need for it, students may resent having to take a library course more than other required courses." Mignon S. Adams and Jacquelyn M. Morris, *Teaching Library Skills for Academic Credit* (Phoenix, AZ: Oryx Press, 1985), 8.

7. In Fall 1998, CSUH had a total enrollment of 12,888 students, 770 of whom were first-time first-year students and 1,462 of whom were new transfer students. Institutional Research and Analysis, California State University, Hayward, *Most Requested Census Information* (2000).

8. Judith Faust, "Teaching Information Literacy in 50 Minutes a Week: The CSUH Experience," *Journal of Southern Academic and Special Librarianship* 2, no. 3 (2001).

9. Howe and Strauss, 15.

10. Institutional Research.

11. John Ritter, "Calif. Racial Data Shifts, Becomes First Big State with No Ethnic Majority," *USA Today*, 30 March 2001, A1.

12. Mihaly Csikszentmihalyi and Barbara Schneider, *Becoming Adult: How Teenagers Prepare for the World of Work* (New York: Basic Books, 2000), 88-90.

13. Howe and Strauss, 264. Gen Y spending seems to be escalating: Gen Yers spent $94 billion in 1999, up $10 billion from 1997. Cristina Merrill, "The Ripple Effect Reaches Gen Y," *American Demographics* (1999).

14. Marcy Gordon, "Senate Rejects Credit Card Limits for Minors," *San Francisco Chronicle*, 14 March 2001, B4.

15. A survey of incoming first-year students at the University of California, Los Angeles, found that a "record number"–one in four–reported "some" or a "very good" likelihood of getting a full-time job while in college. Leo Reisberg, "Student Stress Is Rising, Especially among Women: Annual Survey of Freshmen Also Finds Declines in Drinking and Smoking," *Chronicle of Higher Education* 46, no. 21 (2000). Seventy percent of all CSU students work, with one in three working at least thirty hours per week while taking an average of 12 credits. One in four students also has children. California State University, *Visions, Plans, New Realities* (Long Beach, CA: CSU, 1998), 7.

16. Howe and Strauss, 46.

17. Howe and Strauss, 7.

18. Elliot Soloway, "How the Nintendo Generation Learns," *Communications of the ACM* 34, no. 9 (1991): 23-28. Hype over new or improved technologies pervades contemporary life and shapes expectations. People "are bombarded daily with the possibilities of the Internet, multimedia CD-ROMs, interactive television, and distance learning . . . [They] may not always be computer literate, but you can bet they're going to be technologically demanding." Cheryl LaGuardia, Michael Blake, Laura Farwell, Caroline M. Kent, and Ed Tallent, *Teaching the New Library: A How-To-Do-It Manual for Planning and Designing Instructional Programs* (New York: Neal-Schuman, 1996), 27. cf. Kimberley Robles Smith, "Great Expectations: Or, Where Do They Get These Ideas?" *Reference and User Services Quarterly* 40, no. 1 (2001, 27-31).

19. According to this same survey, eighty-nine percent of teens claimed to use computers several times a week, and sixty one percent surfed the Internet. "Teenagers and Technology: A Newsweek Poll Shows Familiarity and Optimism," *Newsweek* 129, no. 17 (1997), 86-87. According to more recent numbers, seventy-five to ninety percent of teenagers have a computer at home, and fifty percent have Internet access at home. Howe and Strauss, 171.

20. It is fundamentally true that "despite their high opinions of their own abilities, students [are] quite unskilled in research techniques that effectively use Internet resources." Deborah J. Grimes and Carl H. Boening, "Worries about the Web: A Look at Student Use of Web Resources," *College and Research Libraries* 62, no. 1 (2001): 12. Because the "Internet makes readily available so much information, . . . students think research is far easier than it really is." Bradley L. Schaffner, "Electronic Resources: A Wolf in Sheep's Clothing," *College and Research Libraries* 62, no. 3 (2001): 243.

21. Philip J. Calvert, "Web-Based Misinformation in the Context of Higher Education," *Asian Libraries* 8, no. 3 (1999): 93-91. Another study found that even students who rated themselves as novice Web searchers expressed complete satisfaction with the Web as an information source, and nearly all had confidence that they could find needed information on the Web and that the information would be accurate and correct. Bradley P. Tolppanen, "A Survey of World Wide Web Use by Freshman English Stu-

dents: Results and Implications for Bibliographic Instruction," *Internet Reference Services Quarterly* 4, no. 4 (1999): 43-53. In yet another study, eighty-five percent of students were found to rate the accuracy of web resources as excellent. Susan Davis Herring, "Faculty Acceptance of the World Wide Web for Student Research," *College and Research Libraries* 62, no. 3 (2001): 251-258.

22. In Fall 2000, information equity in relation to the Web was also brought within the realm of students' experience, thanks to insights gained from a presentation by Angelynn King at LOEX of the West. King used "Hobson's Choice" [Web page]; available on the World Wide Web at http://www.realchangenews.org/hobson_intro.html to introduce her students to the difficulties that a homeless person–in the various situations described in the "game" on this site–would have in accessing information from the Internet or libraries. Angelynn King, *Disconnected: Teaching Information Equity to Undergraduates* (Unpublished manuscript, 2001).

23. David W. Allan and Lisa A. Baures, "B.I. Instructional Design: Applying Modes of Consciousness Theory," in *The Impact of Technology on Library Instruction* (Ann Arbor, MI: Pierian Press, 1995), 78.

24. Lisa K. Miller, "Cooperative Learning Users Groups: Modeling Cooperation," in *New Ways of "Learning the Library"–and Beyond* (Ann Arbor, MI: Pierian Press, 1996), 127.

25. cf. Jamie F. Baker, "Give It to Them the Way They Want It," *The Masthead* 51, no. 3 (1999): 21; Bradley Dilger, "The Ideology of Ease," *Journal of Electronic Publishing* 6, no. 1 (2000); Alexandra Rand, "Technology Transforms Training," *HR Focus* 73, no. 11 (1996): 11-14; Lorie Roth, "Educating the Cut-and-Paste Generation," *Library Journal* 124, no. 18 (1999): 42; and Don Tapscott, *Growing Up Digital: The Rise of the Net Generation* (New York: McGraw Hill, 1999), 62. Indeed, books are now being designed to appeal to Gen Yers by imitating the graphics and layouts of Web sites and computer games. Susan Dodge, "Tech-Savvy Teens Still Read Books," *Chicago-Sun Times*, 15 February 2000.

26. Patricia Senn Breivik, *Student Learning in the Information Age* (Phoenix, AZ: Oryx Press, 1998), 27. Students' affinities for visual over textual information also reflect their preferences for "ease" and "speed." cf. Dilger. Many Gen Yers "perceive reading as 'slow, painful, and torturous,'" while TV is described as "fast and exciting, with changing visuals and colors that kept them awake." Sharon Curcio, "Finding Modern Ways To Teach Today's Youth," *Corrections Today* 57, no. 2 (1995): 28-30. Indeed, seventy-one percent of teens say they "would prefer to talk into their computers rather than type." Wendy Murray Zoba, *Generation 2K: What Parents and Others Need To Know about the Millennials* (Downers Grove, IL: InterVarsity Press, 1999), 44.

27. Jakob Nielsen, "How Users Read on the Web," *Alertbox* (1997).

28. Kirk McElhearn, "Click Me (Or, the Ubiquity of Hypertext)," *TidBITS* no. 534 (2000). cf. Zoba, 49.

29. Herbert R. Kohl, *"I Won't Learn from You"–and Other Thoughts on Creative Maladjustment* (New York: New Press, 1994), 6. cf. R. W. Burniske, "In Defense of Computer Illiteracy: The Virtues of Not Learning," *Teachers College Record* (2000).

30. An added benefit of the visual directions was their accessibility to students whose native language was not English. "For students with limited English proficiency, having to take performance tests in English automatically puts them at a major disadvantage." Geneva Gay, "Educational Equality for Students of Color," in *Multicultural Education: Issues and Perspectives* (Boston: Allyn and Bacon, 1997), 214.

31. Roth; cf. Jeremy Rifkin, *The Age of Access: The New Culture of Hypercapitalism Where All of Life Is a Paid for Experience* (New York: Jeremy P. Tarcher|Putnam, 2000), 187; Tapscott, 142.

32. Curcio. cf. Allan and Baures, 77.

33. *Graphic Organizers* (No Date).

34. Russell Freeland, "WonderWorks," *Data Based Advisor* 8, no. 3 (1990): 146-148.

35. Rifkin.

36. Baker; Rand; Tapscott, 10.

37. Mel Elfin, "The College of Tomorrow," *U.S. News & World Report*, 113, no. 12 (1992): 110-112.

38. Victor Dwyer, "A Crash Course in Reality 101: Generation Y Asks Universities To Deliver for Their Futures," *Maclean's* 109, no. 48 (1996), 50-55. This article also quotes the president of the University of Manitoba Students' Union as saying, "The university has got to learn some priorities. It has to zero in on what it does well, what it doesn't, and what exactly its tuition-paying clients need to survive in the outside world."

39. Another benefit of giving students choice is the fact that "treating different individuals identically is inherently discriminatory. Their differentness demands variability in treatment . . . sameness of educational resources for diverse individuals and groups does not constitute comparability of quality or opportunity." Gay, 196, 211.

40. Michael Garry, "Training for the Nintendo Generation," *Progressive Grocer* 75, no. 4 (1996): 87-90.

41. Freeland; Rifkin, 187.

42. Howe and Strauss, 93.

43. Garry; Tapscott, 147-148.

44. Howe and Strauss, 257. The outlook for Gen Yers varies, with some questioning whether young people who grew up in front of computer screens will have the extended attention spans necessary to form coherent frames of reference for understanding and adapting to the world around them; others suggest that Gen Yers will free up the human consciousness to be more playful, flexible, and even transient in order to accommodate fast-and ever-changing realities. Rifkin, 12-13.

45. Baker; Roth; Tapscott, 73.

46. Rifkin, 21.

47. Kipp Cheng, "Setting Their Sites on Generation 'Y,'" *Mediaweek* 9, no. 31 (1999): 46.

48. Patricia Senn Breivik, *Planning the Library Instruction Program* (Chicago: American Library Association, 1982), 92. cf. Eileen E. Allen, "Active Learning and Teaching: Improving Postsecondary Library Instruction," *The Reference Librarian* no. 51/52 (1995): 95.

49. Ruth V. Small, "Designing Motivation into Library and Information Skills Instruction," *School Library Media Quarterly Online* (1998).

50. Tapscott, 87.

51. Small.

52. Breivik, *Student Learning*, 39.

53. Soloway; Rand.

54. Breivik, *Student Learning*, 24. cf. Allen, 92, who writes that "Lecture meets the needs of only a portion of highly self directed individuals who learn well by listening and reading."

55. Miller, 127.

56. Garry.

57. Small.

58. As Drueke, points out, some theorists of active learning claim that real active learning must involve acting on material things and social collaboration. Jeanetta Drueke, "Active Learning in the University Instruction Classroom," *Research Strategies* 10, no. 2 (1992): 78.

59. Diana Bagnall, "The Y Factor," *The Bulletin with Newsweek* 117, no. 6165 (1999): 14-20.

60. Csikszentmihalyi and Schneider, 14.

61. Csikszentmihalyi and Schneider, 14.

62. Howe and Strauss, 131.

63. Howe and Strauss, 181.

64. Academic librarians have begun utilizing peer-tutoring and-advising more in recent years to reach these Gen Yers. Bruce Harley, Megan Dreger, and Patricia Knobloch, "The Postmodern Condition: Students, the Web, and Academic Library Services," *Reference Services Review* 29, no. 1 (2001): 23-32; Elizabeth Blakesley Lindsay, "Undergraduate Students as Peer Instructors: One Way to Expand Library Instruction and Reference Services," *LOEX News* 27, no. 4 (2000): 7, 13.

65. Csikszentmihalyi and Schneider, 14. Polls show that teens like school less with each passing grade-level while simultaneously accepting it more as necessary for their futures. Howe and Strauss, 162. Gen Yers are particularly fond of seeing themselves as players not workers, as creative not industrious. Rifkin, 187.

66. Breivik, *Student Learning*, 7.

67. Breivik, *Student Learning*, 6.

68. Unrealistically high expectations could themselves be said to characterize Gen Yers. Three in five of today's twelve-to-seventeen-year-olds think they could be elected president some day. Howe and Strauss, 230. Eighty percent expect to be professionals. Csikszentmihalyi and Schneider, 4-5. Over fifteen percent expect to be doctors or lawyers, occupations currently held by only slightly over one percent of the population. Csikszentmihalyi and Schneider, 45. They expect to earn $75,000 by the age of thirty; as the actual median earnings of a thirty-year old in 1999 were $27,000, the inflation rate would have to reach 278% for Gen Yers to realize this figure. Howe and Strauss, 318. What form Gen Yers' reaction to the inevitable frustration of these expectations will take is as yet unknown. Cf. Zoba, 52.

69. Howe and Strauss, 184.

70. Howe and Strauss, 162.

71. "National Survey of Student Engagement," *The College Student Report* (2001).

72. Cheng; cf. Garry; Andrew Marlatt, "Yen for E-tail," *Internet World* 5, no. 26 (1999): 39; Tapscott, 197.

73. Mary I. Piette, "Library Instruction: Principles, Theories, Connections, and Challenges," *The Reference Librarian* no. 51/52 (1995): 78.

74. Melvina Azar Dame, *Serving Linguistically and Culturally Diverse Students: Strategies for the School Library Media Specialist* (New York: Neal-Schuman, 1993), 16.

75. Breivik, *Planning the Library Instruction Program*, 54.

76. cf. Breivik, *Planning the Library Instruction Program*, 55.

BIBLIOGRAPHY

Adams, Mignon S. and Jacquelyn M. Morris. *Teaching Library Skills for Academic Credit*. Phoenix, AZ: Oryx Press, 1985.

Allan, David W. and Lisa A. Baures. "B.I. Instructional Design: Applying Modes of Consciousness Theory." In *The Impact of Technology on Library Instruction*. Ann Arbor, MI: Pierian Press, 1995.

Allen, Eileen E. "Active Learning and Teaching: Improving Postsecondary Library Instruction." *The Reference Librarian* no. 51/52 (1995): 89-103.

Bagnall, Diana. "The Y Factor." *The Bulletin with Newsweek* 117, no. 6165 (1999): 14-20.

Baker, Jamie F. "Give It to Them the Way They Want It." *The Masthead* 51, no. 3 (1999): 21.

Beck, Mary Ellen. "The ABC's of Gen X for Librarians." *Information Outlook* 5, no. 2 (2001): 16-20.

Beloit College. "Beloit College's Class of 2003 Mindset List." [Web page], 2000. Available on the World Wide Web at http://www.beloit.edu/~pubaff/releases/mindsetlist.html.

Breivik, Patricia Senn. *Planning the Library Instruction Program*. Chicago: American Library Association, 1982.

_____. *Student Learning in the Information Age*. Phoenix, AZ: Oryx Press, 1998.

Burniske, R. W. "In Defense of Computer Illiteracy: The Virtues of 'Not Learning.'" *Teachers College Record* (2000). Available on the World Wide Web at http://www.tcrecord.org/printidkwparam.asp?@IdNumer=10526.

California State University. *Visions, Plans, New Realities*. Long Beach, CA: CSU, 1998.

Calvert, Philip J. "Web-Based Misinformation in the Context of Higher Education." *Asian Libraries* 8, no. 3 (1999): 83-91.

Cheng, Kipp. "Setting Their Sites on Generation 'Y.'" *Mediaweek* 9, no. 31 (1999): 46.

Csikszentmihalyi, Mihaly and Barbara Schneider. *Becoming Adult: How Teenagers Prepare for the World of Work*. New York: Basic Books, 2000.

Curcio, Sharon. "Finding Modern Ways To Teach Today's Youth." *Corrections Today* 57, no. 2 (1995): 28-30.

Dame, Melvina Azar. *Serving Linguistically and Culturally Diverse Students: Strategies for the School Library Media Specialist*. New York: Neal-Schuman, 1993.

Davidson, Jeanne R. "Faculty and Student Attitudes toward Credit Courses for Library Skills." *College and Research Libraries* 62, no. 2 (2001): 155-163.

Dilger, Bradley. "The Ideology of Ease." *Journal of Electronic Publishing* 6, no. 1 (2000). Available on the World Wide Web at http://www.press.umich.edu/jep/06-01/dilger.html.

Dodge, Susan. "Tech-Savvy Teens Still Read Books." *Chicago-Sun Times*, 15 February 2000. Available on the World Wide Web at http://www.suntimes.com/output/news/read15.html.

Drueke, Jeanetta. "Active Learning in the University Instruction Classroom." *Research Strategies* 10, no. 2 (1992): 77-83.

Dwyer, Victor. "A Crash Course in Reality 101: Generation Y Asks Universities To Deliver for Their Futures." *Maclean's* 109, no. 48 (1996): 50-55.

Elfin, Mel. "The College of Tomorrow." *U.S. News & World Report* 113, no. 12 (1992): 110-112.

Faust, Judith. "Teaching Information Literacy in 50 Minutes a Week: The CSUH Experience." *Journal of Southern Academic and Special Librarianship* 2, no. 3 (2001). Available on the World Wide Web at http://southernlibrarianship.icaap.org/content/v02n03/faust_j01.htm.

Freeland, Russell. "WonderWorks." *Data Based Advisor* 8, no. 3 (1990): 146-148.

Garry, Michael. "Training for the Nintendo Generation." *Progressive Grocer* 75, no. 4 (1996): 87-90.

Gay, Geneva. "Educational Equality for Students of Color." In *Multicultural Education: Issues and Perspectives*. Boston: Allyn and Bacon, 1997.

Gordon, Marcy. "Senate Rejects Credit Card Limits for Minors." *San Francisco Chronicle*, 14 March 2001.

"Graphic organizers." [Web page]. No Date. Available on the World Wide Web at http://www.writedesignonline.com/organizers/.

Grimes, Deborah J. and Carl H. Boening. "Worries about the Web: A Look at Student Use of Web Resources." *College and Research Libraries* 62, no. 1 (2000): 11-23.

Harley, Bruce, Megan Dreger, and Patricia Knobloch. "The Postmodern Condition: Students, the Web, and Academic Library Services." *Reference Services Review* 29, no. 1 (2001): 23-32.

Herring, Susan Davis. "Faculty Acceptance of the World Wide Web for Student Research." *College and Research Libraries* 62, no. 3 (2001): 251-258.

Howe, Neil and William Strauss. *Millennials Rising: The Next Great Generation*. New York: Vintage Books, 2000.

Institutional Research and Analysis, California State University, Hayward. "Most Requested Census Information." [Web page]. 2000. Available on the World Wide Web at http://www.aba.csuhayward.edu/ira/.

King, Angelynn. *Disconnected: Teaching Information Equity to Undergraduates*. Unpublished manuscript, 2001.

Kohl, Herbert R. *"I Won't Learn from You" –and Other Thoughts on Creative Maladjustment*. New York: New Press, 1994.

LaGuardia, Cheryl, Michael Blake, Laura Farwell, Caroline M. Kent, and Ed Tallent. *Teaching the New Library: A How-To-Do-It Manual for Planning and Designing Instructional Programs*. New York: Neal-Schuman, 1996.

Lee, Catherine A. "Teaching Generation X." *Research Strategies* 14, no. 1 (1996): 56-59.

Lindsay, Elizabeth Blakesley. "Undergraduate Students as Peer Instructors: One Way to Expand Library Instruction and Reference Services." *LOEX News* 27, no. 4 (2000): 7, 13.

Marlatt, Andrew. "Yen for E-Tail." *Internet World* 5, no. 26 (1999): 39.

McElhearn, Kirk. "Click Me (Or, the Ubiquity of Hypertext)." *TidBITS* no. 534 (2000).

Merrill, Cristina. "The Ripple Effect Reaches Gen Y." *American Demographics* (1999).

Miller, Lisa K. "Cooperative Learning Users Groups: Modeling Cooperation." In *New Ways of "Learning the Library" –and Beyond*. Ann Arbor, MI: Pierian Press, 1996.

National Survey of Student Engagement. "The College Student Report." [Web page]. 2001. Available on the World Wide Web at http://www.indiana.edu/~nsse/.

Nielsen, Jakob. "How Users Read on the Web." *Alertbox* (1997). Available on the World Wide Web at http://www.useit.com/alertbox/9710a.html.

Piette, Mary I. "Library Instruction: Principles, Theories, Connections, and Challenges." *The Reference Librarian* no. 51/52 (1995): 77-88.

Rand, Alexandra. "Technology Transforms Training." *HR Focus* 73, no. 11 (1996): 11-14.

Reisberg, Leo. "Student Stress Is Rising, Especially among Women: Annual Survey of Freshmen Also Finds Declines in Drinking and Smoking." *Chronicle of Higher Education* 46, no. 21 (2000). Available on the World Wide Web at http://chronicle.com/weekly/v46/i21a04901.htm.

Rifkin, Jeremy. *The Age of Access: The New Culture of Hypercapitalism Where All of Life Is a Paid for Experience*. New York: Jeremy P. Tarcher|Putnam, 2000.

Ritter, John. "Calif. Racial Data Shifts, Becomes First Big State with no Ethnic Majority." *USA Today*, 30 March 2001.

Roth, Lorie. "Educating the Cut-and-Paste Generation." *Library Journal* 124, no. 18 (1999): 42.

Schaffner, Bradley L. "Electronic Resources: A Wolf in Sheep's Clothing." *College and Research Libraries* 62, no. 3 (2001): 239-249.

Small, Ruth V. "Designing Motivation into Library and Information Skills Instruction." *School Library Media Quarterly Online*. 1998. Available on the World Wide Web at http://www.ala.org/aasl/SLMQ/small.html.

Smith, Kimberley Robles. "Great Expectations: Or, Where Do They Get These Ideas?" *Reference and User Services Quarterly* 40, no. 1 (2001): 27-31.

Soloway, Elliot. "How the Nintendo Generation Learns." *Communications of the ACM* 34, no. 9 (1991): 23-28.

Tapscott, Don. *Growing Up Digital: The Rise of the Net Generation*. New York: McGraw Hill, 1999.

"Teenagers and Technology: A Newsweek Poll Shows Familiarity and Optimism." *Newsweek* 129, no. 17 (1997): 86-87.

Tolppanen, Bradley P. "A Survey of World Wide Web Use by Freshman English Students: Results and Implications for Bibliographic Instruction." *Internet Reference Services Quarterly* 4, no. 4 (1999): 43-53.

Zoba, Wendy Murray. *Generation 2K: What Parents and Others Need To Know About the Millennials*. Downers Grove, IL: InterVarsity Press, 1999.

Buoyed by a Rising Tide:
Information Literacy
Sails into the Curriculum
on the Currents of Evidence-Based Medicine
and Professional Competency Objectives

Richard B. Kaplan
Julia S. Whelan

SUMMARY. This paper discusses how the information literacy efforts at the Massachusetts College of Pharmacy and Health Sciences (MCPHS) have been supported by national trends within health science education to incorporate evidence-based medicine and problem-based learning into the curriculum. In addition, both accreditation agencies and national commissions have published documents supporting information literacy education for health science students. These trends and mandates in academic medicine have re-enforced faculty and administration support. Unlike many college and university libraries, the librarians at MCPHS are now in the position of being asked to provide more instruction than they can support. Responses to this situation have included an increase in reference staff, change in emphasis from reference

Richard B. Kaplan is Associate Dean for Instructional Resources and Director of Sheppard Library, Massachusetts College of Pharmacy and Health Sciences, 179 Longwood Avenue, Boston, MA 02115.

Julia S. Whelan is Head of Reference Services, Massachusetts College of Pharmacy and Health Sciences, 179 Longwood Avenue, Boston, MA 02115.

[Haworth co-indexing entry note]: "Buoyed by a Rising Tide: Information Literacy Sails into the Curriculum on the Currents of Evidence-Based Medicine and Professional Competency Objectives." Kaplan, Richard B., and Julia S. Whelan. Co-published simultaneously in *Journal of Library Administration* (The Haworth Information Press, an imprint of The Haworth Press, Inc.) Vol. 36, No. 1/2, 2002, pp. 219-235; and: *Information Literacy Programs: Successes and Challenges* (ed: Patricia Durisin) The Haworth Information Press, an imprint of The Haworth Press, Inc., 2002, pp. 219-235. Single or multiple copies of this article are available for a fee from The Haworth Document Delivery Service [1-800-HAWORTH, 9:00 a.m. - 5:00 p.m. (EST). E-mail address: getinfo@haworthpressinc.com].

219

services to teaching, learning and creating computer-based instruction programs, and enhanced collaboration and involvement with teaching faculty. The future, molded by these forces, holds the potential of offering librarians an opportunity to be key members of the evidence-based health care team; to allow librarians to adopt the same quantifiable research techniques into the practice of "evidence-based librarianship"; and to continue to boost information literacy efforts. *[Article copies available for a fee from The Haworth Document Delivery Service: 1-800-HAWORTH. E-mail address: <getinfo@haworthpressinc.com> Website: <http://www.HaworthPress.com> © 2002 by The Haworth Press, Inc. All rights reserved.]*

KEYWORDS. Information literacy, evidence-based medicine, pharmacy, medical libraries, health science libraries, instruction

INTRODUCTION

Academic librarians have long debated and agonized over their role as teachers and their attempts at integrating library instruction into the curriculum. Some libraries are able to organize extensive instruction programs that are tied to a freshman experience program or one that covers the basics of research theory including online search concepts. More specific subject instruction is usually coordinated with a sympathetic faculty member, who graciously provides the librarian a class period for library instruction. Few libraries have been able to fully develop a comprehensive program that is fully integrated into the curriculum and offers required instruction throughout the degree program. Indeed, a survey of Canadian academic libraries in 2000 found that first year students are the focus of instruction at 84.6 percent of libraries.[1] Sheppard Library at the Massachusetts College of Pharmacy and Health Sciences has successfully implemented an information literacy program, which requires all students to take a mandatory series of modules that ultimately will coordinate with all years of the curriculum. This paper will discuss the development of this program and examine trends in health science education and accreditation standards that helped to contribute to a receptive environment that allowed the librarians to initiate a comprehensive information literacy program.

MCPHS BACKGROUND

The Massachusetts College of Pharmacy and Health Sciences (MCPHS) is a private college founded in 1823 and is located in Boston, Massachusetts. MCPHS is one of the largest pharmacy schools in the nation with a total enrollment of approximately 2,000 students. Last year, a branch campus was started in Worcester, Massachusetts offering the Doctor of Pharmacy degree in an accelerated format. MCPHS-Boston is the second oldest school of pharmacy in the nation and now offers additional health science-related degrees in nursing, physician assistant studies, radiological sciences, pharmaceutical sciences, chemistry, health psychology and graduate programs in medicinal chemistry, pharmaceutics and pharmacology.

GROWTH AND CHANGES IN THE PHARMACY PROGRAM

Until the late 1990s, pharmacy programs nationwide offered a 5-year BS degree with an optional 6-year program leading to the Doctor of Pharmacy or Pharm. D. degree. In 1990, the American Association of Colleges of Pharmacy decided that the Pharm. D. should be the entry-level degree for the profession and mandated that all pharmacy schools begin the process of switching over to a full Pharm. D. program. This decision had a major impact on both the College and the Library. Previously, the small number of students enrolled in the Pharm. D. program were given advanced training in the use of drug information resources and research skills in a Drug Literature Evaluation course. The librarians and the faculty collaborated in the teaching of this course. When this degree became mandatory for all pharmacy students, the enrollment in the course increased ten fold. Moreover, the additional year of the program provides the students with a higher concentration of clinical and therapeutic coursework. During a several year transition period, class sizes greatly increased and the curriculum changed from a bachelors to a clinically focused Doctor of Pharmacy degree.

IMPACT ON THE LIBRARY AND ITS RESOURCES

Class enrollment is now over 150 and this presents many challenges and opportunities for the library. Sheppard Library has undergone many changes in order to respond to larger enrollments, a new pharmacy curriculum, and new health science programs. In the early 1990s, the library employed two reference librarians, maintained a core collection of reference material, and had two CD-ROM computer workstations that accessed two databases. Collections were strong in pharmacology, pharmaceutical sciences, and pharmacy education and also provided the College with a small core collection of clinical titles. Between Sheppard Library's collection and access to area medical school libraries, the number of requested interlibrary loans was relatively small. In fact, in the late 1980s, the library did not have a need to even use OCLC or Docline to transmit outgoing requests.

Today's library is significantly different from a decade ago. Part of this change can be attributed to the "sign of the times," where most academic libraries have substantially increased, and continue to increase the numbers of electronic databases, e-journals and e-books and incorporate the use of the Internet into both teaching and research. Also, like many academic libraries, instruction has changed from small groups huddled around reference books or indexes to PowerPoint™ presentations and computer classrooms.

As the technologies and curriculum changed, library staff had to rethink many aspects of its operation including collections, space, staffing, and service priorities. In order to handle large class research assignments, the library purchased multiple copies of many of the major clinical medicine and drug information texts. Single user licenses for databases converted into site licenses. (Timing was very fortunate as this shift coincided with the development of Web-accessible databases.) As the need to supply more clinical information became apparent, the library conducted journal surveys and compiled usage statistics. Consequently, the restructured journal collection is better suited to the new curriculum. The library initiated new document delivery options and money was reallocated to offer a free (for the most part) interlibrary loan service. Interlibrary loan has grown from 145 requests per year in the 1991/1992 academic year to over 2,290 in 2000/2001.

The size of the staff and job assignments needed to change to reflect the new emphasis on access to information rather than ownership and the exponential growth in the demand for library instruction. A copy cataloger position became coordinator for the expanding document delivery service. Through numerous budget requests, the number of reference librarians has expanded from two to four. Space in the library has been reallocated with the addition of a computer laboratory and learning resources center. The reference room was also rearranged with the reference desk now in close proximity to the research computers, the computer lab and the learning resources center. As teaching has taken a more prominent role for the librarians, our hiring practices have also changed. A strong emphasis on communication and teaching skills is a main qualification for all reference positions. Each candidate conducts a class on an assigned topic and is judged on teaching style, innovation, and clarity of the presentation.

INFORMATION LITERACY PROGRAM–
HISTORY, DEVELOPMENT, AND EXPANSION

In 1993, the MCPHS librarians faced the same problems that many academic libraries confront: how to deliver basic library instruction, including research methodologies and the use of online databases, to a large undergraduate class. Given the difficulties of trying to incorporate library instruction into freshman English classes and finding a time to "catch" third-year transfer students, the library decided to develop a series of computer-assisted modules using new authoring software that was coming out on the market, in this case, HyperCard™. A proposal was presented to the College-wide curriculum committee to create a series of sequential, mandatory instruction modules in information seeking skills. A key selling point of these modules was that they would not "interfere" or take time away from regularly scheduled classes. In fact, the first three compliment the existing liberal arts curriculum and provide direct support for the Expository Writing courses. The computerized modules would also be available on the library computers and students can access the modules anytime and as often as needed. It was hoped that these modules would provide students the ability to learn in an interactive, self-paced environment. Additionally, each module would have an associated examination that would be graded by library staff. The proposal was accepted and the program became mandatory for all pharmacy students. This model of non-credit bearing, mandatory graduation requirements has also been successfully used by the College to administer competency requirements for writing and oral proficiency and medical terminology.

In order to develop and implement a successful information literacy program, infrastructure needs to be in place. The Library, as part of the Division of Instructional Resources, provided access to a number of valuable resources that helped to create the Information Literacy Program. The College's first computer laboratory was located in the Library and the first computerized instruction program was written by a chemistry professor in HyperCard™ for Macintosh computers through a National Science Foundation grant.[2] In the process of implementing and running this program, library staff gained valuable experience and insight into the difficulties of developing early computer-assisted instruction. In 1994, the Division hired an instructional design specialist for the College. This provided the library with both a computer facility and expertise to assist in the development of these computer-assisted library modules. Money from an internal grant funded the purchase of the SuperCard™ authoring software and the services of a consultant who provided additional assistance with more of the complex program development issues.

With a team comprised of a librarian, an instructional designer, and a consultant, the task of creating a series of computer-assisted library modules was underway. In 1995, the first three modules came online. The modules have since undergone many changes. Despite repeated, substantial investments in software training, the library has been forced to switch from SuperCard™ to Authorware™ and eventually to HTML and Java Web-based access. The exams are now fully electronic using the testing module on Blackboard's™ courseware package. Today, the first three modules are a graduation requirement for all undergraduate and clinical degree programs at the College. For the pharmacy program, Sheppard Library offers two additional modules using both computer and traditional instruction. In addition, the library also teaches a 1-credit Survey of the Chemical Literature course and a 3-credit Medical Informatics course for students in the pharmaceutical sciences program. Our success and reputation has faculty from all programs wanting additional classes.

FACTORS LEADING TOWARD SUCCESS

As mentioned at the onset, librarians have struggled with their role as educators in academia and with efforts to gain acceptance from faculty and entrance into the classroom. In fact, the current emphasis on the "Information Literacy Movement" can be seen as a response to this struggle. In a recent article, Canadian librarians Katherine Chiste, Andrea Gover and Glenna Westwood do an excellent job portraying the different viewpoints academic librarians have on this conflict. Their metaphors extend from introspection and friendly alliances to military infiltration and conquest.

They list:

- Familiarity with the type of institution . . . mandates and purposes of our institutions vary . . . [librarians need] "an acute and growing awareness of current developments in post-secondary education . . . "
- Seeing the librarian playing the role of educator as an integral part of the educational process
- Acceptance of librarians, both introspectively and externally, as professional colleagues and peers of the teaching faculty
- Understanding by librarians and faculty that information literacy and library research involve skills that are not innate in students and faculty but rather need to be taught
- Believing that librarians are the most qualified people to teach information literacy.[3]

Several factors have made the establishment of an information literacy program particularly easy and effective. Generally, the major reasons relate to the acceptance of librarians as faculty, the Evidence-Based Medicine movement within academic medicine, and most importantly the endorsement of information literacy by the pharmacy accrediting body.

In the following section, we are going to examine specific factors that have allowed this transformation to occur at the Massachusetts College of Pharmacy and Health Sciences.

1. *History of librarians teaching at the College.* Sometimes tradition is the best foundation on which to build. As early as the 1960s, the library director was actively involved in team-teaching a required course for graduate students. Her expertise and success helped to set the framework and establish the librarians in the role of teacher.
2. *Faculty status.* Librarians have long discussed the pros and cons of having faculty status. At MCPHS, all faculty are non-tenured. Librarians have full faculty status and serve on all major College-wide committees and each school's curriculum committee. While committee activities can be time consuming, these duties afford librarians many opportunities to contribute to both the administrative and academic branches of the College. In a small college environment, when librarians work closely with the teaching faculty on committees and interact with them at meetings, they are able to develop a positive reputation as members of the instructional team and are accepted as peers. The combination of faculty status, combined with a rich tradition of library instruction, helped allow the librarians to gain institutional approval and a mandate for its information literacy program.
3. *The Library's position in the administrative hierarchy at the College.* The library director is also responsible for administrating the Division of Instructional Resources. In addition to the library, this division provides the College with media, Web and instructional technology services. This division also initially developed the college's first computer network and e-mail service. (This function has subsequently been transferred to a separately established Information Technology department.) Because of these past and present functions, the Library has been able to establish a reputation as a technology leader and provider. Through this structural alliance with instructional designers and Web personnel, the library has been able to integrate these resources more easily into its library instruction modules.
4. *Mission of the College.* Another condition that could be a factor in creating a supportive atmosphere for the development of an information literacy program is the mission of the institution. While the Massachusetts College of Pharmacy does offer graduate degrees and provides support for research, the College's primary mission is teaching. A teaching-intensive environment is usually, in our opinion, more open to interdisciplinary collaboration and consequently, team teaching with librarians. Pharmacy programs have strong mandates from professional organizations to incorporate information-seeking skills into its curriculum. (The next section will discuss this in greater depth.) A "student-centered

learning" environment, faculty recognition of the need for information-seeking skills, and a history of respect and understanding of the role of the librarian in the teaching process, all helped create the climate necessary to establish and support an information literacy program.

5. *Support from accreditation bodies, professional standards and commissioned reports.* Even though many previously mentioned factors helped to foster the library's program, it is not always easy to get full cooperation from all teaching faculty. There is additional ammunition in the library's arsenal to battle the reluctant faculty member or administration. Generally, in a professional education program, the curriculum is highly structured and sequential. Required courses and distribution electives leave little room for additional library-based courses. Often faculty can be reluctant to relinquish class time for librarians to teach instructional sessions. Accrediting bodies, professional standards, and commissioned reports can be important allies in the fight for information literacy competency requirements. Each of these groups can provide valuable recommendations and the basis for strong arguments when proposing library instruction programs to departments, curriculum committees and administrators.

Regional accrediting organizations differ in their standards for library services. The Middle States Association of Colleges and Schools is an excellent example of a pro-information literacy commission. Under its standards for library and learning resources, the Middle States Association states: "Each institution should foster optimal use of its learning resources through strategies designed to help students develop information literacy . . . It is essential to have an active and continuing program of library orientation and instruction in accessing information, developed collaboratively and supported actively by faculty, librarians, academic deans and other information providers."[4]

The Southern Association of Colleges and Schools also provides strong support for library instruction: "Libraries . . . must provide students with opportunities to learn how to access information in different formats so that they can continue life-long learning . . . This should be consistent with the goal of helping students develop information literacy–the ability to locate, evaluate, and use information to become life-long learners."[5]

Other very useful arguments for the development of information literacy programs come from our own library associations, such as the *Information Literacy Competency Standards for Higher Education* written by the Association of College and Research Libraries.[6] Another report that is helpful to cite is the Boyer Commission Report, *Reinventing Undergraduate Education.*[7]

More specific to the Massachusetts College of Pharmacy and Health Sciences, and perhaps the strongest external force supporting our information literacy efforts, are the competencies promulgated by the pharmacy accrediting agencies. The American Association of Colleges of Pharmacy (AACP) is the accrediting agency in pharmacy. As mentioned earlier, AACP mandated a universal change in pharmacy education in 1990, converting 5-year BS programs to 6-year Pharm. D. programs. A new vision for the profession based on the concept of "pharmaceutical care" was the impetus for these changes.

> Pharmaceutical care is truly a revolutionary concept in the practice of pharmacy in which all practitioners assume responsibility for the outcomes of drug therapy in their patients. It encompasses a variety of services and functions–some new to pharmacy, others traditional, which are determined and provided by the pharmacists serving individual patients. Finally, it espouses caring . . . [8]

In defining the curricular outcomes and competencies graduating students need in order to provide pharmaceutical care, AACP placed itself squarely behind information literacy. The following competencies and outcomes related to information literacy, written by the Commission to Implement change in Pharmaceutical Education, were adopted by AACP in 1990.

> . . . pharmaceutical education must facilitate the acquisition by entry-level students of a relevant knowledge base, skills, attitudes, ethics and values . . . pharmacy graduates . . . must be able to use epidemiologic and demographic data to reach conclusions regarding a variety of issues ranging from the effectiveness of therapies to identifying areas of practice needs.
>
> Although critical thinking is a universally desired educational outcome, professionals particularly need a repertoire of thinking strategies that will enable them to acquire, evaluate and synthesize information and knowledge.
>
> Graduates must have a sufficient understanding of information systems to integrate computer technologies into their practices.
>
> Entry-level pharmacy graduates must recognize the need to increase their knowledge to advance the profession through systematic, cumulative research on problems of theory and practice.
>
> Pharmacy practitioners expand personal, civic and professional knowledge and skills throughout their careers.
>
> In order that practitioners be successful in rendering pharmaceutical care, they must have the skills of inquiry, abstract logical thinking and critical analysis to separate real from illusionary problems, make judgments and decisions based on available data or identify additional data that may be required to:

    A. gather and organize data and information pertinent to specific patients under their care; and

    B. interpret and analyze data.

Entry-level practitioners must use the health-related, professional and disciplinary literature as a means of acquiring a continuing flow of new knowledge.

Students must understand that to become educated is to know what questions to ask and where the answers may be found.

Students . . . must have the ability to identify, locate, obtain and evaluate missing information: the ability to learn on one's own . . .[9]

Table 2 illustrates how these objectives for pharmacy education correlate with the ACRL information literacy standards and outcomes[10] as well as the evidence-based medicine process discussed in the next section of this paper.

Reinforcing these objectives is the pharmacy board examination. All pharmacy graduates must pass a board examination (NABPLEX) in order to receive licensure. As early as 1996, the official study guide, A Candidate's Review Guide for the National Association of Boards of Pharmacy Licensure Examination,[11] includes a competency statement related to information literacy. "The candidate shall identify, interpret, or evaluate sources of information for clarifying or answering questions related to prescriptions, medications, or health care." These competency statements fueled the creation of a new curriculum at MCPHS which included faculty approval of a full sequence of library modules and which made the Drug Literature Evaluation course (team-taught by librarians and pharmacy faculty) a required course.

It should be noted that pharmacy educators do not perceive these changes in the curriculum as simply dictated from above. A study published in 1999 reported the results of a survey on curricular goals sent to all colleges of pharmacy. The study looked at 33 topics in pharmacy curricula, how much these topics are presently emphasized, and their ideal emphasis. Use of electronic information systems was rated 4th in current emphasis and respondents felt that it should be emphasized even more.[12]

Looking at the national response to these mandates, a survey of the pharmacy literature reveals that pharmacy educators have worked diligently to incorporate information literacy into their programs. Recent efforts to develop innovative ways to teach information literacy skills to pharmacists are documented at Auburn,[13] University of Michigan,[14] University of Tennessee,[15] Hampton University,[16] University of Iowa,[17] University of Washington,[18] University of the Sciences Philadelphia,[19] and North Dakota State.[20] What is not clear from this literature is the role that librarians are playing in these efforts.

6. *The nature of health information and health science librarianship.* The very history of medical information fosters cooperation between health care professionals and librarians. The health fields have always needed quick access to very current information. The Surgeon General of the United States considered it a public health priority to establish a print index of the medical literature as early as 1879.[21] The National Library of Medicine created the first searchable literature database (Medline) in 1966.[22] This development fostered strong connections between the health professional and the librarian since the early databases required expert, specially trained searchers. Consequently, health education has a history and inclination towards willingness to value library instruction. Many disciplines contribute to this climate. For example, in nursing, "the curriculum [is] designed with the assumption that information literacy components will continue [to be included]."[23]

In an informal survey of libraries associated with the Association of Academic Health Sciences Libraries, two questions were queried. What percentage of time do librarians spend on traditional reference assistance and what percentage on course preparation and teaching? Has there been an increase in formal teaching by librarians? Over 91% of the health science libraries experienced an increase in instruction, with several libraries also pointing out that they are now doing less general orientations and more course-integrated instruction. While the percentage varied greatly in the time spent performing reference assistance versus formal instruction, most felt they are spending considerably more time in course preparation than in previous years. Many larger academic health science libraries have actually divided staff into two departments, one for reference and the other for education/instruction.[24] The trend towards a much larger teaching responsibility is particularly true at MCPHS where librarians spend more time preparing and teaching information literacy than ever before. (Please see Table 1 for data on the growth in the number of classes taught.) In fact, in order to provide the two reference librarians with the time needed for the preparation and teaching of classes, it was necessary for others to cover many of their former duties. Until the current academic year, when the library received funding to hire additional reference staff, technical services staff and part-time library science graduate students covered the majority of reference desk hours.

As with most academic fields today, the medical "information explosion" is still growing exponentially. Every Saturday approximately 8,000 new records are added to the Medline database.[25] In the last twenty years, a new movement

TABLE 1. Number of Sessions Taught per Year

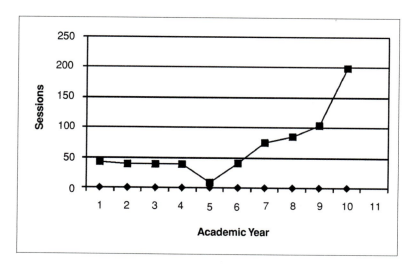

has grown in the realm of medical information, the evidence-based medicine (EBM) movement. This movement might be considered the information literacy movement of medical education. Table 2 demonstrates the correlation between the steps of EBM, the ACRL Information Literacy Standards and the standards for pharmacy education.

7. *Health Education and the Emergence of Evidence-Based Medicine.* Evidence based medicine (EBM) is best defined as " . . . the conscientious, explicit, and judicious use of current best evidence in making decisions about the care of individual patients."[26] Its practice involves five steps that are summarized below:

- Step 1–converting the need for information (about prevention, diagnosis, prognosis, therapy, causation, etc.) into an answerable question
- Step 2–tracking down the best evidence with which to answer the question
- Step 3–critically appraising the evidence for its validity (closeness to the truth), impact (size of the effect), and applicability (usefulness in our clinical practice)
- Step 4–integrating the critical appraisal with our clinical expertise and with our patient's unique biology, values and circumstances
- Step 5–evaluating our effectiveness and efficiency in executing steps 1-4 and seeking ways to improve them both for next time[27]

TABLE 2. A Table of Comparisons: Information Literacy Standards

ACRL Info Lit Standards	Evidence-Based Medicine Steps	AACP
The information literate student determines the nature and extent of the information needed.	The health care professional "convert[s] the need for information (about prevention, diagnosis, prognosis, therapy, causation, etc.) into an answerable question."	[Practitioners] . . . must have the skills of inquiry, abstract logical thinking and critical analysis to separate real from illusionary problems, make judgements and decisions based on available data or identify additional data that may be required. . . . students must understand that to become educated is to know what questions to ask and where the answers may be found.
The information literate student accesses needed information effectively and efficiently.	The health care professional "track[s] down the best evidence with which to answer the question (selects the best evidence resource and searches it efficiently and effectively."	[Practitioners] must gather and organize data and information pertinent to specific patients under their care . . . entry-level practitioners . . . must have the ability to identify, locate, obtain and evaluate missing information.
The information literate student evaluates information and its sources critically and incorporates selected information into his or her knowledge base and value system.	The health care professional "critically apprais[es] the evidence for its validity (closeness to the truth), impact (size of the effect), and applicability (usefulness in our clinical practice)."	[Practitioners] must interpret and analyze data . . . and they will integrate new material with information already known . . . [they] must use the health-related professional and disciplinary literature as a means of acquiring a continuing flow of new knowledge.
The information literate student, individually or as a member of a group, uses information effectively to accomplish a purpose.	The health care professional "integrat[es] the critical appraisal with our clinical expertise and with our patient's unique biology, values and circumstances."	Pharmaceutical care involves a series of problem-solving exercises to achieve the outcomes of care . . .
The information literate student understands many of the economic, legal, and social issues surrounding the use of information and accesses and uses the information ethically and legally.	The health care professional "evaluat[es] our effectiveness and efficiency in executing steps 1-4 and seeking ways to improve them both for next time."	Pharmacy practitioners expand personal, civic, and professional knowledge and skills throughout their careers. They must demonstrate effective self-assessment; and in areas of knowledge, skills, habits, and attitudes needing remediation, propose a strategy to remedy the situation. (Ability Based Outcomes 2)

ACRL (Association of Colleges and Research Libraries)
EBM (Evidence-Based Medicine)
AACP (American Association of Colleges of Pharmacy

In recent years, health care professionals have realized that the harried clinician does not have time to follow these steps to satisfy the information needed to treat each patient encountered. Consequently, resources containing critical evaluations of the literature on clinical topics or practice guidelines, based on these summaries, have developed. Examples include the international Cochrane Library of Systematic Reviews (http://www.update-software.com/Cochrane/default.HTM); the National Guideline Clearinghouse of the Agency for Healthcare Research and

Quality (http://www.guideline.gov/STATIC/about.asp?view=about); and the American College of Physicians Journal Club database of critical reviews (http://www.acponline.org/journals/acpjc/jcmenu.htm).

EBM is based on an effort to counteract the reliance of health care professionals on didactic teaching, expert opinion of senior staff, and reliance on tertiary literature. There are numerous examples of outdated treatment plans and ineffective medicine which can be eradicated by EBM. These range from treatment of severe head trauma to prevention of sudden infant death syndrome.[28] EBM has grown exponentially within the medical community. In 1992, a Medline search on the topic found 1 publication; in 1998, there were more than 1000, and in 2001 there are 5,516 items indexed to this subject heading. There are more than six medical journals devoted to EBM with a circulation over 175,000.[29]

Librarians have been involved with EBM since the 1970s when the clinical librarianship movement began.[30] The clinical librarian attended hospital rounds with the medical team. The librarian conducted computer searches, did literature evaluations, and provided clinicians with important review and/or "best practice" articles. In addition, these librarians began educating the health care professionals they served. These efforts had a measurable effect in educating health care professionals to use the medical literature as part of their practice and there was some evidence that they produced measurable improvements in patient care.[31] Additional studies proving that their presence improves patient outcomes and cuts medical costs are being planned.[32]

THE FUTURE: ASSESSMENT AND NEW SKILLS

Assessment of information literacy efforts is a longstanding challenge and a continuing project. Both the Information Literacy and Evidence-Based Medicine movements have strong constituencies working on assessment. In our local arena, assessment is also a priority. Student evaluations are administered in courses, which are team-taught. Working with the faculty to improve the evaluation instrument, specific questions dealing with content, effectiveness, and clarity of presentations of the librarians were added. Within the Drug Literature Evaluation course, we have also administered 10-question pre-tests and post-tests. These tests focus on Medline searching skills and understanding of the Medical Subject Heading vocabulary, which are important learning objectives for this course. Student performance on homework assignments and on the questions we contribute to the mid-term and final exams are additional sources of feedback and evaluation.

One of the implications of the MCPHS experience is the conviction that librarians need to be taught how to teach. Although most graduate programs in library science offer a course in bibliographic instruction, we worry this is not sufficient preparation. Exposure to educational theory, learning styles, ESL (English as a Second Language) methodology, computer interface design, active teaching techniques, and case-based learning, all seem appropriate but missing from most basic bibliographic instruction courses. In addition, public speaking and presentation skills, especially those utilizing technology, are essential. How many librarians have knowledge of or experience in writing test questions that are easy to understand yet accurately assess specific competencies? Internships and mentoring for librarians by experienced educators seem appropriate but are rarely offered.

The librarians at MCPHS are very fortunate to be at a college that offers creative teaching seminars and workshops. Having an instructional designer on staff with expertise in incorporating technology into the curriculum is an added benefit. Additionally, there is a very active local ACRL special interest group, NELIG (New England Library Instruction Group), which provides both a wonderful support network and resource for sharing information on innovative instruction programs. The Medical Library Association has also responded with support by offering continuing education programs on evidence-based medicine.

CONCLUSION

Information literacy is a growing trend and responsibility of academic librarians. The successful development and implementation of a program depends on many factors including infrastructure (both personnel and technology) and the cooperation of teaching faculty and administrators. While the academic health science instruction model may not directly apply to all libraries, it is our hope that we have provided some useful insights, ideas, and tools that can be used to create the right mix of arguments, allies, and resources on your campus for an information literacy program.

NOTES

1. Heidi Julien, "Information Literacy Instruction in Canadian Academic Libraries: Longitudinal Trends and International Comparisons," *College & Research Libraries* 61, no. 6: 1-14.
2. VC Lopresti, AR Garafalo, and K. Ondhia, "Multi-tier Question Groups for an Integrated HyperCard Natural Science Stack Library," *The Journal of Computers in Mathematics and Science Teaching* 13, no. 3 (1994): 303-20.
3. Katherine Beaty Chiste, Andrea Glover, and Glenna Westwood, "Infiltration and Entrenchment: Capturing and Securing Information Literacy Territory in Academe," *The Journal of Academic Librarianship* 26 (2000): 202-208.

4. Commission on Higher Education, Middle States Association of Colleges and Schools, *Characteristics of Excellence in Higher Education–Standards for Accreditation* (Philadelphia, PA: Middle States Association of Colleges and Schools, 1994), 15.

5. Commission on Colleges, Southern Association of Colleges and Schools, *Criteria for Accreditation* (Decatur, Georgia: Southern Association of Colleges and Schools, 1997), 55.

6. Association of College and Research Libraries, "Information Literacy Competency Standards for Higher Education," [Web page], November 28, 2000 [cited July 11, 2001]; available on the World Wide Web at http://www.ala.org/acrl/ilintro.html.

7. The Boyer Commission on Educating Undergraduates in the Research University, "Reinventing Undergraduate Education: A Blueprint for America's Research Universities," [Web page], June 21, 2001 [cited July 19, 2001]; available on the World Wide Web at http://notes.cc.sunysb.edu/Pres/boyer.nsf/.

8. The Commission to Implement change in Pharmaceutical Education, "Background Paper II: Entry-level, Curricular Outcomes, Curricular Content and Educational Process," *American Journal of Pharmaceutical Education*, 57 (Winter 1993): 377.

9. Ibid., 379-383.

10. Association of College and Research Libraries, *Information Literacy Competency Standards*.

11. NABPLEX Review Committee, *A Candidate's Review Guide for the National Association of Boards of Pharmacy Licensure Examination* (Park Ridge, Illinois: National Association of Boards of Pharmacy, 1996), 16, 68.

12. David R. Graber, Janis P. Bellack, Carol Lancaster and Catherine Musham, Jean Nappi, and Edward H. O'Neil, "Curriculum Topics in Pharmacy Education: Current and Ideal Emphasis," *American Journal of Pharmaceutical Education* 63 (Summer 1999): 148.

13. SM Buring, "Using Newsletter Publishing as a way to Encapsulate Multiple Concepts in a Drug Literature Course," Paper presented at the American Association of Colleges of Pharmacy Annual Meeting, 101, (July 2000): 164.

14. F. Ascione, T Thompson, T. Knox and R. Siden, "Use of Web-based Instruction to Teach Scientific Literature Evaluation Skills," Paper presented at the American Association of Colleges of Pharmacy Annual Meeting, 101, (July 2000): 250.

15. GE Bass, "Pharmacy Informatics: Web Centric Clinical Practice Approach," Paper presented at the American Association of Colleges of Pharmacy Annual Meeting, 101, (July 2000): 19.

16. TM Jenkins and AR Howard, "Integrating a Biostatistics and Literature Evaluation Course," Paper presented at the American Association of Colleges of Pharmacy Annual Meeting, 101, (July 2000): 229.

17. C Catney, H Seaba and K Moores, "Implementing Team Learning to Improve Students' Participation in a Drug Literature Evaluation Course," Paper presented at the American Association of Colleges of Pharmacy Annual Meeting, 101, (July 2000): 165.

18. TA O'Sullivan, M Gibaldi, P Odegard, E Harvey, and J Watkins, "Team Approach to Teaching Students How to Evaluate the Medical Literature," Paper presented at the American Association of Colleges of Pharmacy Annual Meeting, 100, (July 1999): 54.

19. LA Bowman, "Information Needs and Resources of Nontraditional PharmD Students," Paper presented at the American Association of Colleges of Pharmacy Annual Meeting, 100, (July 1999): 11.

20. DR Miller, "Assessment of Critical Thinking in a Drug Literature Evaluation Class," Paper presented at the American Association of Colleges of Pharmacy Annual Meeting, 95, (July 1997): 93.

21. Mary C. Gillett, "The Army Medical Department: Chapter 1: View from the Top," (Center for Military History, United States Army, Washington, D.C. 1995). Available on the World Wide Web at http://www.armymedicine.army.mil/history/booksdocs/spanam/gillett3/ch1.htm.

22. United States National Library of Medicine, "Fact Sheet Medline®" [Web page], May 22, 2001 [cited August 22, 2001]; available on the World Wide Web at http://www.nlm.nih.gov/pubs/factsheets/medline.html.

23. Lisa Blankenship and Lynne M. Fox, "Information Literacy–the Next Generation: Evolving with the Curriculum," *Colorado Libraries* 24 (Winter 1998): 22.

24. Various responses, "AAHSL: Library Instruction," [Listserv postings] July 2001; available via email at AAHSL@AAMCINFO.AAMC.ORG.

25. Fact Sheet Medline®.

26. Ann McKibbon, *PDQ Evidence-Based Principles and Practice* (Hamilton, Ontario: B.C. Decker, 1999), 2.

27. David L. Sackett, *Evidence Based Medicine: How to Practice and Teach EBM* (Edinburg: Churchill Livingstone, 2000), 3-4.

28. A wide range of examples are provided at Mark H. Ebell, "The Introduction to Evidence Based Medicine Course, Limitations of Current Practice," [Web page] [cited August 22, 2001]; available on the World Wide Web at http://www.poems.msu.edu/InfoMastery/Intro/Base.htm.

29. David L. Sackett, *Evidence Based Medicine*, 2.

30. Robert Veenstra, "Clinical Medical Librarian Impact on Patient Care: A One-Year Analysis," *Bulletin of the Medical Library Association* 80 (January 1992): 19.

31. Ibid.

32. Loraine F. Schacher, "Clinical Librarianship: Its Value in Medical Care" *Annals of Internal Medicine* 134 (April 17, 2001): 720.

Index

Page numbers followed by *App.* indicate an Appendix; those followed by *fig.* indicate figures; and those followed by *n* or *nn* indicate note(s).

American Association of Higher
 Education, 133
American Association of School
 Librarians (AASL), 25
American Library Association (ALA),
 25,148
 continuing education, defined, 147-148
 Information Literacy Community
  Partnerships Assembly of,
  28-29
 Special Presidential Committee on
  Information Literacy
  Community Partnerships of, 28
Assessment of library instruction
 programs. *See* ACRL
 *Information Literacy
 Competency Standards for
 Higher Education,* assessment
 using
Association of College and Research
 Libraries
 Bibliographic Instruction Section
  Task Force of, 147
 collaboration through, 25
 Immersion Institute for Information
  Literacy, 76-77,84
 *Information Literacy Competency
 Standards for Higher
 Education,* 9,10,25,58,77,
 84-88,87*fig.,*109-119*App.*
 (*See also* ACRL *Information
 Literacy Competency
 Standards for Higher
 Education,* assessment using)
 information literacy defined by, 2*n. 1*
 Institute for Information Literacy,
  Immersion Program of, 9
 See also ACRL *Information
 Literacy Competency
 Standards for Higher
 Education,* assessment using;
 Information Literacy
 Immersion program

Barker, Joel, 49
Baron, Sara, 71,143
Bechtel, Joan, 12-13
Bibliographic instruction, participatory
 approach to
 barriers to implementation of, 172-173
 discussion leadership skills, 173
 Paulo Freire principles of, 174
 instructor's role, 170-172
 less taught, more learned concept, 171
 limitations of, 172
 objectives of, 168
 participatory methodology, 168-170
 problem, statement of, 168
 student reactions to, 173-174
 summary regarding, 167,175
 timeline of, 168-170
 vs. active learning, 172,172*table*
Bibliographic instruction, transition
 from, 5
 *ACRL Information Literacy
 Competency Standards for
 Higher Education,* 9,10,12,58,
 85,87*fig.*
 action plan, goals, 8-9
 administrative support, 11
 collaborative support and, 4-5,9-11,
  14-15,18*n. 21*
 collaborative support and,
  challenges to, 7-8,11-12
 cultural landscapes and, 7,14-15
 Earlham model of bibliographic
  instruction and, 3,4,5,6,
  16-17*n. 1,*17*n. 4*
 Gustavus Adolphus College
  experience and, 6,12-14
 history regarding, 5-6
 internal steps, 9
 librarian status and, 7
 literature regarding, 6-8
 National Leadership Grant, 12-14
 resources, competition for, 8,12
 St. Olaf College experience and, 5,8-9
 summary regarding, 3-4,15-16
Breivik, Patricia Sean, 33,34

Integrating Total Quality Management in a Library Setting, edited by Susan Jurow, MLS, and Susan B. Barnard, MLS (Vol. 18, No. 1/2, 1993). *"Especially valuable are the librarian experiences that directly relate to real concerns about TQM. Recommended for all professional reading collections." (Library Journal)*

Leadership in Academic Libraries: Proceedings of the W. Porter Kellam Conference, The University of Georgia, May 7, 1991, edited by William Gray Potter (Vol. 17, No. 4, 1993). *"Will be of interest to those concerned with the history of American academic libraries." (Australian Library Review)*

Collection Assessment and Acquisitions Budgets, edited by Sul H. Lee (Vol. 17, No. 2, 1993). *Contains timely information about the assessment of academic library collections and the relationship of collection assessment to acquisition budgets.*

Developing Library Staff for the 21st Century, edited by Maureen Sullivan (Vol. 17, No. 1, 1992). *"I found myself enthralled with this highly readable publication. It is one of those rare compilations that manages to successfully integrate current general management operational thinking in the context of academic library management." (Bimonthly Review of Law Books)*

Vendor Evaluation and Acquisition Budgets, edited by Sul H. Lee (Vol. 16, No. 3, 1992). *"The title doesn't do justice to the true scope of this excellent collection of papers delivered at the sixth annual conference on library acquisitions sponsored by the University of Oklahoma Libraries." (Kent K. Hendrickson, BS, MALS, Dean of Libraries, University of Nebraska-Lincoln) Find insightful discussions on the impact of rising costs on library budgets and management in this groundbreaking book.*

The Management of Library and Information Studies Education, edited by Herman L. Totten, PhD, MLS (Vol. 16, No. 1/2, 1992). *"Offers something of interest to everyone connected with LIS education–the undergraduate contemplating a master's degree, the doctoral student struggling with courses and career choices, the new faculty member aghast at conflicting responsibilities, the experienced but stressed LIS professor, and directors of LIS Schools." (Education Libraries)*

Library Management in the Information Technology Environment: Issues, Policies, and Practice for Administrators, edited by Brice G. Hobrock, PhD, MLS (Vol. 15, No. 3/4, 1992). *"A road map to identify some of the alternative routes to the electronic library." (Stephen Rollins, Associate Dean for Library Services, General Library, University of New Mexico)*

Managing Technical Services in the 90's, edited by Drew Racine (Vol. 15, No. 1/2, 1991). *"Presents an eclectic overview of the challenges currently facing all library technical services efforts. . . . Recommended to library administrators and interested practitioners." (Library Journal)*

Budgets for Acquisitions: Strategies for Serials, Monographs, and Electronic Formats, edited by Sul H. Lee (Vol. 14, No. 3, 1991). *"Much more than a series of handy tips for the careful shopper. This [book] is a most useful one–well-informed, thought-provoking, and authoritative." (Australian Library Review)*

Creative Planning for Library Administration: Leadership for the Future, edited by Kent Hendrickson, MALS (Vol. 14, No. 2, 1991). *"Provides some essential information on the planning process, and the mix of opinions and methodologies, as well as examples relevant to every library manager, resulting in a very readable foray into a topic too long avoided by many of us." (Canadian Library Journal)*

Strategic Planning in Higher Education: Implementing New Roles for the Academic Library, edited by James F. Williams, II, MLS (Vol. 13, No. 3/4, 1991). *"A welcome addition to the sparse literature on strategic planning in university libraries. Academic librarians considering strategic planning for their libraries will learn a great deal from this work." (Canadian Library Journal)*

Personnel Administration in an Automated Environment, edited by Philip E. Leinbach, MLS (Vol. 13, No. 1/2, 1990). *"An interesting and worthwhile volume, recommended to university library administrators and to others interested in thought-provoking discussion of the personnel implications of automation." (Canadian Library Journal)*

Library Development: A Future Imperative, edited by Dwight F. Burlingame, PhD (Vol. 12, No. 4, 1990). *"This volume provides an excellent overview of fundraising with special application to libraries. . . . A useful book that is highly recommended for all libraries." (Library Journal)*

Library Material Costs and Access to Information, edited by Sul H. Lee (Vol. 12, No. 3, 1991). *"A cohesive treatment of the issue. Although the book's contributors possess a research library perspective, the data and the ideas presented are of interest and benefit to the entire profession, especially academic librarians." (Library Resources and Technical Services)*

Training Issues and Strategies in Libraries, edited by Paul M. Gherman, MALS, and Frances O. Painter, MLS, MBA (Vol. 12, No. 2, 1990). *"There are . . . useful chapters, all by different authors, each with a preliminary summary of the content–a device that saves much time in deciding whether to read the whole chapter or merely skim through it. Many of the chapters are essentially practical without too much emphasis on theory. This book is a good investment." (Library Association Record)*

Library Education and Employer Expectations, edited by E. Dale Cluff, PhD, MLS (Vol. 11, No. 3/4, 1990). *"Useful to library-school students and faculty interested in employment problems and employer perspectives. Librarians concerned with recruitment practices will also be interested." (Information Technology and Libraries)*

Managing Public Libraries in the 21st Century, edited by Pat Woodrum, MLS (Vol. 11, No. 1/2, 1989). *"A broad-based collection of topics that explores the management problems and possibilities public libraries will be facing in the 21st century." (Robert Swisher, PhD, Director, School of Library and Information Studies, University of Oklahoma)*

Human Resources Management in Libraries, edited by Gisela M. Webb, MLS, MPA (Vol. 10, No. 4, 1989). *"Thought provoking and enjoyable reading. . . . Provides valuable insights for the effective information manager." (Special Libraries)*

Creativity, Innovation, and Entrepreneurship in Libraries, edited by Donald E. Riggs, EdD, MLS (Vol. 10, No. 2/3, 1989). *"The volume is well worth reading as a whole. . . . There is very little repetition, and it should stimulate thought." (Australian Library Review)*

The Impact of Rising Costs of Serials and Monographs on Library Services and Programs, edited by Sul H. Lee (Vol. 10, No. 1, 1989). *". . . Sul Lee hit a winner here." (Serials Review)*

Computing, Electronic Publishing, and Information Technology: Their Impact on Academic Libraries, edited by Robin N. Downes (Vol. 9, No. 4, 1989). *"For a relatively short and easily digestible discussion of these issues, this book can be recommended, not only to those in academic libraries, but also to those in similar types of library or information unit, and to academics and educators in the field." (Journal of Documentation)*

Library Management and Technical Services: The Changing Role of Technical Services in Library Organizations, edited by Jennifer Cargill, MSLS, MSed (Vol. 9, No. 1, 1988). *"As a practical and instructive guide to issues such as automation, personnel matters, education, management techniques and liaison with other services, senior library managers with a sincere interest in evaluating the role of their technical services should find this a timely publication." (Library Association Record)*

Management Issues in the Networking Environment, edited by Edward R. Johnson, PhD (Vol. 8, No. 3/4, 1989). *"Particularly useful for librarians/information specialists contemplating establishing a local network." (Australian Library Review)*

Acquisitions, Budgets, and Material Costs: Issues and Approaches, edited by Sul H. Lee (Supp. #2, 1988). *"The advice of these library practitioners is sensible and their insights illuminating for librarians in academic libraries." (American Reference Books Annual)*

Pricing and Costs of Monographs and Serials: National and International Issues, edited by Sul H. Lee (Supp. #1, 1987). *"Eminently readable. There is a good balance of chapters on serials and monographs and the perspective of suppliers, publishers, and library practitioners are presented. A book well worth reading." (Australasian College Libraries)*

Legal Issues for Library and Information Managers, edited by William Z. Nasri, JD, PhD (Vol. 7, No. 4, 1987). *"Useful to any librarian looking for protection or wondering where responsibilities end and liabilities begin. Recommended." (Academic Library Book Review)*

Archives and Library Administration: Divergent Traditions and Common Concerns, edited by Lawrence J. McCrank, PhD, MLS (Vol. 7, No. 2/3, 1986). *"A forward-looking view of archives and libraries. . . . Recommend[ed] to students, teachers, and practitioners alike of archival and library science. It is readable, thought-provoking, and provides a summary of the major areas of divergence and convergence." (Association of Canadian Map Libraries and Archives)*

Excellence in Library Management, edited by Charlotte Georgi, MLS, and Robert Bellanti, MLS, MBA (Vol. 6, No. 3, 1985). *"Most beneficial for library administrators . . . for anyone interested in either library/information science or management." (Special Libraries)*

Marketing and the Library, edited by Gary T. Ford (Vol. 4, No. 4, 1984). *Discover the latest methods for more effective information dissemination and learn to develop successful programs for specific target areas.*

Finance Planning for Libraries, edited by Murray S. Martin (Vol. 3, No. 3/4, 1983). *Stresses the need for libraries to weed out expenditures which do not contribute to their basic role–the collection and organization of information–when planning where and when to spend money.*

Planning for Library Services: A Guide to Utilizing Planning Methods for Library Management, edited by Charles R. McClure, PhD (Vol. 2, No. 3/4, 1982). *"Should be read by anyone who is involved in planning processes of libraries–certainly by every administrator of a library or system." (American Reference Books Annual)*